U.S.S. MONITOR

Edward S. S. Morrison
819 Wavecrest Lane
Houston, Texas 77062

i

U.S.S. MONITOR

The Ship That Launched A Modern Navy

By LT Edward M. Miller, USN

Copyright © 1978 by

LEEWARD PUBLICATIONS, INC.
                    Annapolis, Maryland

Library of Congress Catalog No. 78-61684
ISBN No. 0-915268-10-8

Designed by Robert F. Sumrall
Jacket illustration by Alan B. Chesley
Composition by Leeward Publications, Inc.
Printing by Collins Lithographing and Printing Co., Inc.
                    Baltimore, Maryland

Foreword

The momentuous engagement between the USS *Monitor* and the CSS *Virginia* on 9 March 1862 may well be the one event in naval history most familiar to the American people. For those of us who have been involved in the search for the final resting place of the *Monitor*, this interest is displayed by the constantly recurring question, "When will she be raised?" Although the details of the great battle and the subsequent history of the two participants are not always understood by the general public, there remains a realization that the *Monitor* and its opponent, the ex-USS *Merrimack*, were involved in the beginning of a great technological change in naval warfare. To most people, the ultimate fate of these ships has been of less interest.

The details of the deliberate destruction of the *Virginia* and the unexpected loss of the *Monitor* at sea are well known to naval historians. The wreckage of the *Virginia* was distributed as souvenir paper weights and canes. The *Monitor*, lost for years, is now known to lie on the bottom of the sea off Cape Hatteras. While the problem of her recovery still remains to be solved, the story of her design evolution, construction, operation, loss, and eventual discovery is told by Lieutenant Miller in a comprehensive narration of the events leading to positive identification of the *Monitor's* wreck site.

In *USS Monitor—the Ship That Launched a Modern Navy*, an extension of a three-volume study of the *Monitor* (Project CHEESEBOX) by midshipmen of the U.S. Naval Academy in 1974, the author brings together for the first time a clear understanding of the several configurations of the ship, a definitive account of her sinking, and an extensive review of the personalities, techniques, and expeditions that led to the final discovery of the century-old wreck.

The approximate position of the wreck site has existed in public records—the log of the towing vessel *Rhode Island*—since the day the *Monitor* sank. Through improved techniques in sonar and magnetic anomaly detection, remote underwater photography and real-time video recordings from underwater, surface, and airborne platforms, a new capability has become available to search large areas of the ocean where the use of divers would be inefficient or precarious. The story of the use of these new techniques and equipment that allowed the search to be reduced to reasonable dimensions of time and space is recounted in the final chapter. That chapter recalls men's efforts to explore the past with the hope of recapturing for the American people a better understanding of an exciting event in our historical heritage.

The establishment in 1975 of the *Monitor Marine Sanctuary* commemorates the history of the ship and protects it for the future. Although the mystery of the location of the wreck has been solved, and its identity has been verified, the future of the *Monitor* poses a challenge to archeology, technology, and the resources to be devoted to its preservation. This book stands as a colorful epiloque to the century-old story of the *Monitor*.

Ernest W. Peterkin
28 February 1978

Capt. Ernest W. Peterkin, USNR.
Capt. Peterkin is employed by the Naval Research Laboratory in Washington, D.C. He is the Technical Project Manager of the SOLRAD project which has launched several satelites to monitor solar activity. He assisted the National Armed Forces Museum Advisory Board at the Smithsonian Institution in studying the design/engineering details of the salvage of the *Tecumseh*, a Civil War Monitor sunk in Mobile Bay, Alabama. On the basis of his work for the Smithsonian and his participation in PROJECT CHEESEBOX, he has been recognized as an expert on Monitor design, construction, and engineering. He is a fellow of the Company of Military Historians and a long-time student of American military history.

To the Jack Tars of the U.S. Navy who called themselves
"The Monitor Boys"

Diorama by Sheperd Paine

Acknowledgements

In an endeavor such as Project Cheesebox it is difficult to point to a single fact, circumstance, or individual that attributed solely to successful completion. The project, just as the reader will recognize in the entire *Monitor* search, was the result of the interaction of a great number of people and series of circumstances. The project continually evolved in scope and importance as events unfolded. What started as individual seminar papers grew into a collective effort producing a three volume research manuscript of over a thousand pages. In retrospect, it is obvious to see that the project would not have been successful but for the great number of people who freely gave of themselves to help the Midshipmen.

The large number of people preclude individual recognition, however, several must be mentioned. Project Cheesebox would never have gotten started if it wasn't for the early support of Bill Andahazy, Professor William Darden and Dr. Richard Mathieu. Also, Mr. Ernest W. Peterkin was a constant source of encouragement, and his friendship is one of the most rewarding experiences of the project.

After graduation in June of 1974, the manuscript was just a pile of papers and scribbled notes. I was assigned temporary duty at the Naval Historical Center, Washington Navy Yard to complete it. I am deeply indebted to Vice Admiral E. B. Hooper for this opportunity and for his support of our project.

Of course, much of the work behind the scenes was done by our faithful and patient secretary, Mrs. Gloria Ceznek. She filled many a crucial role from receptionist to den mother and her interest and skill at deciphering our writing proved to be a major factor in the production of the manuscript.

Finally, the patience and encouragement of my mother and my wife Jeannie has to be acknowledged. They put up with me burying my head in books and papers weekend after weekend trying to complete this narrative.

Edward M. Miller

MIDSHIPMEN PARTICIPANTS OF PROJECT CHEESEBOX

Frederick Christensen	Edward Miller
David Clites	Douglas Rau
Herbert Hribar	Charles Richner
John Meyer	William Snook

The Author

LT. Miller, upon graduation from the U.S. Naval Academy in June, 1974 was assigned temporary duty at the Naval Historical Center under the direction of Vice Admiral E. B. Hooper, Historian of the Navy. As Project Officer he completed the Project Cheesebox manuscript and assisted in coordinating the Navy's participation in establishing the Monitor Marine Sanctuary. In February, 1975 he was assigned to the Naval School of Diving and Salvage in Washington, D.C. for training as a HeO_2 Deep Sea Diving and Salvage Officer. Upon graduation in September of 1975, he was assigned to the USS *Ortolan* (ASR-22), one of the Navy's newest catamaran-hulled submarine rescue vessels equipped with the Mark II Deep Dive System. Subsequently, he was sent to Submarine Development Group One in San Diego, California for training as a Saturation Diving Officer. He is presently serving aboard the *Ortolan* as Assistant Engineer and Saturation Diving Officer.

x

Contents

Foreword v

Preface xiii

Introduction 1

Chapter 1—John Ericsson, Inventor 3

Chapter 2—Genesis of the Monitor Concept 13

Chapter 3—Design & Construction 21

Chapter 4—Journey to Hampton Roads 37

Chapter 5—The Loss of U.S.S. Monitor 53

Chapter 6—The Search for the Monitor 87

Epilogue 107

Appendix 111

Bibliography 113

Index 121

℘reface

The fall and winter of 1973 proved to be a veritable morass of video tape records, microfilms, and historical documents. After the Research Vessel *EASTWARD* returned from Cape Hatteras and a two week search for the remains of the ironclad USS *MONITOR*, identification of one of the wreck sites located during the project became a consuming obsession. Features of the vessel documented in video tape records and photographs were compared to construction details of the *MONITOR* preserved in surviving historical sources. The strategy demanded monotonous hours analyzing video tape data and laborious historical research.

My first contact with the author was a result of these research activities. At the National Archives, Library of Congress, New York Historical Society, Swedish-American Historical Society, and Stevens Institute, inquiries about manuscript collections containing material related to the *MONITOR* engendered a virtually identical response: contact Midshipman Edward M. Miller at the United States Naval Academy. At more than one repository detailed interrogations resulted in a candid confession that Midshipman Miller was more familiar with *MONITOR* related collections than the staff. It seemed that the mysterious midshipman was more than one step ahead at every source.

The results of "Project Cheesebox" reflect the extent of this research. The three volume "Cheesebox" publication represents the most comprehensive treatment of the *MONITOR*'s origins, construction, service record, loss, and discovery available. Lt. Miller has drawn heavily on that research in weaving the historical narrative for this volume. In chapters related to the celebrated contest at Hampton Roads and the dramatic loss of the *MONITOR* off Cape Hatteras, extensive contemporary source material has been utilized to afford a direct contact with the officers, engineers, and crew of the vessel. The technique captures an intensity that might otherwise be lost in interpretation.

In presenting the complex scenario of discovery, the author relies on both documentary records and his own experience as a principal in the "Great *MONITOR* Sweepstakes." The final chapter effectively sorts out the complicated series of events which led to the *ALCOA SEAPROBE* investigation and confirmation that the USS *MONITOR* had indeed been found. Fortunately, neither the book nor Lt. Miller's participation ends here, for the story of the *MONITOR* may be only beginning.

In January, 1975 a cooperative effort between the State of North Carolina and the United States Department of Commerce resulted in the designation of the *MONITOR* as our first Marine Sanctuary. Under this program the National Oceanic and Atmospheric Administration and the North Carolina Division of Archives and History are working in concert to develop a management policy and research guidelines that will ensure the systematic scientific investigation of the wreck. Because of this protection, the *MONITOR* represents an unparalleled opportunity for historians, archaeologists, oceanographers, and engineers to marshal available resources for a well conceived and supported state-of-the-art investigation designed to collect the data required to assess the feasibility of recovery, conservation, and display options. With a resource as historically significant and unique as

the *MONITOR*, anything less than a systematic scientific approach is extremely difficult to justify.

Today the remains of the *MONITOR* represent an exciting legacy from the past. We have a responsibility to preserve what we inherit from the past for the future. If we respond positively to that responsiblity, the celebrated "Cheesebox-on-a-Raft" may indeed be restored to the nation it was constructed to preserve.

Gordon P. Watts, Jr.
28 February 1978

Gordon P. Watts, Jr.

Gordon Watts is a Marine Archaeologist at the Division of Archives and History of the State of North Carolina. He was one of the principle investigators on the *EASTWARD* cruise that located the wreck of the *MONITOR* and was principally responsible for the identification of the hulk. He has obtained his Masters Degree from East Carolina University and his theisis was on the construction of the *MONITOR*.

He has obtained a wealth of experience diving on the numerous wrecks of Civil War blockade runners off the North Carolina coast. Additionally, he has conducted a special summer seminar in Marine Archaeology for the past three summers in which students are taught the field principles of marine archaeology and are given the opportunity to work in the Marine Archaeological Program and the Marine Preservation Laboratory.

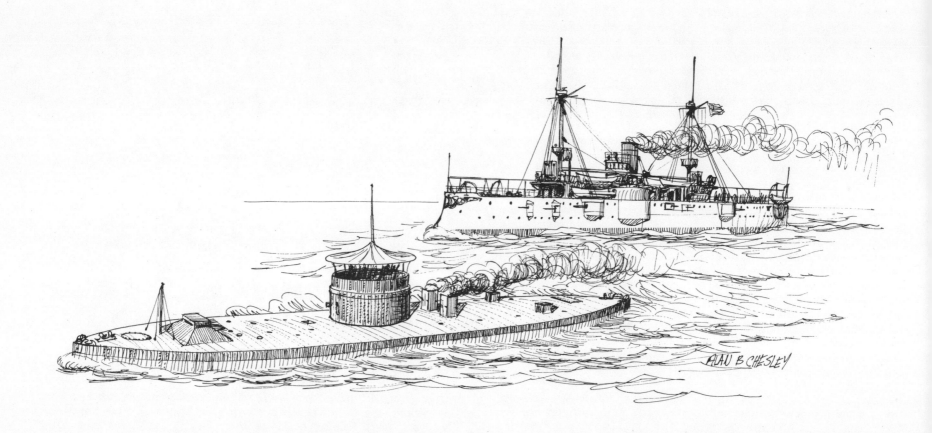

The ship that transformed naval warfare, the Monitor *was the forerunner of the modern navy, with heavy* **armor** *and a revolving turret. This artist's concept shows the* Monitor *in column with the battleship* Texas, *the first modern battleship in the U.S. Navy, although the two ships never operated together; the* Texas *was not commissioned until nearly thirty years after the* Monitor *sank.*

INTRODUCTION

FEW SHIPS IN U.S. naval history have been as highly acclaimed or as controversial as the Civil War Ironclad, USS *Monitor*. Her historic battle with the CSS *Virginia* marked a new era in naval warfare. The story of how the *Monitor* was hurriedly built and arrived at Hampton Roads in time to turn one of the blackest days of U.S. naval history into victory will continue to intrigue historians and school children alike.

Built out of necessity to meet the challenge of Southern ironclad construction, the *Monitor* has been shrouded in controversy ever since. While she was being built she was called "Ericsson's Folly," and many wondered if the Navy Department had gone mad spending money on such an unconventional design which could not possibly carry the weight of iron her designer, John Ericsson, was placing on her. If she did float, it would be pure insanity to send such a small warship carrying only two guns against such a behemoth as the resurrected USS *Merrimack,* renamed the CSS *Virginia* by the Confederates, which would carry up to ten guns.

Even after meeting the CSS *Virginia* on 9 March 1862 and proving her invulnerability to Confederate shell, the results of the battle have been an unending controversy containing some of the biggest "ifs" in history with both sides claiming victory.

Because of hesitancy to again risk the *Monitor* in combat with the *Virginia* and the eventual destruction of the *Virginia* by her own crew, the two ironclads would never meet again. Nevertheless, the two ships had left their indelible mark on naval history, for the world had taken notice that the age of steam and iron had begun. From then on, every modern warship would be built of iron and propelled by steam.

Nine months after the historic duel, the *Monitor* foundered in a gale off Cape Hatteras, North Carolina. As the shouts of desperate men faded into the blackness of that stormy December night in 1862 and the *Monitor* disappeared beneath the waves, a new controversy arose out of the events of that evening. How could the Navy lose its most famous ironclad at sea?

Was it poor seamanship? Or was it a flaw in her design? Did her hull separate from the upper raft? How was it that the monitor *Passaic* survived the storm when the *Monitor* foundered? These question have never been answered.

The controversy did not end with the storm at sea. After 111 years of being one of the sea's best kept secrets, the final resting place of the *Monitor* has been found, ending a quarter of a century of modern search filled with controvertible claims of discovery.

Only now can the complete story of the USS *Monitor* be written. Heretofore, all histories have been incomplete in that they merely indicate that the *Monitor* was lost somewhere south of Cape Hatteras. For the first time the complete story of the ship, beginning with John Ericsson in Sweden and ending with the photographs which positively identify her sunken hulk, can be told. The final resting place of the historic ship will be marked on all navigational charts of the area. The *Monitor* is no longer one of the forgotten mysteries of the sea.

The material presented here is based on research conducted under *Project Cheesebox* at the United States Naval Academy. In the spring of 1973 a team of eight midshipmen organized themselves to document the history of the *Monitor,* conduct engineering tests on her design and to make a search for the lost ironclad. This research into the history of the *Monitor* brought to light many little-known details; how she was conceived, built, fought and foundered. As a result of their works, and that of many others including John Newton of Duke University, chief scientist of the expedition that first photographed the wreck, and Gordon Watts who identified the hulk as that of the *Monitor,* her final resting place is protected as the first Marine Sanctuary in the United States—a fitting memorial to the deeds of this famous warship and a reminder that the fate of the Navy and possibly the nation once depended on the outcome of one battle.

Captain John Ericsson, as he appeared in 1861. A quick tempered, self-centered perfectionist, he was nevertheless a genius at mechanical inventions.

1

JOHN ERICSSON, INVENTOR

The history of the Civil War ironclad *Monitor* necessarily begins with the engineering master who conceived and designed the ship. The *Monitor* was not conceived in a single flash of genius, but was the result of more than forty years engineering experience. Her development is only one among many achievements credited to Ericsson.

John Ericsson was born in Langbanshyttan, Sweden in the province of Vërmland on 31 July 1803. In that same year Robert Fulton launched his first steam-powered paddlewheel of which Napoleon I of France remarked that the face of the globe would be changed as a result. The age of steam was about to begin and John Ericsson was destined to play a vital role in the development of steam technology.

John Ericsson was the youngest of three children and his education commenced early under the guidance of his father, Olaf, who was a mine inspector. The Ericsson family had been involved in Swedish mining for four generations and it was through his father's work that young Ericsson developed his keen interest in, and first showed his ability for mechanical invention. At five years of age he was drawing, using a compass made from birch twigs and his mother's sewing needles. He disassembled clocks and watches for their gears and springs and melted down his mother's spoons for the construction of a windmill. It was at this early age he developed his intense feeling of rivalry and pride in perfecting his work; everything he did was in competition with his older brother Nils.

When John Ericsson was eight years old, his family moved to Forsvik where his father was given a new job on the Göta Canal, a gigantic project that would bisect Sweden. The other engineers on the project continued John's education in English, French, Latin, architectural drawing, chemistry, and mechanical draftsmanship. It was not long before the Ericsson boys were working beside the other engineers; Nils as a carpenter and cement maker and John as leveler and assistant surveyor. At the age of

sixteen, John was promoted and given charge of six hundred men while also being charged with drawing plans for the complete 30-mile long canal, and all the machinery and tools used in its construction.

In 1820, at the age of seventeen John Ericsson became eligible for military service and elected to join the Twenty-third Rifle Corps of the Swedish Army stationed in remote Jämtland, in the northernmost part of Sweden. It was during this service that the young officer fell in love with Carolina Lilierköld, daughter of one of his senior officers. It was a misguided romance, with John eventually forbidden to see her again. Abruptly, Lt. Ericsson was ordered to Stockholm with letters of introduction to the Minister from England, unknowing that he had fostered an illegitimate son. Ericsson's brother, Nils, later discovered the fact and sought out his nephew, who had been placed in a foster home, to raise as his own son. It would not be until 1872 that Hjalmar Ericsson, the forty-eight year old son of John Ericsson would write to his father who by then was world-known and living in New York.

While in Jämtland, Ericsson was assigned to prepare maps of the military areas and communities. These are preserved today in the Royal Archives in Stockholm as masterpieces in cartographic art.

Ericsson also designed steam engines to drain ditches. While employed in this he experimented with his "Caloric engine." The theory of operation was that very hot air could be used to run the engines instead of expending the large quantity of heat energy required to change water into steam to drive an engine. He was invited to demonstrate his engine before the Swedish Engineering Society in Stockholm and the Minister from England. The demonstration went well, his engine producing ten horsepower. After this showing, it was arranged for Ericsson to travel to England to demonstrate his engine before the newly organized Society of Civil Engineers in London, and he was given a one year leave of absence from the Army. Ericsson borrowed 10,000 Swedish crowns and having made his decision to forsake his love for his work, left Sweden, never to return.

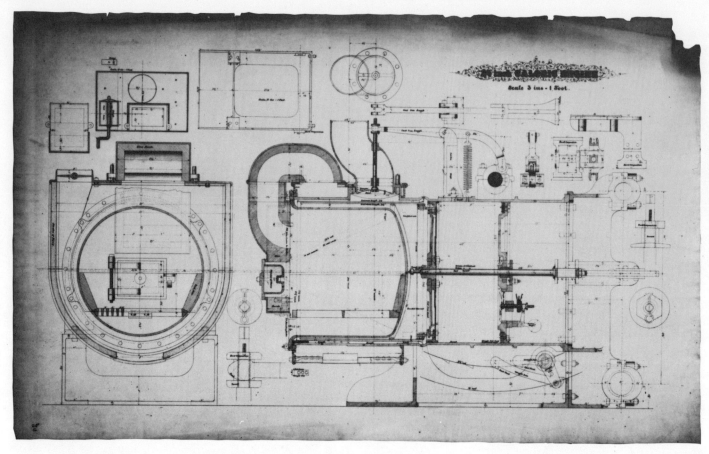

Ericsson's caloric engine operated on the expansion of hot air instead of steam. He believed this invention was his greatest contribution to mankind, as Horace Greeley acclaimed "The age of steam has closed, the age of caloric opens..."

John Ericsson arrived in London on 18 May 1826 and presented a paper before the Institute of Civil Engineers located at 15 Buckingham Street on the Strand which is still on file at the Institute; No. 119, "A Description of a Method of Employing the Combustion of Fuel as a Moving Power." The demonstration failed, due to his use of a slow burning coal that produced too much heat and destroyed the engine. The young inventor was left discredited and nearly penniless. However, John Braithwaite, a prominent engineer who had witnessed the demonstration was suitably enough impressed with Ericsson despite the failure and offered him a partnership. So at age twenty-three, John Ericsson joined in a very productive partnership which in ten years produced thirty inventions.

Some of the most interesting of these were an evaporator to remove salt from water, a depth-finder for ships, cutting files, a hydrostatic weighing machine, engines with a higher fuel efficiency, forced draft blowers and centrifugal blowers for furnaces, a high capacity steam driven water pump and a steam engine with a surface condenser. One of the foremost inventions at this time was a steam fire engine which incorporated the "Braithwaite" pump, capable of pumping a stream of water through a hose that could reach the top of the tallest buildings in London. It was rejected by the London Fire Brigade because the engine took twenty minutes to get up steam and would have had to be maintained continually on the line to be of use in emergencies. Two more "Braithwaite" steam fire engines were built. One was used at the Liverpool docks for many years, while the other was ordered by Frederick William III of Prussia for use by the Berlin Fire Brigade. One of the engines was demonstrated in New York City in 1840, a full decade before the steam fire engine was in general acceptance and use in America.

Ericsson, having become deeply involved in his work in the new partnership, had forgotten all about his military obligation. In 1827 he received a letter from his Commanding Officer informing him that his one year leave of absence had expired and he was now considered a deserter. Because of his fine work in representing Sweden in England and a few hasty letters

The Ericsson steam fire engine, built for the London Fire Brigade in 1840.

The steam locomotive "Novelty," designed by Ericsson and built in England in 1829, set a new land speed record, covering a mile in 53 seconds.

to influential friends in Sweden, Ericsson was reinstated and promoted to Captain. He immediately resigned his commission but retained the title of Captain for life.

Perhaps one of the most important and controversial inventions by Ericsson during this period in England was the steam locomotive "Novelty." In August of 1829, Ericsson read of the contest sponsored by the Liverpool and Manchester Railway for the most improved steam locomotion engine. The prize was five hundred pounds sterling. Ericsson and Braithwaite designed and built the "Novelty" in just seven weeks.

The contest was held on 6 October 1829 at Rainhill, England. Five entries were received, but the competition was soon reduced to the "Novelty," and the "Rocket," built by George Stephenson, a renowned British engineer. The contest ran in heats over successive days ending on 16 October 1829. On the first run the "Novelty" attained the speed of thirty miles per hour. A reporter for the *Mechanics Magazine* said, "The great lightness of the 'Novelty,' its great compactness, its beautiful workmanship, excited universal admiration."

On her second run, the "Novelty" covered a mile in fifty-three seconds, a land speed record. Stephenson's "Rocket" attained only twenty-four miles per hour. However, the hard luck of the young inventors was not to be broken. The "Novelty" had performed too well for the Directors of the Liverpool and Manchester Railway. In an effort to remove the "Novelty" from the competition, the Directors changed the rules in the middle of the competition, forcing Ericsson and Braithwaite to make hasty alterations that taxed the engine beyond its design limitations. The engine finally faltered. The Directors promptly disqualified the "Novelty" despite numerous complaints. Ericsson and Braithwaite had lost the much-needed prize money, but all of England had taken notice of John Ericsson, whose engine designed and built in barely seven weeks, had out-performed the one built by George Stephenson, England's foremost locomotive engineer. But an engineer must sell his inventions for a livelihood, and they were not successful at that. So virtually penniless and full of frustration, young Ericsson returned to his work.

Patent model of the first screw propeller designed by John Ericsson. A similar propellor was first used in the U.S. Navy on the U.S.S. Princeton *in 1843.——Courtesy U.S. Naval Academy Museum.*

Ericsson was aided in the development of the first screw propeller boat by an American, Francis B. Ogden, who was serving as United States Consul at Liverpool and was an inventor in his own right with an interest in steam locomotion. Ogden had heard of the two young inventors and offered them financial assistance. With Ogden's help, Ericsson and Braithwaite designed and built a tugboat which featured Ericsson's newly invented screw propeller.

The *Francis B. Ogden* was launched on the Thames River on 19 April 1837. She had a length of 45 feet, a beam of eight feet, a three-foot draft, and was driven by two propellers five feet three inches in diameter. An earlier loss of power through gear linkages was overcome by directly connecting the engine and propellers. On her first trial run the boat exceeded ten knots and was nicknamed the "Flying Devil" because of the way she looked in operation. "This miniature steamer had such power . . . that she towed a schooner of one hundred and forty tons burden at the rate of seven knots, and the American packet ship *Toronto* at the rate of more than four and a half knots against the tide."

Technical publications and newspapers in mid-1837 contained warm reports of the *Ogden,* but the British Admiralty, contrary to Ericsson's expectation, showed no interest in his latest invention. Undaunted by this apparent indifference, Ericsson invited the Lords of the Admiralty to be towed in their barge from Somerset House to Blackburn and back by his *Ogden.* The journey was made at better than ten knots, but the Lords were scarcely enthusiastic. Sir William Edward Perry, Comptroller of Steam Machinery for the Royal Navy thought that the vessel would have little practical use. In spite of this demonstration, the Surveyor of the Navy, Sir William Symonds added his judgment on this new means of propulsion; "Even if the propeller had the power of propelling a vessel, it would be found altogether useless in practice, because the power being applied to the stern, it would be absolutely impossible to make the vessel steer." Such ridicule and incomprehension disheartened Ericsson. The *Francis B. Ogden* had placed the two inventors deeply in debt, and to make matters worse, Ericsson's other debts were large enough to send him to debtor's prison. Fortunately, his brother Nils came to his rescue and secured his release from prison.

At this time, Ericsson met a person that would have the greatest single impact on his life. Captain Robert F. Stockton, USN, had heard of Ogden's investment in the experimental craft and wanted to study the possibility of such a vessel to be used as a carrier of goods on the Delaware and Raritan Canal. Stockton requested and received overseas assignment in England and arrived shortly after the *Ogden*'s failure to impress the Admiralty officials. A meeting was arranged between John Ericsson, Francis B. Ogden and Robert F. Stockton at the Trafalgar Tavern in London. A trial cruise was arranged on the *Ogden* and Stockton was much impressed. As a result, Stockton and Ogden provided a thousand pounds for the construction of two iron ships of similar design. "I do not want," said Captain Stockton, "the opinions of scientific men: what I have seen this day satisfies me." Once converted to full approval of Ericsson's ideas, Captain Stockton promised not only his personal support but strenuous efforts to interest the American government. It seemed as though John Ericsson had at last found an influential official from a country progressive enough to appreciate his work. This news could not have been better for Ericsson. He had just received another setback.

The Ericsson screw propeller had gone unchallenged until 1835 when Francis Petit Smith's propeller was first employed. Ericsson's propeller had been used commercially since 1831, but Ericsson had failed to secure a patent on it until 13 July 1836, six weeks after Smith's patent. The British patent office refused to recognize Ericsson as the sole inventor of the propeller, thus making Great Britain a sworn enemy of Ericsson's for the rest of his life. Ericsson gave up his efforts to promote his maritime ideas in England and prepared to depart for the United States, a country that appeared likely, if Captain Stockton was a representative American, to be more receptive to his ideas.

Before leaving Great Britain, however, Ericsson built a small steamer for Stockton. Naming it after him, it was intended for use on the canal Stockton owned in New Jersey. The *Stockton* was seventy feet long and operated with a crew of five. She crossed the Atlantic successfully and arrived in late May of 1838, an operating example of Ericsson's ability.

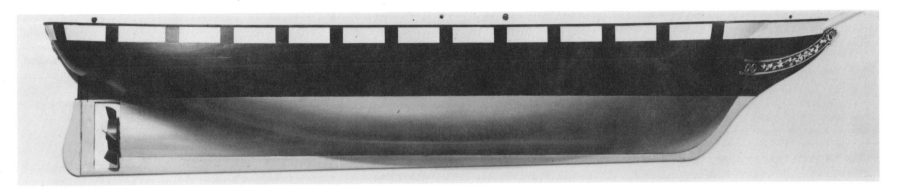

Half model of the U.S.S. Princeton, *the first ship in the U.S. Navy to utilize a screw propeller.* ——*Courtesy U.S. Naval Academy Museum.*

USS Princeton

Meanwhile, Stockton, who immediately saw the potential of such a vessel in the U.S. Navy, had returned to Washington to intercede for Ericsson in trying to convince the Navy Department of the worth of the Ericsson propeller. This proved to be no easy task. The United States had experimented with steam engineering as early as 1814 when Robert Fulton designed and built the *Demologos,* the world's first steam warship. She was propelled by a partially enclosed paddle wheel amidships on the centerline of the vessel. She attained speeds of six and a half knots, and with her battery of twenty 32-pounders and armor of nearly five feet of oak promised to serve well in harbor defense against a blockading British squadron. However, the death of Fulton on 24 February 1815 in New York City, slowed final commissioning so much that the *Demologos* was never tested in combat. She was placed in ordinary at the Brooklyn Navy Yard in June 1815, housed over and used as a receiving ship. On 4 June 1829 her magazine exploded, killing 30 men and totally destroying the ship. Although she marked a break with traditional design, the *Demologos,* untested as an effective warship, had little impact upon contemporary naval planning. England experimented rather more energetically with the possibilities of maritime steam plants, encouraged perhaps by the rising interest in steam locomotion ashore. By 1840 there were several paddle-wheel steamers in British service. The United States failed to follow up the tentative lead afforded by the *Demologos.* The *Fulton II,* built in the early 1830s, was more the result of political pressure, rather than a sincere spirit of technical curiosity on the part of the naval hierarchy.

On 3 March 1839, Congress appropriated funds for three new naval vessels. Captain M. C. Perry used his family influence to secure the construction of the USS *Mississippi,* a ten-gun paddle frigate that met with "great success as a cruising vessel; comfortable, fast, steady gun platform." The second, the USS *Missouri* was along similar lines. The third vessel was

not yet decided upon and Stockton went to work using his influence in Washington circles to try and secure the funds for the third vessel which he hoped would be designed by Ericsson.

A certain number of steam craft were used commercially, the Ericsson's *Stockton* among them, but technical limitations slowed any vigorous development of this new motive power. "The heavy, clumsy machinery of that day reduced both the space available in the hold, and the weight that might be allotted to the guns and the sail power, while the big paddle boxes encumbered the gun deck and impaired the sailing qualities of the ship. Without producing satisfactory speed, steam increased the risk of fire. Excessive coal consumption limited radius of action; and the vulnerability of their boilers, engines, and paddle boxes confined the steamers for the most part to service as tugs, transports, and dispatch vessels."

There existed, further, the conservatism somehow inherent in military bodies. Tradition and a certain unprogressive sentimentality blocked with considerable success the scattered suggestions that such realistic naval design, as envisioned by Ericsson, could surpass the sailing ship. Funnels and coal smoke had no more right aboard a properly-run man-of-war than the beating paddle wheels. "Sailors were not only incompetent to handle machinery, but considered it beneath their professional dignity to learn," refusing to dirty their hands in cinders and ashes. The resentment was even stronger among the officer corps of the day.

In October of 1839, Captain Stockton sent for Ericsson who was still in England to come to the United States prepared to present his "idea of constructing a formidable steam-ship-of-war, with all her machinery below the water-line, and capable of carrying such an armament as would make her invincible for defense and the most destructive of all known instruments of war." Ericsson drew plans for a 2,000 ton vessel. He boarded the *British Queen,* bound for America, on 3 November 1839, saying good-bye forever to Great Britain. Ericsson brought with him his "Ericsson gun" model and a working model of his new warship, which was named *Princeton,* in honor of Stockton's birthplace. Stockton immediately took Ericsson to the Brooklyn Navy Yard where he arranged for several introductions and demonstrations. Their arguments fell on deaf ears as Stockton was unable to convince the naval commissioners of the desirability of a vessel incorporating Ericsson's ideas. Angered by what he interpreted as a betrayal of Democratic principles under President Van Buren, Stockton took a two year leave of absence from the Navy and actively campaigned for the Whig political party. In the meantime John Ericsson was an unemployed engineer with only two models and some drawings.

Stockton's apparent abandonment left Ericsson in comparatively the same situation he had faced in 1826 in London when his model caloric engine failed in its demonstration. Now in 1839, he was again without friends, in a new country and living on borrowed money. However, Ericsson never lost his unflagging optimism and most important his faith in his own ability in moments of utter frustration and possible ruin. Characteristic of Ericsson was his reaction to the gloomy future in the new country. Staying in a shabby apartment in the Brooklyn Navy Yard, Ericsson decided it was time to change his surroundings and decided to move. With seven hundred and fifty dollars borrowed from Francis B. Ogden, he moved to the expensive Astor Hotel in New York City. When things were going poorly, he never hesitated to spend what money he had on a new suit of clothes or some other luxury. In fact, while in London his tailor bill was so high that it contributed to his arrest and imprisonment in the debtor's prison.

Not far from the Astor Hotel was the Phoenix Foundry, recently acquired by William Hogg and Cornelius H. DeLamater. Ericsson went to work for the Phoenix Foundry which proved to be good fortune for all three men. Their association was very profitable and a lifelong friendship developed between John Ericsson and "Harry" DeLamater.

In February of 1841, one month from the day of his inauguration, William Henry Harrison died of pneumonia, elevating John Tyler to the Presidency. President Tyler, in appreciation for his vigorous campaigning, offered Stockton the cabinet post of the Secretary of the Navy. Stockton, whether from expediency or righteousness, chose to decline the post and requested instead Tyler's support for the construction of the *Princeton.* Captain Stockton re-entered the Navy and once more took up the cause of convincing Congress that the Navy needed the screw propeller.

Abel P. Upshur assumed the post turned down by Stockton and helped secure permission to construct the Ericsson-designed warship. After months of neglect, John Ericsson received a message from Stockton in July of 1841 stating that Congress had given the go-ahead for his ship and asking him to come to Washington. Jubilant that his ideas had finally been recognized and accepted, Ericsson sped to the Capitol. Stockton wasted no time giving Ericsson directions; "You must at once prepare

drawings for a screw frigate of six hundred tons." Ericsson replied, "I know, I know, it is not a ship of the size we planned. I have remonstrated against it vigorously, I may tell you. I like yielding to no man, but I must be discreet and cannot presume the council further. Thus sir, we must do with what we have, and that quickly. Time is of the essence." Ericsson was not about to quibble, he had gotten permission to build his ship.

By means of continued persistence, then, Stockton had finally cleared the way for Ericsson to build something more formidable than a tugboat. Ericsson sketched preliminary plans immediately and agreed to draw up detailed plans of the ship and its steam plant. Within a week Ericsson provided the requested plans and the estimated cost of $75,000. Ericsson was drawing on all his experience and constrained frustrations as he hurriedly turned out the 124 drawings that were needed.

Actual construction of the *Princeton*'s hull took place at the Philadelphia Navy Yard while her engines were being built in New York. From the keel-laying in early 1842 until completion two years later, Ericsson divided time between the tasks of designing the ship and superintending her construction. The ship was launched in 1843, but a considerable length of time was spent in outfitting her. "Of the numerous screw steamers planned by Ericsson, the *Princeton* was the only one built under his superintendence. . . . He was extremely particular about the quality of both materials and workmanship." Throughout this period, while devoting his professional skill and a good deal of expense to his position as builder, Ericsson made no direct arrangement with either Stockton or the government for payment for his services or patented devices. "Stockton gave his assurance over and over again that if the vessel succeeded there would be no difficulty about pay." Ericsson desired only to see his brainchild become a reality. He cared nothing about monetary gain or his rights as inventor of the ship. He carried out the project without qualms, trusting the promise of appropriate financial adjustment. On 2 February 1844, Ericsson received payment of $1,150 from Stockton.

The *Princeton,* finally completed, was, in fact, a warship unlike any previously known. Her hull was of white oak. "The peculiarity of her model consisted in a very flat floor amidships, with great sharpness forward and excessive leanness aft." Carrying a maximum load in a hull 164 feet long with a 36½ foot beam, she drew better than nineteen feet. A power plant weighing 85 tons had been designed to turn Ericsson's screws. In comparison, the HMS *Arrogant,* built five years later, contained a steam system of comparable power but of much greater weight, and its volume of some 2800 cubic feet far exceeded the 1700 cubic feet occupied by the *Princeton*'s engine. On the *Princeton,* a six-bladed propeller was directly linked to the engine. Placed below the waterline, the *Princeton*'s engines were relatively invulnerable to enemy gunfire. The absence of the cumbersome paddle wheels and their trunks made increased space available for topside ordnance, favorably lowered the ship's center of gravity, and reduced underwater drag.

Steam remained, because of limited coal capacity, an auxiliary power source; the *Princeton* was rigged for sail. Although soft coal was normally used in commercial steam craft, she burned anthracite, thereby eliminating the tell-tale plume of black smoke. Fan blowers, located in the bilges, helped to produce better combustion and hotter furnace temperatures, a development that made possible rapid warming up of the plant, obviously advantageous on a man-of-war. Ericsson replaced the previous smokestack with a telescoping funnel. This removed one target for enemy gunfire, and the blowers were capable of replacing the normal stack draft. Further, the stack, ordinarily a somewhat ungainly structure, could be gotten entirely out of the way while the ship was under sail. Stockton pointed out in a letter to the Secretary of the Navy that the *Princeton* could attack "making no noise, smoke or agitation of the water (and, if she chooses, showing no sail)."

In armament the *Princeton* likewise was a progressive design, her twelve 42-pound carronades were of conventional manufacture, but the experimental main battery consisted of two 12-inch guns capable of firing balls of 220 pounds. Both were guns "of greater caliber than had previously been known in naval history." One of them, later named the "Oregon," had been designed and forged by Ericsson in England and subsequently brought to the United States. Finding the wrought-iron transversely weak, Ericsson devised the idea of shrinking iron hoops onto the breech as a safety measure. Captain Stockton was by this time becoming rather convinced of his own technical prowess, and he undertook the construction of a similar gun, "forged at Hamersely Forge, and bored and finished under Ericsson's directions." This was the ill-fated "Peacemaker." "It was of the same caliber as the imported gun, . . . but a foot more in diameter at the breech, and much heavier. . . . Great confidence was placed in its strength because of the supposed superiority of American iron." These guns produced results without precedent in naval gunnery; they penetrated 57 inches of oak timber and four inches of wrought iron, making the *Princeton* the most formidable warship of the day.

Even before being outfitted with her guns, the *Princeton* was taken on trial runs. Her performance equalled Stockton's most enthusiastic claims. "Wherever she appeared, immense crowds gathered to witness her evolutions and inspect her machinery." Perhaps no clearer indication of the ship's capabilities exist than the description of her race of 19 October 1843, with the highly publicized *Great Western:*

> The Battery and the piers were thronged with an expecting multitude. At her appointed hour the *Great Western* came plowing her way down the East River, under circumstances, which manifested more than ordinary effort. She was enveloped in clouds of steam, and of dense black smoke; her paddle wheels were revolving with unusual velocity, leaving a white wake behind her, that seemed to cover half the river with foam; and with her sails all set, she was evidently prepared to do her best in the anticipated race. As she passed the Battery she was greeted with three hearty cheers. . . .

> She had left Castle Garden about a quarter of a mile behind her, when a fine model of a sailing ship, frigate-like, appeared gliding gracefully down the East River, against the tide, without a breath of smoke or steam to obscure her path—with no paddle wheels or smoke-pipe visible—propelled by a noiseless and unseen agency, without a rag of canvas on her lithe and beautiful spars—but at a speed which soon convinced the assembled thousands that she would successfully dispute the palm with the gallant vessel, celebrated throughout the world, and everywhere admitted to be the queen of the seas. Such is the march of improvement in the arts. The newcomer was the United States War Steamer *Princeton.* The agent by which she was moved was Ericsson's propeller. She soon reached the *Great Western,* went round her, and passed her a second time before they had reached their point of separation. In a moment, practical men began to speak lightly of their hitherto favorite paddle wheel, and the propeller that they had shrugged their shoulders at, and amused themselves with for some years of doubtful experiment rose into altogether unexpected favor.

On 5 February 1844, Stockton, in command of the ship at Philadelphia, sent a description to Secretary of the Navy Henshaw, concluding that, because of improvement embodied in the *Princeton,* "the ocean may again become a neutral ground, and the rights of the smallest as well as the greatest nations may once more be respected."

With the process of equipping and arming finally at an end, Stockton proudly took the *Princeton* to Washington for display to her most critical audience. Stockton's dual position of promoter and captain was sufficient to make him something of a hero in the eyes of press and public, and he was not a man to reject praise. There is no evidence to suggest that Stockton made an effort to secure due recognition for Ericsson. The members of the House of Representatives were taken for a voyage down the Potomac on 20 February during which the Congressmen were entertained with a feast and gunfiring.

Such was the success of this first cruise, in fact, that a second was arranged for 28 February. President Tyler, his Cabinet, and various lesser notables were aboard for an outing similar to that of the previous week. "The day was spent in feasting, romping, dancing, and singing, with music that was almost unceasing, and mirth that was infectious and uncontrollable. During the passage down, one of her large guns . . . was frequently fired, to the enjoyment of all on board." Late in the afternoon as the *Princeton* once again headed upstream for Washington, the new Secretary of the Navy, Thomas W. Gilmer, suggested a final firing of the main battery. Captain Stockton went on deck to command the crew of his "Peacemaker," and a group of yet-curious passengers clustered about the big gun. As the powder charge ignited, the gun burst at its breech, killing Secretary of State Upshur; Secretary of the Navy Gilmer; Captain Kennon, Chief of the Bureau of Construction and Equipment; Virgil Maxey, a former diplomat; a Colonel Gardiner of New York; and one of Tyler's black servants. Stockton, members of the gun crew, and some of the other spectators were injured by fragments of the gun or by the powder flames.

Newspapers of the time announced the explosion with the proper amount of lurid description and consternation. Beneath a headline "MOST AWFUL AND MOST LAMENTABLE CATASTROPHE," for example, the *National Intelligencer* of Washington stated the following day, "In the whole course of our lives it has never fallen our lot to announce to our readers a more shocking calamity." Both military services ordered an appropriate display of honors for the dead. On 2 March funeral services were held at the White House.

During the period of building and pre-explosion displays, Stockton's once extreme enthusiasm for "the one man he had hunted the world over to find, who could build a complete ship" had perceptibly cooled. It had been agreed that Ericsson would accompany the *Princeton* to Washington. "He proceeded accordingly to the foot of Wall Street at the appointed time, expecting to be taken aboard there, but the vessel carrying his fortunes, not less than those of Stockton, steamed by without stopping for him." Ericsson became increasingly annoyed by these slights.

Investigation of the explosion quickly followed the accident. Faced with the prospect of a court of inquiry, Captain Stockton called upon Ericsson to testify in his support in Washington. "If Stockton was not disposed to share the credit of his success with him, he was quite ready to give him full measure of responsibility for failure." Ericsson replied that Stockton had the gun's plans and knowledge of its operation on February 28 in his possession; Ericsson could personally add nothing. Ericsson was a man of deep sensitivity and a rather quick temper and the snubs by Stockton and the lack of proper payment for his services would seem sufficient to justify his behavior. Captain Stockton, accustomed to the obedience expected by a man of power, was greatly angered by this refusal.

The court of inquiry dismissed the incident as an accident, but Stockton remained bitter toward Ericsson. In March when Ericsson submitted a bill for $15,080 for his services and patents, Stockton advised the Secretary, "I cannot approve of his bill; it is direct violation of our agreement as far as it is to be considered a legal claim upon the Department." From this time on Ericsson was called "a mechanic of some skill" or an "ingenious but presumptuous mechanic." The degree of Stockton's responsibility for the non-payment of Ericsson's claim and his motivation may be judged from his remark; "If Ericsson had not been a damned coward, there would have been no trouble about his getting his money for the vessel." Contention over the unpaid claim continued. In 1857 the United States Court of Claims approved a payment of $13,930, but although Congress recognized the obligation, no payment was ever made.

The *Princeton* remained in service until 1847, performing well during the Mexican War, and was subsequently sent to the Mediterranean. Her influence upon European naval thinking was heavy; both the British and French designed steamers along similar lines. In 1848 she was condemned as rotten and broken up at the Boston Navy Yard.

The *Princeton* was a significant vessel in terms of naval technical evolution. She was the first warship of any Navy to use an underwater screw propeller rather than paddle wheels. The *Princeton*'s performance was sufficient to demonstrate the screw's superiority for new construction, however, the explosion of the "Peacemaker" had marred her record, somehow overshadowing her numerous other contributions to the development of steam engineering. The explosion, subsequent investigation and harsh treatment by the press left a scar on John Ericsson which he would never forget. He would be hesitant to present his ideas before Washington and the Navy Department again.

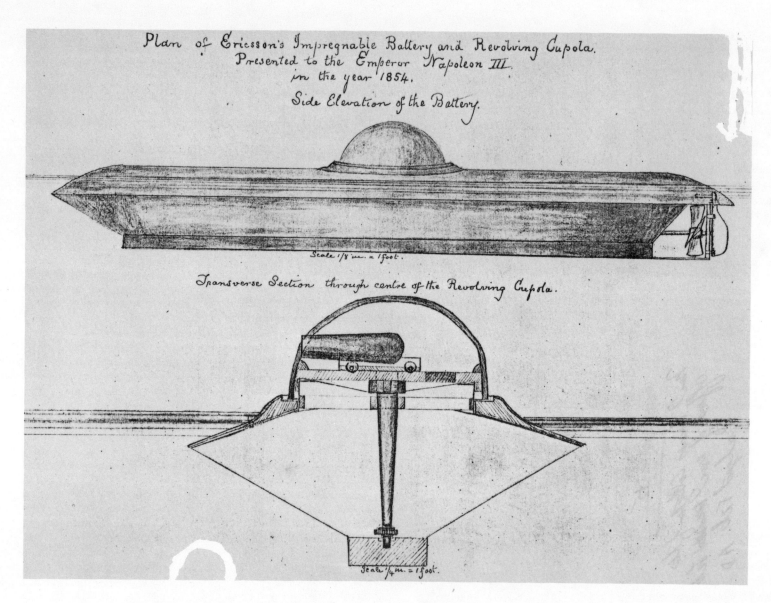

Ericsson's proposal to Napoleon III for an ironclad warship (1854). This design shows the basic characteristics of the "Monitor concept" evolving in the inventor's mind. ——*Courtesy U.S. National Archives.*

2

GENESIS OF THE MONITOR CONCEPT

In the decade following the disaster aboard the *Princeton,* Ericsson resigned himself to working for Harry DeLameter at the Phoenix Foundry in New York designing steam engines for use on a wide variety of ships. He could not, however, put completely aside his ideas on a new theory of naval warfare; what Ericsson referred to as his system of "sub-aquatic warfare" which had been germinating in his mind since 1826. If Ericsson cannot be credited as the originator of many of these concepts and developments, he most certainly can be said to be a forerunner in their particular application in a period of rapidly expanding technology both in the United States and abroad.

The monitor concept for his system of "sub-aquatic warfare" as he called it was in modern terminology a semi-submersible warship of shallow draft having a minimum profile for the enemy to aim at. He placed the guns on a turntable creating a revolving armored cupola or gun turret which could be trained in any direction. He placed the turret on a gun platform or hull which provided stability for the guns and afforded protection for the engines, propeller, magazines and other vital spaces below the waterline. He fully intended to have the decks awash in any type of sea other than a flat calm. The idea of the revolving gun turret, as Ericsson would be the first to say, was nothing new to warfare as were many of his other ideas. However, his application of these various principles to a single concept did create a novel vessel singularly unique in contemporary naval architecture giving credence to the adage that "the whole is greater than the sum of the parts".

In 1846, the U. S. Congress sent out a circular letter to several engineers in an effort to find out "the practicability on rendering an iron vessel shot-proof". Ericsson submitted plans for a partially submerged iron warship whose description bears strong resemblance to his later "impregnable battery"—the *Monitor.* In fact, there is strong evidence to suggest a gradual evolution and refinement of this concept. The designs he submitted in 1846 are filed as *Report No. 681, H.R. 29th Congress.* When the Crimean War erupted in Europe, Ericsson was anxious to humiliate Russia, an ancient foe of his native Sweden, and sent a proposal to Napoleon III in 1854 to construct a warship along the lines of the monitor concept having a domed cupola and more conventional ship hull. The usual practice when inventors sent proposals to the Emperor was for one of his aides to transmit the papers to the Ministry concerned, which then reported its opinion. An intensive search has failed to reveal any reference to this proposal of Ericsson's in the archives of the French Ministry of Marine. However, Cornelius Bushnell states in his memoirs that Ericsson had shown him the gold medal and a letter of appreciation from Napoleon III when he visited his home in the fall of 1861.

Further evidence of the evolution of the monitor concept is found in the MacCord Collection of Ericsson drawings at the Stevens Institute of Technology. This design was for a human-propelled gunboat with a later version having a small steam auxiliary titled "Swedish gunboat" by the draftsman. It has an armored raft with minimum freeboard and armored semi-cupola. The guns were fixed in relation to the ship's centerline, the train of fire being controlled by the "bow thruster" located in the forward section of the ship. In general concept, shape, and layout of the ship this undated early design of Ericsson's was, in essence, an ironclad monitor vessel.

The development of ironclads was not an interest solely of the United States, for as early as 1819 with the development of the shell gun by General Henri-Joseph Paixhans of France the race between armor and shell had begun. Paixhans developed a system of firing an explosive shell on a flat trajectory that would wreak havoc on the heaviest wooden ships afloat. Both France and England experimented with the new guns and protected warships until the Crimean War when the Turkish fleet at Sinope

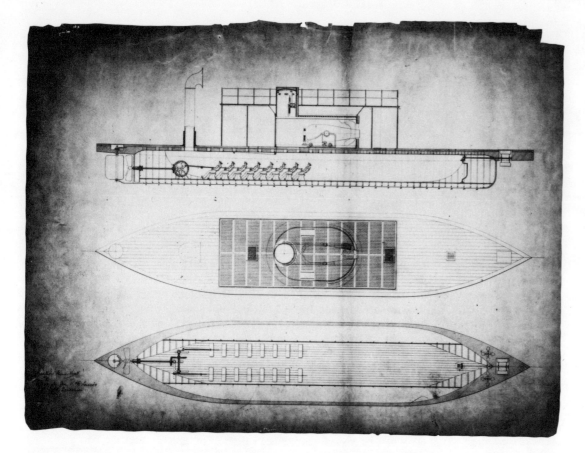

A Swedish gunboat designed by Ericsson that was hand-powered by a crew of men working on connecting rods fastened to a drive wheel. The turret was fixed with the centerline of the ship. The train of the gun was controlled by moving the bow of the ship with a bow thruster.
——Courtesy Stevens Institute of Technology.

was annihilated on 30 November 1853 by the heavy-shell guns of a Russian fleet, focusing world attention on the power of the new shell guns. Consequently, both France and Great Britain embarked on an ambitious ironclad program with France building *La Gloire* and others less notable and Great Britain building the *Warrior* and several others. Until, ultimately at the time of the battle at Hampton Roads, there were more than forty seagoing ironclads, thirty armored coast-defense vessels, and eighteen partially protected gunboats already built, building or authorized in Europe.

Watching these developments and pushing for an ironclad policy of his own was Senator Stephen R. Mallory, Chairman of the Naval Committee in the U. S. Senate, who would later become Secretary of the Navy for the Confederacy and be responsible for the early construction of ironclads in the South.

The only ironclad project in the United States while Europe was so busy building ships of iron was the ill-fated *Steven's Battery* which was contracted to the founder of Stevens Institute of Technology in 1843 as a result of the war scare of 1841–42 with Great Britain. Intended primarily for coastal defense and the protection of New York harbor the project was plagued with under-estimates and cost over-runs with the size and design being changed many times before finally being broken up, and sold as scrap in 1881 for lack of funds to complete her.

Ericsson during this relatively quiet period in the 1850's was working on what he felt was his greatest gift to mankind, his caloric engine. He had convinced a group of financiers of the desirability of a new type of commercial ship propelled by this economical caloric engine. His concept was to use hot air rather than hot steam as the expansive force in the cylinders, with an arrangement for reusing the heat wasted in the exhaust of a steam engine. Ericsson conceived of a ship to be used as a test platform for his theories on the adaptability of the caloric engine for propulsion. The caloric would be smaller, lighter, and more economical than the conventional steam engine. His new ship, the *Ericsson* was 260 feet long and had a 40-foot beam. Of her $500,000 cost, $130,000 went into the engines. On 11 February 1853 prominent engineers, merchants and editors were invited to inspect the new 2,200-ton ship. On a trial run the *Ericsson* attained just under ten knots and all aboard were amazed at the clean, quiet, and cool engineering spaces. Ericsson, with pride, showed members of the inspecting party his caloric engine with its huge cylinders moving slowly up and down vertically in their casing. While explaining the engines operations, Ericsson nimbly mounted one of the huge pistons and invited the press to do likewise, assuring them it was entirely safe. Many members climbed on for the ride, "passing up and down with the motion of the pistons and finding the temperature . . . cool and parlor-like." "The sensation of a ride upon a piston of a first class marine engine without danger to life and property was certainly novel and attractive." However, in a speed trial, the *Ericsson* could not match the 16 knots of a conventionally steam-powered competitor, but she was more economical—the *Ericsson* had consumed only six tons of coal in 24 hours compared to fifty-eight tons in the same period by the competition. Horace Greely proclaimed in his newspaper that, "the age of steam is closed, the age of caloric opens. Fulton and Watt belong to the past. Ericsson is the great mechanical genius of the present and future."

Ericsson experimented with several modifications to get more work out of his engines but to no avail and so just as rapidly as the age of caloric opened, it ended. Some critics clamored that Ericsson was trying to achieve perpetual motion and in an age that worshiped speed instead of economy, the *Ericsson* was a poor investment. Operating at a temperature of 444 degrees Fahrenheit, the engine destroyed its lubricants in a manner that contemporary technology could not correct. The final blow came in an eerie foreshadowing of what was to come when the *Ericsson* foundered off Sandy Hook in a sudden gale with gusts up to eighty miles an hour. The subsequent salvage operations were successful, but the cost and labor for reconditioning her experimental engines proved too costly for her financiers who wanted a return on their investment, so they converted her to conventional steam.

Having incurred a substantial debt, Ericsson was forced to return to less enlightened, though more profitable work at the Phoenix Foundry. Even though forced to abandon it, he would always refer to his caloric engine as his single most notable contribution to mankind and he would later affectionately remark about his namesake; "There was more engineering in that ship than in ten monitors—it was simply a mechanical marvel."

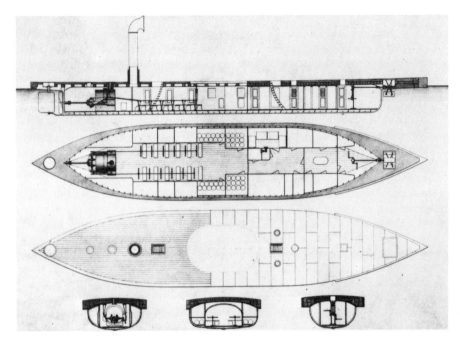

A Swedish gunboat equipped with a steam auxiliary designed by John Ericsson. ——Courtesy Stevens Institute of Technology.

The layout of this Swedish gunboat designed by Ericsson was very similar to that of the Monitor. *This drawing shows the location of the magazine, shell room, and various staterooms, with all captions in Swedish. ——Courtesy Stevens Institute of Technology.*

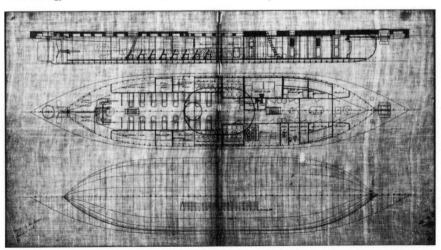

When Lincoln took his oath of office on 14 March 1861, the nation waited anxiously as the words from his inauguration address echoed across the land.

"In your hands, my dissatisfied fellow-countrymen, and not in mine, is the momentous issue of civil war. The government will not assail you. You can have no conflict without being yourselves the aggressors."

For months, tension had run high as extremists from both North and South had played their firebrand game of state politics, pushing the country to the brink of civil war. Reason yielded to incensed emotions as many decided that compromise was no longer possible. The seeds of the conflict had been sown long before Lincoln took office and yet with him alone rested the prospects of the grim harvest.

Even before Lincoln assumed office, seven states had already seceeded from the Union and consequently federal buildings, forts, and arsenals in the rebellious states were being seized daily. Many called for federal retaliation; Lincoln showed restraint and understanding, knowing full well that those states as yet undecided were watching his every move. Confidential messages and letters immediately became known to the secessionists because of spies and unfaithful couriers. Southern sympathizers in the Federal government had for months been secretly abetting the Southern cause by allowing agents to purchase military supplies from Northern manufacturers and to secretly stockpile war materials. Thus in addition to being swamped with the normal number of people with disputable ability seeking political appointments, Lincoln was surrounded by those determined to destroy the Union. In this atmosphere of uncertainty and mistrust, Lincoln was forced to form his government and establish policy.

Lincoln's cabinet had factions of extreme political views, ranging from Secretary of State William H. Seward's conservatism to Secretary of the Treasury Salmon P. Chase's radical abolitionism. Lincoln had been saddled with these choices out of political necessity at the nominating convention. The cabinet had been selected with an eye toward conciliating the South and when the pressure of those first few weeks of Lincoln's presidency was brought to bear, no agreement on any policy could be reached. As a result Lincoln had to stand largely by his own judgment.

Being confronted with the complete disability of the federal bureaucracy due to the resignations of many important figures, Lincoln filled the vacancies as best he could, overlooking many deficiencies if the person held promise of functioning properly. In many departments the resignations elevated those of little experience to positions of responsibility. In the Bureau of Ordnance and Hydrography every person save a draftsman and the messenger resigned at the outbreak of the war.

Of particular concern to Lincoln and his Cabinet was the loyalty of those in the Army and Navy. In the gathering storm, they more than any other would determine the outcome. Southern politicians in Congress had maneuvered many officers sympathetic to their cause to command important forts, vessels, or arsenals in the South so that only a demand for a surrender was sufficient to secure it. Gradually, Lincoln's policy of conciliation and restraint hardened and the South learned that they had to deal with a persistent administrator determined to save the Union.

Lt. Colonel Gardner had been in command at Charleston Harbor, South Carolina and reported the preparations for war by the secessionists as early as November, 1860. He applied to Washington for reinforcements, and at the request of Southern members of Congress, the then Secretary of War, a native of Virginia, relieved Gardner of his command and appointed Major Robert Anderson to command at Charleston believing that this officer's Kentucky origin would make him sympathetic to the South.

In this they were mistaken because Major Anderson would remain loyal to his oath if he received his government's support. Abandoning Fort Moultrie on the shore of Charleston Harbor as untenable, Anderson deceptively, under the watchful eyes of the Confederates, moved his entire command of sixty-one artillerymen, thirteen musicians, and eight officers to Fort Sumter and secretly transported all their supplies to the fort in the middle of Charleston Harbor. Learning that their scheme had failed, the Confederates under the command of General Beauregard, who had instructed Anderson at West Point, made preparations to reduce the fort. Anderson waited, he would not fire the first shot. He had been assured by Lincoln that he had his support, appeasement had ended.

Similarly at Fort Pickens in Florida Captain Adams was operating under an agreement negotiated by the Buchanan administration by which the federal government would not reinforce the Fort provided the Confederates did not attack it. Lincoln and Welles decided to instruct Adams to disregard the agreement, to reinforce at once, and to hold the Fort. The courier that brought the request for instructions from Florida could not return the reply as he was resigning from the Navy. He had been loyal enough to deliver the message and his wish was granted. Lieutenant John L. Worden whose loyalty was certain was selected to memorize and deliver the reply. Worden did this and Fort Pickens was reinforced the night of 12 April. On his return north, Worden took the same route and was captured and put into prison, but later released in an exchange of prisoners.

Meanwhile in Charleston, Major Anderson had been denied access to the markets of the city and food was in short supply inside the Fort as Charlestonians grew more antagonistic.

On 6 April, Lincoln sent a dispatch to the governor of South Carolina, stating in part: "I am directed . . . to notify you to expect an attempt will be made to supply Fort Sumter with provisions only, and that, if such attempt be not resisted, no effort to throw in men, arms, or ammunition, will be made, without further notice, or in case of an attack upon the Fort."

Jefferson Davis immediately called an emergency meeting in Montgomery. The Confederate Secretary of State, Robert Tombs prophetically spoke at this session: "The firing on that fort will inaugurate a civil war greater than any the world has yet seen . . . you will wantonly strike a hornet's nest which extends from mountains to ocean; legions, now quiet, will swarm out and sting us to death. . . ." His words went unheeded. The shouts of excited men had drowned out the veneration for reason, and Jefferson Davis gave the order to attack the Fort.

Luckily for Major Anderson and his small garrison, a relief expedition had been organized under Captain Gustavus Fox, the Assistant Secretary of the Navy. When the shells exploded over Fort Sumter on 12 April 1861, the ships that would rescue Anderson were a day away. The small garrison left after a gallant defense on 13 April; witnessing the gala jubilation of the city of Charleston as the Southern banner was raised above the Fort. When the relief expedition returned to New York harbor they received a heroes welcome, but Major Anderson had serious news of particular note to the Navy Department. The Confederates in Charleston had used a strange floating battery with sloping sides plated over with iron on which the 32-pound guns of the Fort had no effect.

The situation rapidly deteriorated. On 14 April, Lincoln issued a proclamation for 75,000 volunteers to join the Army. On 17 April, Virginia seceded from the Union. The status of Maryland was questionable. Lincoln expected a small band of rebels to take the capitol at any moment. What few troops were available barricaded the Capital and other public buildings. On 19 April a mob attacked the 6th Massachusetts volunteers in Baltimore and Lincoln issued the hollow proclamation of the blockade of the Gulf States in answer to Jeff Davis' "letters of marque" authorizing commerce raiders.

To fulfill Lincoln's proclamation, Secretary of the Navy Gideon Welles had only twenty-three steam men-of-war in a neglected fleet of seventy-six vessels, of which only forty-two were in commission and those scattered in two oceans. He was expected to blockade 185 registered harbors along almost 2,500 miles of shoreline. In addition to this serious material shortage, in order to commission the thirty-four vessels that were inactive, Welles had only 207 seamen in the ports and receiving ships of the Atlantic seaboard.

The situation in the Army was not much better. The strength of the Regular Army had dwindled to a mere 16,400 men, mostly scattered on the Indian frontier. These professionals would form the cadre for both armies as the ranks swelled with recruits answering the call to arms.

Lincoln, soon to have an army, needed a general and a special courier was sent to Robert E. Lee, a professional soldier of 36 years, offering him command of the Union Army. Lee declined stating that he could never draw his sword against his native state. General Scott told Lincoln that he had lost a commander worth 50,000 men.

Fall of Gosport Navy Yard

The ninety-acre Gosport Navy Yard at Norfolk, Virginia was the largest in the United States. It included repair facilities, storage warehouses and the first and largest stone drydock in the country.

In the spring of 1861, Commodore Charles S. McCauley, commanding the Navy Yard, was in the unenviable position of having to defend the yard, knowing that any action on his part might lead to war. He was warned by the Navy Department not to take any steps to raise needless alarm in the populace. The result was that few preparations were made to prepare the yard for war. The situation gradually worsened as Virginia edged toward secession.

When Fort Sumter was fired upon, Secretary of the Navy Gideon Welles realized the immense importance of the supplies, ammunition, guns and shipping at Norfolk to the Southern cause. Perhaps the greatest prize was the steam frigate *Merrimack* which was at the yard for overhaul. Welles immediately dispatched Engineer-in-Chief Benjamin Isherwood to Norfolk to get the *Merrimack*'s old engines working and Commander James Alden to take her to sea. As they hurriedly worked to re-assemble the engines and to gather a skeleton crew, the local Confederate commander feinted a build-up of soldiers and artillery to storm the yard. McCauley ordered work stopped so as not to force a confrontation. He argued that he had only sixty Marines and two dozen watchmen to oppose the rumored five thousand Confederates.

Isherwood and Alden, realizing that appeasement would no longer satisfy the rebel leaders as their demands for surrender grew louder each day, returned to Washington on 19 April to report to Secretary of the Navy Welles, who with the responsibility of a naval blockade just set in his lap, ordered Commodore Hiram Paulding to relieve McCauley and try to salvage the situation. With the eight-gun Steamer *Pawnee* and one hundred Marines, Paulding set out for Hampton Roads to tow the *Merrimack* to safety and to destroy what could not be carried out.

Paulding arrived in Norfolk after a stop at Fort Monroe to embark 350 infantrymen shortly after eight PM on 20 April. He was a day late. At noon, McCauley had ordered the yard destroyed. All ships, excepting the *Cumberland* were scuttled. Men were scattering combustibles, preparing to set the yard afire.

Paulding took command and set out to complete the destruction, despite an angry mob of concerned citizens who were worried about their homes which surrounded the Yard.

Through the night soldiers and Marines loaded the *Cumberland* with all the powder and ordnance she could carry. One stray shot would have scattered her all over Norfolk.

About 2 PM of 21 April the Marine barracks was set ablaze by accident. Sensing that the mob outside the gates might storm the yard Paulding decided that nothing further could be accomplished and embarked

The Confederate floating battery used in the bombardment of Fort Sumter. This was the first use of armor plating afloat during the Civil War. The Union guns were ineffective against this battery.

The Gosport Navy Yard was burned by Union forces on 20 April 1861. The hulk of the USS Merrimack was salvaged by the Confederates and rebuilt as the CSS Virginia.

his force aboard the *Cumberland*. At 4:20 A.M. a signal flare was seen from the yard by the citizens of Norfolk and all knew that the Union was retiring.

Hurriedly, runners ignited the buildings and powder trains. Commodore John Rodgers and Captain H. G. Wright were assigned to blow up the drydock, but their effort failed, as a sympathetic Union petty officer interrupted the powder train to save the nearby homes of his friends from destruction.

In the morning, the Confederates occupied the yard which was only partially destroyed. They put out many of the fires. The rebels held the machine shops, vast amounts of supplies and munitions and some 1200 heavy guns, including 300 of the modern Dahlgrens. In addition, they had Drydock No. 1 which could accommodate the largest ships in the fleet. They took a $10,000,000 establishment without firing a shot. The North soon felt the consequences of such a defeat as Stephen R. Mallory, the Chairman of the U. S. Senate's committee on Naval Affairs, took office as the Confederate Secretary of the Navy.

Mallory had kept abreast of the developments of ironclad ships in Europe and was convinced that a well armored fighting ship could take on any ship of the period. He soon began to exploit the new facilities. He ordered new machinery from Europe and contracted with the Baker Wrecking Company to raise the *Merrimack* and other hulks. In a letter dated May 10, 1861, Mallory wrote: "I regard the possession of an iron-armored ship as a matter of first necessity. Such a vessel at this time could traverse the entire coast of the United States, prevent all blockades, and encounter, with a fair prospect of success, their entire Navy . . . inequality of numbers may be compensated by invulnerability . . ."

The same day the Confederate Congress appropriated $2,000,000 to build ironclads. In May of 1861 the *Merrimack* was raised and towed to Drydock No. 1. She was in no worse shape than before the fire. Lt. John N. Brooke, CSN and Naval Constructor John L. Porter inspected her and determined that she was suitable for conversion to an ironclad. It was thought that the economy of conversion of an already existing warship instead of building from the keel up warranted such an undertaking. It is ironic that the deep draft of the *Merrimack* is what finally condemned the ship to destruction by her own crew.

By the end of June, Mallory had approved the final plans drawn by Porter. However, from the beginning the work was plagued by the lack of material in the industrial poor South.

Rumors were circulated in Norfolk which gradually drifted north to Washington that the salvaged hulk was worthless and thus began one of the most successful deceptions in the war, as the South shrouded the work on the ironclad in secrecy.

The ruins of the Navy Yard after the Union withdrawal. Much useful war material fell into Confederate hands. ——*Courtesy U.S. National Archives.*

Ericsson worked long into the night with his chief draftsman, Charles W. MacCord, making the drawings necessary for the Monitor. MacCord was later a professor at Stevens Institute of Technology and saved the only original Monitor drawings known to exist.

3

DESIGN & CONSTRUCTION

In July, 1861, the tempo of the war increased. Opposing armies met at Manassas, Virginia, in the Battle of Bull Run. All hopes of a short conflict faded at Manassas. What had begun as a glorious march of Union forces to Richmond turned into a panic-driven flight back to Washington.

Lincoln had to find an officer capable of leading the Army of the Potomac. A general strategy would have to be developed to guide the ensuing campaigns. The Union's general strategy was coined by Winfield Scott, a veteran of the Mexican War. Called the Anaconda Policy, it outlined the gradual strangulation of the industrial-poor South by cutting off commerce and ultimately by dividing and conquering the southern states. This strategy required the establishment and maintenance of a naval blockade, and the preclusion of foreign intervention, especially by Great Britain. A naval blockade proclaimed by the President was held by the pro-Southern press to be a violation of international law. Future events would further aggravate that sentiment.

The burden of much of the success of the plan fell on Secretary of the Navy Gideon Welles, who was fast commissioning every available coastal ship for blockade duty. Again, time was an essential factor. The Secretary of the Confederate States Navy, Stephen R. Mallory, was convinced of the invulnerability of iron warships against the Union Navy's aging wooden fleet; he hurriedly acquired materials needed to construct a fleet of iron ships.

Gideon Welles soon learned by reports from Norfolk that the Confederates had raised the hulk of the USS *Merrimack*, had floated it into the still operational Drydock Number 1, and were busy converting it into an ironclad. Rumors of the power and might of the new warship spread rapidly, creating panic. All northern ports, commerce, ships, even the capitol in Washington itself, would be in range of the ironclad's batteries. She could roam the eastern seaboard, undeterred by the wooden ships of the Union fleet. As concern mounted, there was increasing pressure on Congress and the Navy to meet the new menace from the south.

The naval hierarchy had for years scoffed at the idea of building a warship of iron, to be propelled only by steam, as something ungainly, unmaneuverable, and unreliable. The few benefits of such a ship would not justify its great cost. Experts were sure that a well-handled ship of the line carrying fifty or more guns would be more than a match for anything the South could produce. Captain A. A. Harwood, Chief of the Bureau of Ordnance and Hydrography, expressed the preference for the type of ships that remained unchanged since the days of Nelson: ". . . it would be hazardous to rely upon new models of vessels, however plausible, at a critical time and intend to effect decisive results . . . The experience of the Navy proves beyond a doubt that whenever the construction of vessels of war have been entrusted to persons not ultimately versed in the requirements of a man-of-war, however able in other respects, the result has been uniformly a failure in some vital point . . ."

This thinking pervaded the Bureau of Construction and Repair, even as more than a hundred proposals for ironclads and other warships of new designs flooded into the bureau prior to March 1862. The new designs included warships protected by chain, iron plate, and even natural rubber. The conservative attitude of the Navy Department was revealed in the fact that the first ironclads were constructed on the Western Rivers, outside the jurisdiction of the department, before any "ironclad policy" had been stated in Washington. The field commanders, recognizing the value and operational capabilities of ironclads, were not about to await official approval before including them in their planning.

On 19 July 1861, Senator Grimes of Iowa introduced a bill into Congress directing the Secretary of the Navy to appoint a board of three naval officers to investigate plans for ironclad warships and to appropriate $1.5 million for the construction of one or more such ships if the board reported favorably on them.

The bill passed, and on 7 August 1861, Secretary Welles advertised in the major newspapers of the north for proposals to construct an ironclad battery under the following terms:

> . . . parties who are able to execute work of this kind, and who are engaged in it, of which they will furnish evidence with their offer, for the construction of one or more iron-clad steam vessels of war, either of iron or of wood and iron combined, for sea or river service, to be not less than ten nor over sixteen feet draught of water; to carry an armament of from eighty to one hundred and twenty tons weight, with provisions and stores for from one hundred and sixty five to three hundred persons, according to armament, for sixty days, with coal for eight days. The smaller draughts of water, compatible with other requisites, will be preferred. The vessel to be rigged with two masts, with wire rope standing rigging, to navigate at sea.
>
> A general description and drawings of the vessel, armor and machinery, such as the work can be executed from, will be required.
>
> The offer must state the cost and the time for completing the whole, exclusive of armament and stores of all kinds, the rate of speed proposed, and must be accompanied by a guarantee for the proper execution of the contract, if awarded.
>
> Persons who intend to offer are requested to inform the department of their intention before the 15th of August, instant, and to have their propositions presented within twenty-five days from this date.

Who could possibly design such an unconventional ship in so short a time? Ericsson refused to deal with the Navy Department, but in a letter offered his services directly to the President. In the flood of mail to the chief executive it went unheeded. The North's efforts to build an ironclad all hinged upon one man not officially connected with the government, Cornelius S. Bushnell, an old friend of Gideon Welles from New Haven, Connecticut.

Bushnell was a successful businessman, with many influential friends both inside and outside of government. It was primarily for this reason that Welles sought him out in July, 1861, at Willard's Hotel in Washington. Welles handed Bushnell a draft of the ironclad bill and asked him to use his influence to assure its passage. When the bill passed, Bushnell, a smart businessman and financier, saw the opportunity to benefit from government contracts and promoted a design by Samuel H. Pook for an ironclad named *Galena*.

To handle the proposals for the new construction, Secretary Welles, on 8 August 1861, appointed Commodore Joseph Smith, Chief of the Bureau of Yards and Docks, to be senior officer of the Ironclad Board, with Commodore Hiram Paulding and Commander John Dahlgren as his board members. At Dahlgren's own request, he was relieved of that duty a short time later and Commander Charles H. Davis was appointed in his place. It was then that the story of the *Monitor* began.

Bushnell presented the *Galena* design to the board and worked closely with Welles to secure approval for its construction. With no engineering background, he was unable to convince the Board that the design could carry the heavy iron bars proposed in addition to the armament. Seeking assistance on that point, Bushnell was advised by C. H. DeLameter of New York to consult with John Ericsson. The *Galena* was a 738-ton ship of conventional lines, protected by iron bars attached to her sides. She carried a conventional fixed battery of four nine-inch guns and two one-hundred pounders with a complement of 164 men. Bushnell visited Ericsson and supplied him with the necessary data for his calculations. A short while later Bushnell received his reply: the *Galena* would easily carry the proposed weight. Having his answer, Bushnell was anxious to return to Washington, but Ericsson detained him to show him a design for an "impregnable battery" which he had developed as a proposal to Napoleon III in 1854. The design won him a gold medal and letter of commendation, but no contract. Bushnell recognized the great value of the design and convinced Ericsson to let him take the drawings and crude carboard model of his ship to Secretary Welles, who by coincidence was visiting in Hartford, Connecticut.

Welles was impressed with Bushnell's enthusiasm and Ericsson's engineering, and encouraged Bushnell to secure backing and present the Ericsson design to the Naval Board in Washington. Bushnell secured promises of financial backing from John A. Griswold and John F. Winslow, both of Troy, New York, who were personal friends of the governor of the state and successful businessmen. They agreed to supply the iron and some of the machinery for the ship that still existed only in the inventor's mind. It was a testimonial to Bushnell's extraordinary energy and influence that he was able to secure support for such a speculative business venture in so short a time. The governor provided him a letter of introduction and Secretary of State Seward arranged for him to have a personal meeting with the President. After a great deal of maneuvering and political arm-twisting, Bushnell and his associates were on their way to Washington to meet the President.

The ship model they were to display had been collecting dust since 1854 and represented a concept which had been germinating in Ericsson's mind since 1826. If it could be built in ninety days as Ericsson said, it possibly could save the Union from the dreaded *Virginia*'s guns.

On the night they arrived in Washington, Bushnell and his associates presented the design to Lincoln. He related that his only experience in boat building was on file down at the Patent Office—a canal boat that could run where there was no water—but nevertheless, he was impressed by the earnestness of the men and the simplicity of the plan. Lincoln could not influence the board's opinion, but he agreed to meet Bushnell, Griswold and Winslow at the Navy Department the following morning.

At eleven o'clock the next day Lincoln observed as Bushnell presented the design as best he could. Most were impressed by its novelty. Some advised trying it, while others severely ridiculed it. At the end of the meeting, Lincoln was asked for his opinion. "All I have to say is what the girl said when she put her foot in the stocking, 'It strikes me there's something in it,' " was his reply. However, the Board was not thoroughly convinced and Bushnell was asked to return the following morning so that in the interim the members could have an opportunity to discuss the plan.

Next day Commodore Smith convened the entire Board and asked Bushnell to once again explain the design and its merits. When he had finished, Bushnell carefully noted the remarks of each board member and left the conference room confident of success. Later that afternoon, through friends in the Navy Department, he learned that some high officials were fearful of another Ericsson failure; they had little confidence in a design so radically different from the traditional sail-powered man-of-war.

How were Ericsson's friends to convince senior naval officers, who were familiar only with traditional wooden warships, of the value of his plans? The answer was, they couldn't. They managed at last to get Smith and Paulding to concur in the building of one *trial* battery, provided Davis agreed. But Davis told them that they might take the little thing home and worship it, as it would not be idolatry, because it was made in the image of nothing in the heaven above or on the earth below or in the waters under the earth. There was only one thing left to do; get Ericsson to plead the case himself.

The three associates realized that dealing with adamant naval officers was simple, compared to getting along with the cantankerous Ericsson. They decided that they had better not tell him that his plan had not won favor in Washington. Bushnell described his next meeting with Ericsson in a letter to Welles: "I appeared at his house the next morning precisely at 9 o'clock, and heard his sharp greeting, 'Well, how is it?' 'Glorious,' said I. 'Go on, go on,' said he with much impatience. 'What did they say?' 'Admiral Smith says it is worthy of the genius of an Ericsson.' The pride fairly gleamed in his eyes. 'But Paulding—what did he say of it?' 'He said, "It's just the thing to clean the 'Rebs' out of Charleston with." ' 'How about Davis?' he inquired, as I appeared to hestitate a moment. 'Oh, Davis,' said I, 'he wanted two or three explanations in detail which I couldn't give him, and so Secretary Welles proposed that I should come and get you to come to Washington and explain these few points to the entire board in his room tomorrow.' 'Well, I'll go—I'll go tonight.' "

When the small group arrived at the Navy Department, history failed to record who was more shocked; the Ironclad Board for seeing Ericsson appear before them after having his plan rejected and asking each of the officers what points needed clarification, or John Ericsson himself after learning that the Board had turned down his idea. Not being satisfied with just a negative reply, Ericsson demanded to know why they had rejected him. Bushnell wrote; "You remember how he thrilled every person present in your room with his vivid description of what the little

boat would be and what she could do; and that in ninety days time she could be built; although the Rebels had already been four months or more on the *Merrimack* with all the appliances of the Norfolk Navy Yard to help them." In describing his impregnable battery, Ericsson had become "a full electric battery in himself." He was instructed to proceed at once, with the details of the contract to be worked out with his associates and forwarded for signature at a later date.

Ericsson wasted no time in getting to work. The hull of the vessel would be built by Thomas F. Rowland, agent of the Continental Iron Works at Greenpoint, Long Island. The plate, bars and rivets were to be furnished by the Albany Iron Works of Troy, New York. The steam machinery, boilers, propellers and apparatus for the turret would be manufactured by the DeLameter Iron Works of New York. The port stoppers were to be supplied by Charles D. DeLancy of Buffalo and the turret was to be built by the Novelty Iron Works across the river from Greenpoint.

But in Washington, the great enthusiasm first displayed had waned with fears that the battery would prove a failure and disgrace the members of the board for their action in recommending it. Thus, when the final contract arrived for signature, Ericsson and company were dismayed by the clause requiring them to take all the risk.

The contract for the *Monitor* was dated 4 October 1861, after the first keel-plates had already passed through the rolling mill and other work was several weeks in progress. Ericsson had agreed to construct the ship for $275,000 in a period extended by the board to 100 days. However, the Ironclad Board had agreed to his design only if he and his financial backers would take all the risk by requiring the new warship to be proven in combat before they collected full payment. This lead to the interesting historical extrapolation that the *Monitor* technically still partially belonged to Ericsson and company when she fought the Battle of Hampton Roads. Gideon Welles wrote into the contract himself:

> It is understood between the contracting parties that after the Battery shall be ready for sea and be taken possession of by the government for the purpose of testing her properties as stipulated in the contract, such possession shall be regarded as accepting the vessel so far only as the workmanship and quality of materials are concerned, and that the test of the qualities and properties of the vessel as provided, shall be made as soon thereafter as practicable not to exceed ninety days; the reservation of twenty five per cent to be withheld until the test is made.

This just hardened Ericsson to the task but Winslow and Griswold were wealthy and cautious businessmen and the clause caused them much anxiety. It also concerned Daniel Drew of New York and N. D. Sperry of New Haven, their bondsmen in the contract who signed it without any consideration or reward other than the satisfaction of aiding their government. Needless to say, Bushnell had to use all his ingenuity and

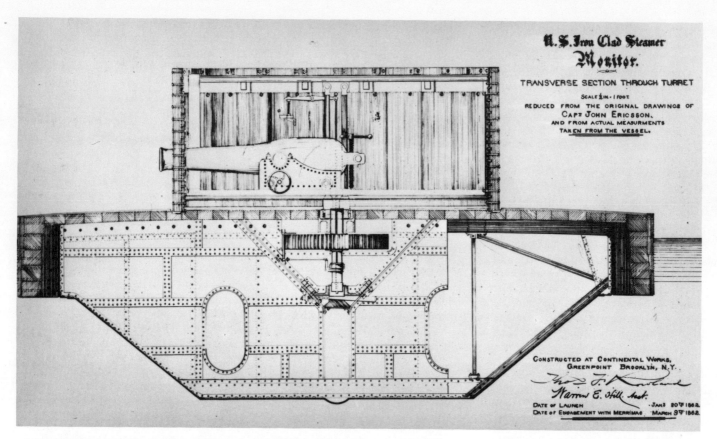

U.S. Iron Clad Steamer
Monitor.

TRANSVERSE SECTION THROUGH TURRET

SCALE ½ IN. = 1 FOOT
REDUCED FROM THE ORIGINAL DRAWINGS OF
CAPT JOHN ERICSSON,
AND FROM ACTUAL MEASUREMENTS
TAKEN FROM THE VESSEL.

CONSTRUCTED AT CONTINENTAL WORKS,
GREENPOINT BROOKLYN, N.Y.

Warren E. Hill. Asst.

DATE OF LAUNCH · JANE 30TH 1862.
DATE OF ENGAGEMENT WITH MERRIMAC · MARCH 9TH 1862.

Transverse section of the Monitor, *showing the iron bulkhead that supported the turret and the large pinion gear that rotated it. Note the screw and wedge used to "jack up" the turret prior to moving it.*

energy to keep the company from foundering as Ericsson was too busy with his draftsman, C. W. MacCord, producing the necessary engineering drawings.

A set of original specifications was sent to the Ironclad Board, but there never was a complete set of drawings for the ship. Ericsson hurriedly made drawings which MacCord finished, but many times his sketches were carried right to the shops for execution. Some of the drawings in the MacCord Collection at the Stevens Institute of Technology in Hoboken, New Jersey, still bear the marks of the men who worked on them. Frequently, Ericsson informed Commodore Smith of changes in the specifications only after they had already been incorporated into the vessel. Accordingly, many of the exact details of how the *Monitor* was actually constructed are found only in the hundreds of letters in the National Archives, the New York Historical Society, and other locations. The great number of letters from Smith was a point of contention with Ericsson, as replying to them only kept him from his work. Occasionally questions were raised in Washington that required Ericsson's reply to dispell the fears of failure. To a letter questioning the stability

of his ship and the weight of armor, Ericsson replied: "Pardon me for saying in conclusion that there is no living man who has tripped me on calculation or proved my figures wrong in a single instance in matters relating to theoretical computation."

And to add a final note of disdain Ericsson pointed out that "If the 'expert naval architect' were right, myself and assistants merit commiseration as we have to pay for the *iron* that is to sink the battery."

Ericsson was to equip the ship "complete in all parts and appointments for service." This included everything from machinery and marine heads (first ever installed below the waterline) to china and drapes. The builders were also to provide "masts, spars, sails and rigging of sufficient dimensions to drive the vessel at the rate of six knots in a fair breeze." This affront to the engineer's temperament Ericsson chose to ignore. No further mention of this requirement was ever made and there is no record of Ericsson's remarks upon reading it in the contract.

The *Monitor* was an engineer's ship, the prototype of a new era in ship construction. She was designed from the keel up to be completely functional—an instrument of destruction. Her name was selected by

Model of the Monitor *showing her prominent turret and cubical pilot house. Her radical profile was in stark contrast to the contemporary broadside warship.* ——Courtesy Smithsonian Institution.

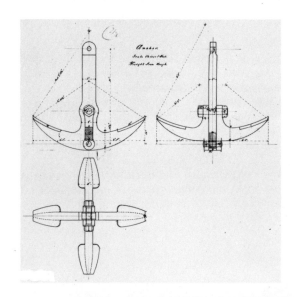

The unique Ericsson four-fluked anchor used on the Monitor. ——Courtesy of Smithsonian Institution.

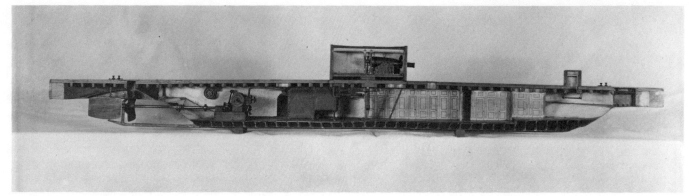

Cut-away model showing interior details of the Monitor. ——Courtesy U.S. Naval Academy Museum.

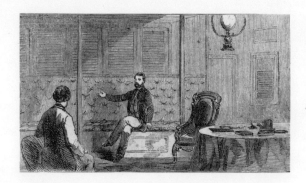

The captain's cabin, showing leather-tufted benches and fine furniture. ——Harper's Weekly, 1862.

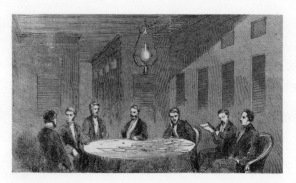

The officer's wardroom. ——Harper's Weekly, 1862.

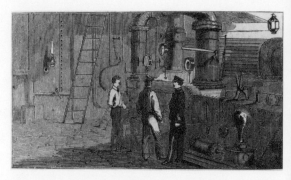

The engine room, showing the boilers and some of the auxiliary pumps. ——Harper's Weekly, 1862.

Ericsson himself to symbolize a warning to Great Britain and to admonish the South. Her silhouette was dominated by the gun turret, twenty feet in diameter and nine feet high, plated with eight courses of armor an inch thick. The turret alone weighed 120 tons, without the two eleven-inch Dahlgren guns. The only other prominent feature of the ship was the cubical pilot house mounted forward where the helmsman and commanding officer controlled the ship. The ship had only a nine-inch freeboard, a minimal target. The revolving turret allowed the two guns to be trained without turning the ship. The ship's shallow draft of only nine feet would be a great advantage in the shallow southern bays and estuaries. The lower part of the hull contained all the machinery and living spaces, below the waterline. The overhang of the raft protected the underwater body from damage by ramming or shellfire.

A single athwartships iron bulkhead supported the great weight of the turret and its machinery. Forward of the bulkhead were the crew's berthing deck, ship's storerooms, powder magazines, and captain's cabin and salon. Forward of all this was the pilot house, anchor windlass room and chain locker. Aft of the bulkhead was the galley and engineering spaces containing the boilers, main engine, auxiliary machinery, pumps, and coal bunkers.

The *Monitor* was not hastily constructed. Her well-conceived design indicated detailed and intricate interior arrangement. A first item of interest was the circular anchor well designed to allow operation of the anchor windlass from below the main deck, without the crew ever being exposed to the enemy. The anchor was well protected when raised; it was a specially designed four-fluke type. The anchor windlass was hand-

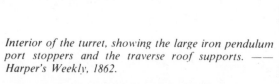

The berth deck looking aft showing the doors leading to the adjacent stowage room. The crew slept in hammocks slung from the overhead. ——Harper's Weekly, 1862.

Interior of the turret, showing the large iron pendulum port stoppers and the traverse roof supports. —— Harper's Weekly, 1862.

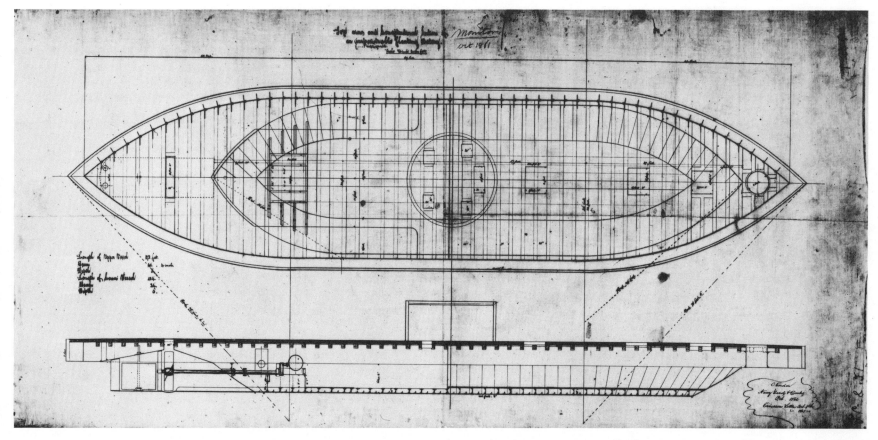

Drawing of framing details of the Monitor's *hull.* ——*Courtesy U.S. National Archives.*

cranked and required several men to power it. The same compartment contained the pilot house which protruded above the main deck. It was constructed of solid nine by twelve-inch wrought iron blocks. Slots in the sides of the pilot house allowed the commanding officer, pilot, and helmsman full view. The slots, only five-eighths of an inch wide, were later widened against Ericsson's wishes, and proved to be a weakness in battle and at sea.

The captain's cabin was aft of the pilot house on the starboard side, and contained a wash basin and head facilities. Across the passageway was a salon where the captain could entertain visiting dignitaries and carry out the ship's business. Ericsson furnished both spaces with expensive furniture and drapes.

The officer's wardroom contained a large dining table and a chair for each officer. Illumination was by oil lamps, augmented by discs of glass set in the overhead. These deck lights were fitted with iron covers to protect them in battle and at sea. Staterooms on each side of the wardroom were each fitted with their own wash basins, personalized bowls and pitchers. Ericsson spared nothing for the officers who would handle the ship; he provided them with fine furniture and monogrammed silverware and dinnerware. An engraving of the wardroom, printed in *Harper's Magazine,* showed the woodwork to be the best that could be provided.

Aft of the wardroom was the berth deck for the crew. Men slept in hammocks which were stowed in the overhead when not in use. Storerooms and supply rooms bordered this area. The powder magazine, forward on the port side, was illuminated from a separate compartment through a glass panel to keep all exposed flame away from the powder. The shell room on the starboard side was of the same design.

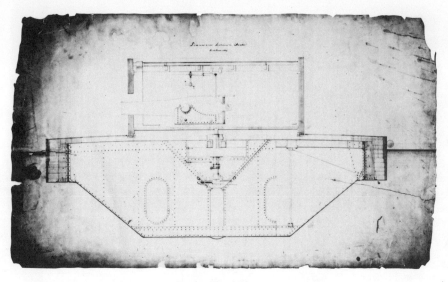

Cross Section

The drawings on page 28 and 29 are copies of the original construction drawings discovered at the Stevens Institute of Technology. Some of the drawings have smudge fingerprints of the workmen still on them.

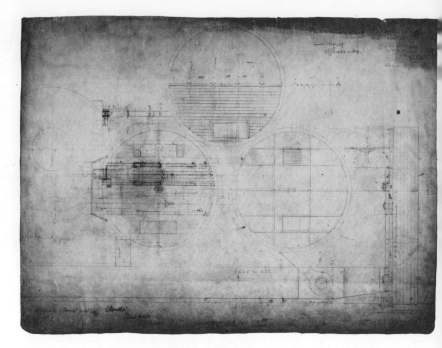

Turret Layout

Turret Design

Details of Armor Belt

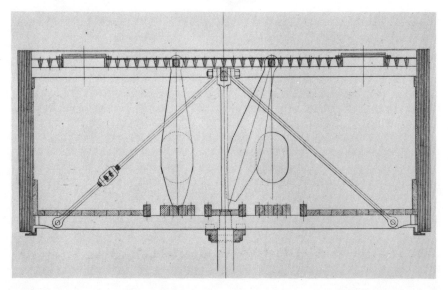

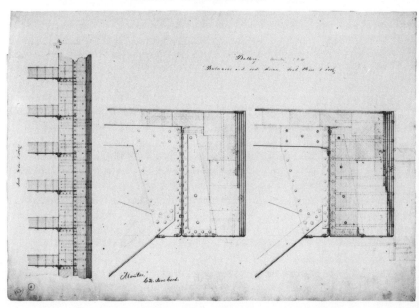

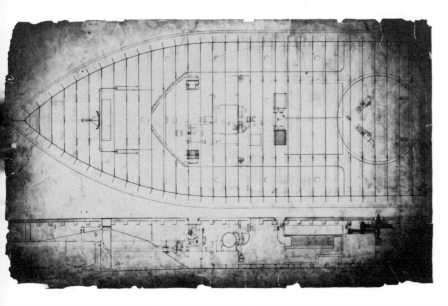

Hull Layout Aft

Stern Arrangement

The drawings on page 28 and 29 are copies of the original construction drawings discovered at the Stevens Institute of Technology. Some of the drawings have smudge fingerprints of the workmen still on them.

Propeller

Boiler Arrangement

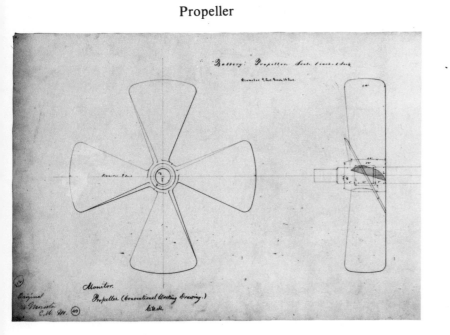

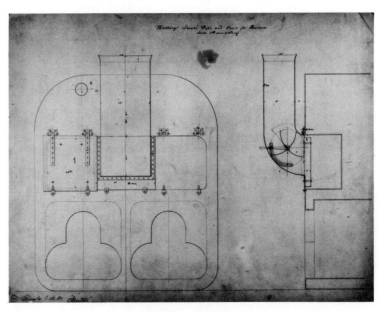

LINES PLAN

U.S.S. MONITOR

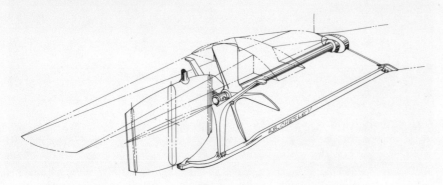

Perspective of the Skeg, Rudder, and Propeller

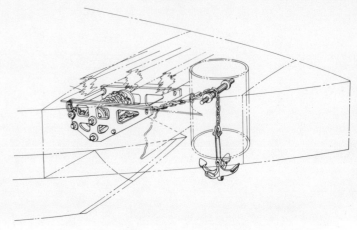

Perspective of the Anchor Well

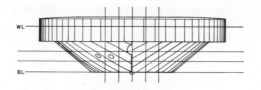

Body Plan

Half Breadth Plan

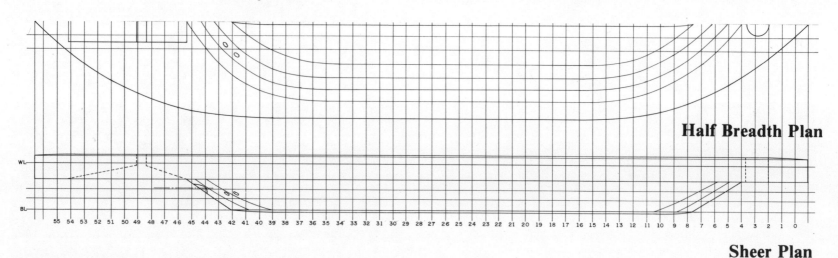

Sheer Plan

Drawing by Alan B. Chesley/Copyright © 1978 by Leeward Publications, Inc.

USS *Monitor* as outfitted December 1862.

SCALE | 0 5 10 15 20   30   40   50 | FEET

Outboard Profile

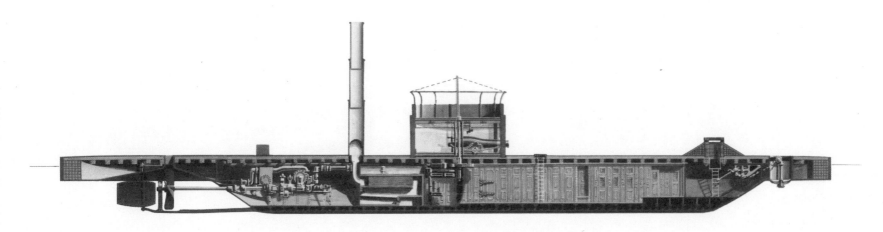

Inboard Profile

Rendering by Alan B. Chesley/Copyright © 1978 by Leeward Publications, Inc.

USS *Monitor* as outfitted June 1862.

U.S.S. MONITOR

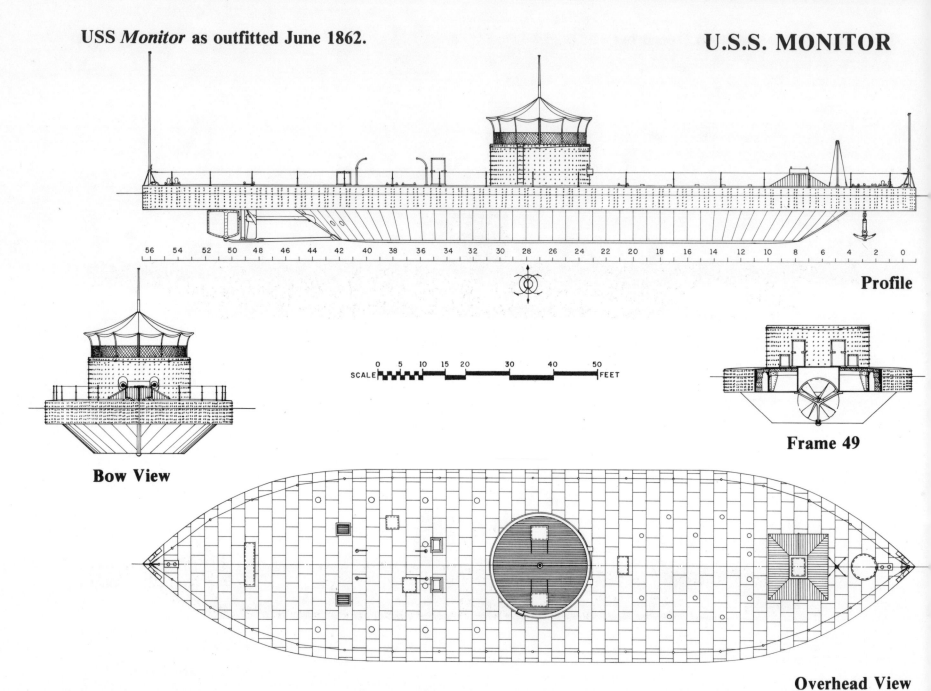

Profile

SCALE 0 5 10 15 20 30 40 50 FEET

Frame 49

Bow View

Overhead View

Drawing by Alan B. Chesley/Copyright © 1978 by Leeward Publications, Inc.

The main bulkhead was reinforced vertically to carry the weight of the large driving gear which was shrunk onto the center shaft of the turret. The turret was revolved by two single-piston donkey engines. The controls, operating a clutch mechanism, were inside the turret. Before the turret could revolve it had to be jacked up by a screw and wedge mechanism at the foot of the bulkhead. With twenty-five pounds of steam pressure per square inch, the turret could make two and a half revolutions per minute, moving the guns in train at the rate of 16 degrees per second.

Two doors in the main bulkhead opened onto the galley and the engineering spaces. The *Monitor* had the first pressurized forced draft system in the Navy. In order to keep up the draft to the fires under the boilers, and keep smoke and fumes out of the living spaces, these doors had to be kept closed. The engine room operated at two pounds above normal atmospheric pressure. The engineering plant consisted of two horizontal fire-tube boilers that supplied steam to the main engine. The boilers were fired with anthracite coal. Jammed into the engineering spaces were Ericsson's own horizontal marine engine, the large capacity Worthington and Adams pumps, the bilge injection pump, and many other pumps and auxiliary machines. In addition, steam was supplied to radiators in a heating system, and, most important, to the turret mechanism. No drawings of the steam plant lay-out have ever been found.

The operation and well-being of the *Monitor* depended upon a new type of officer just gaining recognition in the Navy—the engineers. Engineers were frequently looked down upon by regular line officers, who strolled the quarter deck in clean uniforms and fresh air, and had little sympathy for those who emerged from below decks, covered with oil, grease and coal dust, never having seen the daylight and having no idea of the direction in which their engines were driving the ship. The great disdain of the engineers was well expressed by Chief Engineer Isaac Newton aboard the *Monitor*: "As there are no sails and ropes on the *Monitor*, the spare time this deficiency gives the first Lieut. causes me very great annoyance."

As Ericsson pushed his ship nearer to completion, the men who were working night and day on the ship developed great pride in her. It exists to this day in Greenpoint, Brooklyn, where there is still a Monitor Street and an Ericsson Street. The school children there memorialize the ship with an annual essay contest, and the average person on the street is able to talk about where Ericsson lived and where the ship was built.

Most newspapers of the day closely watched the progress of building the ship, and printed articles ridiculing the project as "Ericsson's folly." In Washington, pressure mounted as daily accounts about the progress of the *Merrimack*, renamed CSS *Virginia* by the Confederates, stirred up more fears. Commodore Smith urged all expediency in completing the ship. It was launched on 30 January 1862, with much fanfare as crowds gathered along the banks of the East River. Bets were made as to whether or not the "iron coffin" would float. When she slid down the ways, Ericsson stood on her deck, in defiance of the small craft in the river

The launching of the Monitor, *30 January 1862. Many doubters felt it would go straight to the bottom of the East River.*

standing by to rescue survivors. To the amazement of everyone except Ericsson, the ship floated within three inches of her predicted waterline. This was a triumph for Ericsson, as he had designed the ship from only pure mathematical calculations; there had been no model testing or computer analysis. Ericsson's calculations, when compared to modern ship design analysis, attest to his great skill as an engineer.

During the next week the new ship held trials. The executive officer was Lieutenant S. Dana Greene, a recent naval academy graduate; the *Monitor* was his first ship. There were seven officers assigned to the ship, including Paymaster William F. Keeler, whose letters to his wife * vividly described life aboard the ship. The ship's company also included Alban C. Stimers, an officer assigned at Ericsson's request to over-see the construction. He was, next to Ericsson, most familiar with her machinery.

Her trials were not without mishap. On her first venture from the dock, the main engine was working in reverse due to faulty valve setting. No one had bothered to inquire whether she had a left- or right-handed propeller. This was easily remedied, however, another problem proved more serious. The steering mechanism was totally out of balance; the area forward of the rudder post was too great in proportion to that abaft it. As a result the helmsman was unable to hold the wheel once it was put

* *Aboard the USS Monitor: 1862.* Annapolis, Maryland, 1964. U.S. Naval Institute.

33

Model of the Monitor, *showing her 20-foot diameter turret. The turret weighed more than 120 tons. ——Courtesy Smithsonian Institution.*

over and lost control of the ship. She rammed a dock, and had to be towed back to the shipyard. Naval authorities proposed hauling her out and replacing the rudder with one of better proportions, but Ericsson forcefully rejected this.

"The *Monitor* is mine, and I say it shall not be done!" he stated. Remembering the terms of the contract he was technically correct. In a tone of contempt he added, "Put in a new rudder! They would waste a month doing that; I will make her steer as easily in three days."

This he proceeded to do by doubling the purchase between the tiller and the wheel ropes. It is well that his objection prevailed, for the delay in fitting a new rudder would have prevented the *Monitor* and *Virginia* meeting when they did, if at all. On 25 February 1862 the *Monitor* was put in commission with Lt. John L. Worden in command—the same officer who had been captured by the Confederates on his return from Florida after delivering instructions from the President to Fort Pickering. His release was secured in an exchange of prisoners. He was personally selected by the Secretary of the Navy to command the ship that had taken Ericsson 147 days to build, from contract to commissioning. This command would prove a severe test of his skills as a naval officer.

On her gun trials at the Palisades both guns were simultaneously disabled due to the lack of understanding of the braking system on Ericsson's gun carriages. The inventor's draftsman, Charles W. MacCord described the incident:

. . . the friction for taking up the recoil was produced by means of two levers, actuated by a screw, with a hand wheel at the side of the gun carriage. Since there were two guns, pointing in the same direction, with very little space between them, the handwheels were, of course, placed on the outer side of the carriages; naturally suggesting the idea that the whole mechanism was right-handed for one and left-handed for the other. But this was not so; in order to save time it was made the same for each, and in serving either gun the compression was effected by turning the top of the wheel to the left. Now screws are ordinarily turned the other way in order to produce pressure; and Chief-Engineer Stimers, by whom the first trial was conducted, would seem not to have made himself acquainted under the construction here adopted. Grasping the handwheel of gun No. 1, he turned it *to the right* until the resistance in his judgment indicated a proper degree of compression, and gave the order to fire. It must next be stated that the first effect of his action was to relieve any pressure that might have existed; the second effect was that the levers, whose movement was quite limited, became jammed in the supporting brackets, thus causing the resistance which had completely deceived the Chief-Engineer. The great weapon gave a sullen roar, and, being entirely free, flew back until it was stopped by the cascabel striking against the interior of the turret.

One would imagine the experience sufficient to inspire caution; but, curiously enough, Engineer Stimers seems to have assumed that the carriages must be rights and lefts, and to have concluded that what was thus proved wrong for one was exactly the correct thing for the other. And so, without looking under the gun to see what was there and make sure of what he was really doing, he at once proceeded to experiment with gun No. 2 in the same manner, and with precisely similar results.

Similar accounts of experimentation with the new machinery exist in the letters and diaries of the officers and crew—some of them humorous. One young officer, much to his chagrin, was taught the importance of positioning the seacock properly when using one of the below the waterline marine toilets, by a geyser of water spurting into his face.

Luckily no serious damage was incurred during this period and on 4 March 1862 a final and successful trial trip was run, guns were satisfactorily fired, and a favorable report was made by the board of naval officers. An interesting entry in the ship's log for that date recorded that two men deserted, taking the ship's cutter with them. This raises a question. Were they members of the gun crew for that ill-fated trial who decided they had had enough of this iron coffin?

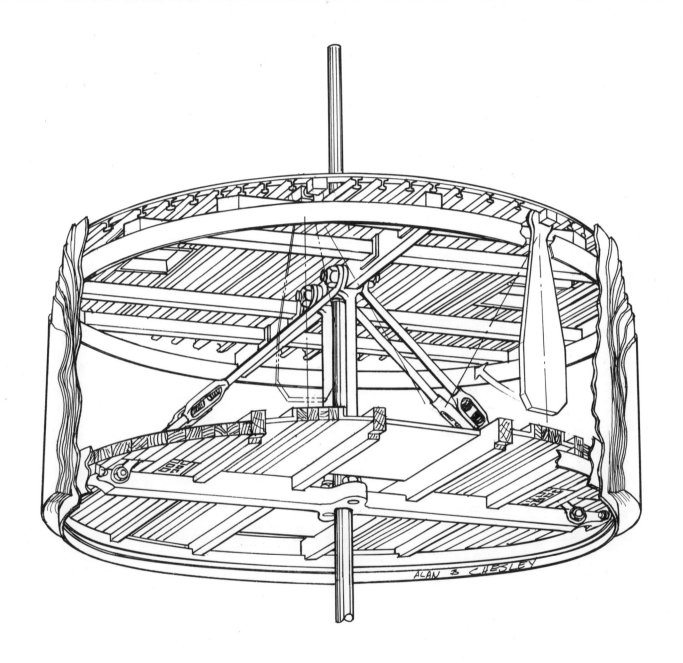

Construction details of Monitor's *turret, showing the large iron pendulums which were swung down to close the gunports when the guns were out of battery.*

The action between the C.S.S. Virginia *and the U.S.S.* Monitor, *9 March 1862. The "Yankee Cheesebox" proved the great advantage of the revolving turret. The* Monitor *was at that time the most advanced warship in the world.*

4

JOURNEY TO HAMPTON ROADS

Under persistent prodding from Washington, all hands made preparations to get underway; mechanics hurriedly finished last minute details and stores and ammunition were loaded aboard. Forty-nine seamen of various rates, volunteers from the *North Carolina* and *Sabine* lying in New York harbor, had been selected by Lt. Worden as the crew for the new and untried vessel. No seaman had ever seen such a ship before. They would be aboard her for less than three weeks before fighting the biggest battle of their career. It is difficult to imagine how they must have felt surrounded by the strange and unfamiliar machines.

For such an experimental ship as the *Monitor* was, the nine days of trials between her commissioning and her sailing for battle were all too few; in the modern navy many months of trials are common. But in 1862 such haste was justified—the fate of the Union hung in the balance. Had the *Virginia* broken the blockade and attacked Northern commerce, Great Britain possibly would have viewed the Southern cause more favorably, and her intervention could have changed the trend of the war, and perhaps the outcome.

Under orders from Welles, Lt. Worden was to take his ship to sea at the first available opportunity. It was feared that the *Virginia* would appear at Hampton Roads any day. Worden prudently delayed a day, waiting for a weather front to pass, with the hope that several days of clear weather would follow.

On Thursday, 6 March 1862 the *Monitor* got underway in the midst of a snow storm, under tow by the tug *Seth Low*. There were no cheering crowds or gun salutes as the two craft left New York harbor. It had been decided that towing the ship would expedite the journey and reduce the risk to an untried vessel of questionable sea-keeping ability.

The tension in Washington reached a fever pitch. Facing the ominous threat of the *Virginia,* few people had confidence in the ability of the *Monitor* to successfully challenge her. A last minute directive was rushed to Lt. Worden instructing him to proceed directly to Washington, not stopping at Hampton Roads. Fortunately, the dispatch arrived too late; the tug sent after the *Monitor* to deliver the message failed to catch her.

The epic journey to Hampton Roads has now become legend. During the passage *Monitor* nearly foundered twice but providentially arrived in time to meet the *Virginia*. A few details of the voyage are still worthy of mention.

On the first day at sea, the weather was calm and the *Monitor* towed well. Worden had prepared his ship for sea by stuffing oakum in every crack and seam. The turret had been jacked up to place a gasket of packed oakum around the base. This was contrary to Ericsson's instructions; he had designed a brass ring set into the deck to form a near watertight seal, metal-to-metal around the turret circumference. The only leaks discovered that first day, on the deck and at the forward main hatch, were easily handled by the pumps. Engineer Stimers, who was aboard to evaluate the ship, reported to Ericsson: "I never saw a vessel more buoyant or less shocked, than she was yesterday. There has not been sufficient movement to disturb a wine glass setting on the table."

As dawn broke on 7 March 1862, the experienced seamen knew they were in for some stormy weather. The sky was gray and overcast, with the wind picking up over an angry sea. The weather continued to deteriorate until the seas were breaking over the *Monitor*'s decks with such force that the whole ship shook. The impact of the waves against the turret dislodged part of the oakum at the base, leaving a large gap for the sea water to flood in.

Lt. Greene, the executive officer, wrote:

> The berth-deck hatch leaked in spite of all we could do, and the water came down under the turret like a waterfall. It would strike the pilot-house with such force as to knock the helmsman completely round from the wheel. The waves also broke over the blower pipes, and the water came down them in such quantities that the belts of the blower-engines slipped, and the engines consequently stopped for lack of artificial draught, without which, in such a confined place, the fires could not get air for combustion.

Albin C. Stimers supervised most of the Monitor's *construction and was the person most familiar with her machinery.*

to save the ship. Fumes were filling the entire ship and the water was rising. Thoughts of abandoning ship were in everyone's mind. Stimers, realizing the seriousness of the situation set the crew to bailing by forming a bucket brigade up the turret ladder. This action calmed the panic more than it reduced the flooding. Stimers also directed attempts to restore ventilation by sending men into the fireroom to do a specific task and then come right out before the fumes reached them. In this manner they got the blowers, engines and pumps going again. The *Seth Low,* seeing that the *Monitor* was in trouble, had altered course in search of calmer seas. It was evident to all on board that Providence was on their side; the seas decreased and fresh air was drawn in below decks. But their journey was not yet over, as Stimers recorded: "I turned in about half past twelve, but in about half an hour, the tiller ropes came off . . ."

The seas had begun to pick up again and again the ship was in trouble, but Stimers knew what to do. He worked for an hour in the cramped spaces around the steering mechanism to restore control of the helm. The knowledge gained by Stimers during the construction of the vessel had helped divert two near disasters, and assured that the *Monitor* would reach Hampton Roads.

Without sufficient steam pressure, the pumps would lose their race with the in-rushing water. The engineers worked feverishly to start the blowers. As they worked on one, the other belt broke and soon a mixture of "hydrogen and carbonic gases" filled the entire engine room. The space had to be abandoned as men started to pass out and scrambled up the turret ladder choking for fresh air. Stimers described the heroic efforts by Isaac Newton, the ship's chief engineer:

> Pretty soon, Newton recovered sufficiently, . . . to feel that he was responsible for doing all in his power, though not enough to use his best judgment, and away he went to the fire room and put a hose in the nozzle for wetting down the fires, but before he could do much, had to leave, arriving at the berth deck door just as he gave out entirely. One of the firemen happened to look in there to see if there was anyone left and brought him out. They got him to the top of the turret and after some fifteen minutes of anxious work on the part of the surgeon, he began to revive, but his case remained doubtful for several hours, so did that of the 3rd Assistant Hand.

With the chief engineer and his assistants unconscious, suffering from smoke inhalation and anoxia, Alban Stimers was the only person aboard who understood the engine and pumps. He knew what had to be done

As the *Monitor* rounded Cape Henry at 4 PM on Saturday 8 March 1862, the crew could hear heavy gunfire from the direction of Hampton Roads, twenty miles away. All feared that the dreaded *Virginia* had ventured forth as expected. The prediction that a "single ironclad, in the midst of a hostile wooden fleet, would resemble a lion amid a flock of sheep" had been proven correct.

That hectic day marked a low point in U. S. naval history. For months the North Atlantic Blockading Squadron had stationed its most powerful warships at Hampton Roads. The crews of these ships had kept a wary eye in the direction of Norfolk expecting to see the dark billowing smoke of the approaching Southern ironclad.

The *Virginia* was constructed from the hulk of the U. S. Steam Frigate *Merrimack*. She had been raised and cut down to the old berth deck and converted to a casemated ironclad. "Both ends for seventy feet were covered over, and when the ship was in fighting trim were just awash. On the midship section, 170 feet in length, was built at an angle of 45 degrees a roof of pitch-pine and oak 24 inches thick, extending from the waterline to a height over the gun-deck of 7 feet. Both ends of the shield were rounded so that the pivot-guns could be used as bow and stern chasers or quartering. Over the gun deck was a light grating, making a promenade about twenty feet wide. The wood backing was covered with iron plates, two inches thick and eight wide. The first tier was put on horizontally, the second up and down, in all to the thickness of four inches, bolted through the wood-work and clinched. The prow was of cast-iron, projecting four feet and badly secured, as events proved. The rudder and propeller were entirely unprotected . . . The motive power was the same that had always been in the ship; both of the engines and boilers had been condemned on her return from her last cruise, and were radically defective. Of course, the fire and sinking had not improved them . . . A more ill-contrived or unreliable pair of engines could only have been found in some vessels of the United States Navy."

The conversion cost was about one hundred and ten thousand dollars, and involved over 1500 workmen over a nine month period. When the *Virginia* engaged the Union fleet, she was uncompleted; she had no gun port covers or sufficient armor below the waterline. Her battery "consisted of two 7-inch rifles, heavily reinforced around the breech with 3-inch steel bands, shrunk on. These were the first heavy guns so made, [the famous Brook's Rifle] and were the bow and stern pivots. There were also 2, 6-inch rifles of the same make and 6, 9-inch smooth-bore broadside— 10 guns in all." Much of the credit for the construction of such a formidable warship with the limited resources available to the South in such a short period of time goes to the inventive genius and foresight of Stephen Mallory, the Confederate Secretary of the Navy, Constructor John Porter, the designer; Chief-Engineer William P. Williamson, who restored the engines; and Lt. John M. Brooke who supervised the manufacture of the armor plates and procurement of the battery. The conversion of the *Merrimack* into an ironclad was one of the most successful deceptions of the war. Inaccurate reports of the progress and the efficacy of the vessel were deliberately planted in the Southern press to stir panic in the North. Secretary Mallory had great visions of the effect of "dashing cruises" by the *Virginia* up the Potomac and even to New York in good weather. However, her designers and the man that would take her into battle recognized that she was not a seagoing vessel as was evident when she steamed into Hampton Roads.

On 24 February 1862 Flag Officer Franklin Buchanan was given command of the Confederate James River Squadron which consisted of several small, unarmored gunboats and the yet to be tried *Virginia*. He flew his flag on the *Virginia*. Buchanan had helped establish the U. S. Naval Academy in 1845 and had served as its first Superintendent. His brother was a Union naval officer aboard the *Congress*, anchored in waiting for his approach. Both officers knew of the others' presence. Such is the tragedy of a nation divided in civil war.

The *Virginia* was just as novel and untried to the Confederates as the *Monitor* was to her crew. "The officers and crew were strangers to the ship and to each other. Up to the hour of sailing she was crowded with workmen. Not a gun had been fired, hardly a revolution of the engines had been made, when we cast off from the dock and started on what many thought was an ordinary trial trip . . . From the start we saw that she was slow, not over five knots [The *Monitor* was capable of 6-9 knots.]; she steered so badly that, with her great length, [310 feet] it took from thirty to forty minutes to turn. She drew twenty-two feet [as compared to the *Monitor*'s eleven feet in battle trim], which confined [her] to a comparatively narrow channel in the Roads."

At eleven o'clock on 8 March 1862 the *Virginia* and her escorts steamed down the Elizabeth River. The shore was crowded with cheering spectators and soldiers. "At anchor at this time off Fort Monroe were the frigates *Minnesota, Roanoke,* and *St. Lawrence* and several gun-boats. The first two were sister ships of the *Virginia* before the war; the last was a sailing frigate of fifty guns." There also was a large fleet of British and French warships at anchor in anticipation of the ensuing engagement. Off Newport News, seven miles above Fort Monroe were the U.S. frigate *Congress* with 50 guns and the *Cumberland* with 30 guns. Buchanan chose the south channel and steered the *Virginia* towards Newport News. "The day was calm and the two ships were swinging lazily by their anchors . . . Boats were hanging to the lower booms, washed clothes in the rigging. Nothing indicated that [the *Virginia* was] expected."

The Union fleet was seemingly unprepared for the encounter everyone had expected for months; thus began a scandal in which the press viewed Secretary of the Navy Gideon Welles solely responsible. Commodore Goldsborough had continually received warnings from Washington about the progress on the *Virginia* and had, the day before, received word that her flags were flying, that she had taken on a crew and was ready for action. When the *Virginia* steamed out of the Roads, Goldsborough was many miles away in the Carolina Sounds overseeing another operation and Captain William Radford of *Cumberland* was attending a court-martial board. Although he returned on horseback, he arrived just as his ship was sinking.

The *Roanoke* had laid at her anchorage for four months with a broken shaft and was 180 men short of her full complement. The tugs which had been ordered for towing the sailing vessels out of danger or into supportive distance were nowhere in sight. Even the vigilance of the watch seemed compromised as the officers on the French sloop-of-war *Gassendi* noticed *Virginia*'s arrival fifteen minutes before a Union gunboat fired the warning signal. The confusion, lack of planning and teamwork on the part of the Union fleet was appalling. The consequence was a heavy toll in lives and ships.

The initial response to the sighting of the *Virginia* was catastrophic for the Union fleet. Almost immediately the *Roanoke, St. Lawrence* and *Minnesota* ran aground as they tried to assist the *Cumberland* and *Congress* without the necessary assistance of steam tugs. The *Virginia* got to within three-quarters of a mile from the *Cumberland* before she had cleared her decks for action and opened fire with her heavy pivot guns.

The *Virginia* exchanged broadsides with the *Congress* as she passed; then steaming directly for the *Cumberland,* fired once with her forward pivot gun before ramming *Cumberland* under the fore-rigging on the starboard side, almost at a right angle. Flag Officer Buchanan was anxious to test the *Virginia* as a ram; he was short of gun powder and shot. Both ships were engulfed in smoke as the *Cumberland*'s guns bore down on the ironclad in a deafening roar. The *Cumberland*'s decks ran red with blood as her gun crews fell before the ironclad's deadly fire.

On the lower gun deck, a shot penetrated the thick oak, dismounting the gun and killing the gun crew and completely severing the leg of the gun captain of the next gun. Lying in a pool of his own blood, he gave commands to place his gun in battery and fire before collapsing. The *Cumberland*'s return fire had little or no effect upon the enemy. Many of the *Virginia*'s shells crashed completely through both sides of the ship without exploding due to faulty fuzes.

Before leaving Norfolk, the *Virginia* had been smeared with grease as thick as it would stick. It was hoped that this might cause shot to glance off her sides. While under fire from the *Congress* and the *Cumberland* with her prow still in the *Cumberland*'s side, men feared that both ships would go to the bottom together. It seemed to the crew that she was literally "frying from one end to the other." One Confederate gunner wrote:

> The smoke from the burning grease on the outside blowing through the ports and mixing with the burning powder on the inside, made it so dense we could hardly breathe. A man at my gun by the name of Hunt, during this pandemonium turned round to a man at Eggleston's

gun, named Jack Cronin . . . "Jack, don't this smell like hell?" And Jack retorted, "It certainly does, and I think we'll be there in a few minutes!"

The smell of gun powder, sizzling grease, flesh, and blood grew strong. As the *Virginia* sluggishly withdrew from the side of *Cumberland,* the great damage was obvious. The ironclad had "opened her side wide enough to drive in a horse and cart." Soon *Cumberland* listed to starboard as her hull filled rapidly. As she settled her crew fought until their guns were under water, many lingering too long to help a wounded shipmate and going down with the ship. When she came to rest on the bottom, completely submerged, the *Cumberland*'s battle colors were still flying. Her rigging was crowded with survivors who had managed to scramble to safety. The surface of the water was littered with the debris of battle and men struggling to save themselves. In less than an hour one of the most powerful ships in the Union Navy had been sent to the bottom with one hundred twenty-one men lost.

The *Virginia* had two men killed, nineteen wounded. The muzzles of two of her guns and her exterior evidenced the test she had undergone. Her smoke stack was riddled, and her boats and anchors were shot away. More importantly she had left her iron prow in the side of her victim, starting a leak. Her crew did not know this.

She had won a great victory. Her armor had proved impregnable, proving once and for all the great superiority of an ironclad over a wooden ship-of-the-line, thus settling that debate and starting another; the contest between armor and shell that had a far-reaching effect in World War II.

Meanwhile, *Congress* had attempted to get underway by slipping her anchor and had run aground in such a manner that she could not bring her broadside to bear on the enemy. Joined by the Confederate vessels *Patrick Henry, Jamestown,* and *Teaser,* the *Virginia* raked the *Congress* fore and aft with hot shot and shell that turned her decks into a shambles. It became evident that the *Congress* would soon meet the fate of the *Cumberland.* Her two deck-mounted pivot guns returned the enemy's fire. As one gun crew was slaughtered another would jump in its place until the guns were dismounted by the *Virginia*'s fire. When Lt. Pendergrast, who assumed command after the death of Lt. Joseph B. Smith, (the son of Commodore Smith of the Ironclad Board) found his ship on fire in several places, and being unable to bring a single gun to bear on the enemy after the dismounting of the pivot guns, he ordered the colors hauled down in surrender.

While the CSS *Beaufort* and CSS *Raleigh* were alongside the *Congress,* removing wounded and prisoners, a heavy fire from Federal infantry on shore drove them off. It is not certain whether or not they recognized that the *Congress* had surrendered, but the action wounded several of the Confederates trying to give assistance, including Buchanan on the *Virginia.* In anger he ordered the ship destroyed by hot shot and incendiary shell and she burned long into the night.

It was now five o'clock with only an hour of daylight remaining. The next target for the *Virginia* would be the *Minnesota*. She was hard aground and with an ebb tide could be left until morning. Lt. Catesby ap Rogers Jones had relieved Buchanan after his injury and had every confidence that the *Virginia* would have an even more decisive triumph next day with the returning of the tide. Besides the loss of her iron prow, and the muzzles of two of her guns, her armor was "somewhat damaged; the anchors and all flag-staffs shot away and smokestack and steam pipes were riddled." This was a small price to pay for the severe defeat inflicted on the Union Navy.

As dusk fell on the battle-strewn water and the smoke of the retiring ironclad still hung in the distance, a strange craft appeared in Hampton Roads. Men in gun batteries on the approach to the Roads thought it was a "Yankee Water Schooner." This was a water-tank mounted on a barge used to replenish the water supply of the ships in the blockading squadron.

As the *Monitor* entered the Roads, Lt. Worden had ordered all the boats cleared away and the ship stripped of her sea-rig, the turret keyed up, and every preparation made for battle. With no sleep in forty-eight hours and very little to eat, the crew stowed the canvas awning, deck stanchions and the ventilating and smoke stacks. All that protruded above the flat deck— just nine inches above the water—was the circular turret, resembling a water-tank to those who had never seen the *Monitor,* and the cubical pilot house.

Monitor anchored in the Roads at 9 PM. The burning *Congress* lit up the sky; great clouds of smoke and sparks created an atmosphere of gloom. Lt. Worden reported to Capt. Marston aboard the *Roanoke,* who had received instructions to send the *Monitor* directly to Washington. Instead, he sent the *Monitor* to the assistance of the *Minnesota.* In his judgment the *Monitor* was the only hope of preventing another attack by the *Virginia.* No pilot was available for the *Monitor,* so Acting Master Sam Howard of the *Roanoke* volunteered. The burning hulk of the *Congress* provided a brilliant beacon to guide them. Lt. Greene wrote:

> An atmosphere of gloom pervaded the fleet, and the pygmy aspect of the newcomer did not inspire confidence among those who had witnessed the day before . . . Reaching the *Minnesota,* hard and fast aground, near midnight, we anchored, and Worden reported to Captain Van Brunt. Between 1 and 2 AM the *Congress* blew up— not instantaneously, but successively. Her powder-tanks seemed to explode, each shower of sparks rivaling the other in its height, until they appeared to reach the zenith—a grand but mournful sight. Near us, too, at the bottom of the river, lay the *Cumberland,* within her silent crew of brave men, who had died while fighting their guns to the water's edge, and whose colors were still flying at the peak.

The crew of the *Minnesota* were throwing overboard everything not secured and essential to fight, in an attempt to lighten their ship. But all efforts seemed futile with the falling tide.

The *Monitor* crew found that the sea water had rusted the turret mechanism and donkey engines. They spent the night lubricating and re-working the gears in order for the turret to operate smoothly. The 120-ton turret had to be jacked up through the center post so that the edge would clear the deck. The screw mechanism and large wedge which accomplished this were at the base of the central bulkhead which directly supported the turret. Freeing the turret was a long and arduous operation. Shot and powder had to be moved into the turret and the gun carriages worked. Even they had rusted.

The atmosphere was tense as the *Monitor*'s crew prepared for battle. The cramped spaces beneath the deck smelled of heavy perspiration. No one got any sleep.

The news of Saturday's disaster reached and alarmed all of Washington early Sunday morning. A Cabinet meeting was immediately called. The atmosphere was tense as the Secretaries arrived in their carriages and entered the room amid hushed conversations. Gideon Welles, Secretary of the Navy, sat quietly in the gloom-filled room, knowing everyone was watching him. Where was his *Monitor*? Had she arrived safely? Why hasn't he heard from Fox, the Assistant Secretary whom he had sent to watch the battle? William H. Seward, Secretary of State, always buoyant and talkative, was quiet, obviously overwhelmed by the turn of events. What effect would this great defeat have on Great Britain and France? Would they decide to lend more active assistance to the Southern cause? The tall, handsome, and humorless Secretary of the Treasury, Salmon P. Chase, itemized in great detail, ship by ship, the casualties of Saturday's battle. Secretary of War Edwin M. Stanton was full of dire predictions. He was certain that the *Virginia* could destroy every vessel in the Union service, demand tribute of the Atlantic coast ports, venture up the Potomac, disperse Congress, and knock the dome off the Capitol. It was clear to him that the "whole character of the war" had been changed. The danger was so imminent that he expected a cannon ball to land in the White House before the end of the meeting. Repeatedly, he and Lincoln went to a window to assure themselves that the *Virginia* was not steaming up the river at that very moment.

The old antagonism between Stanton and Welles came out in the open as Stanton demanded to know what Welles was going to do to check the Southern ironclad and prevent her from reaching Washington. Stanton had a great dislike for the Secretary of the Navy, and felt that the "Navy was secondary and subject to the control and direction" of the War Department. Lincoln, however, supported Welles' view on a departmental equality and often acted as peacemaker. That morning, however, he sat quietly, allowing Stanton to "run his course" of disdain towards Welles. All Welles could do was to reiterate his confidence in the *Monitor* and, in any event, he didn't believe the *Virginia* could survive a trip northward. He had hoped that the *Monitor* would have been ready in time to destroy the *Virginia* in her dry dock, but all that had changed now. Why hadn't he heard from Fox yet? Had another disaster befallen the Union fleet in Hampton Roads?

After much discussion, President Lincoln, weary and troubled, called for his carriage. Leaving the room, head down, he muttered, "Frightful news," and then drove to the Navy Yard to seek the advice of Captain Dahlgren, the Commandant of the Navy Yard. When Commodore Smith at the Navy Yard heard that the *Congress* had been lost, he remarked with restrained emotion, "The *Congress* sunk? then my son must be dead," and retired to his office, the same office where Ericsson and Bushnell had signed the contract for the *Monitor*.

Battle of the Ironclads

As daylight broke over Hampton Roads on Sunday, 9 March 1862 the *Virginia* and her consorts were anchored near Sewell's Point. The *Minnesota* was still fast aground, with the *Monitor* alongside. At about half-past seven the Confederate vessels got underway with great clouds of billowing black smoke and headed for the *Minnesota*. Signals were passed between the Union ships at anchor. Before Captain Van Brunt, of the *Minnesota*, could relay any official instructions to Worden, the *Monitor* was underway and steaming out to meet her adversary, as no instructions were necessary or desired.

Lt. Worden, forty-four years old when he took command of the *Monitor*, had spent twenty-eight years in the naval service. Hospitalized to recover from the effects of Southern prison, he left against the advice of doctors and family to accept the command; for which he had been personally recommended by Commodore Smith. His demonstrated strength and singleness of purpose in the ensuing conflict would prove the wisdom of the selection.

Lt. S. Dana Greene, executive officer of the *Monitor*, was just twenty-two years of age and only a recent graduate of the Naval Academy. He had seen less than three years of active service with the rank of Midshipman. Lt. Worden reported that "he applied himself unremittingly and intelligently to the study of her peculiar qualities and to her fitting and equipment . . ." Despite his limited experience, he went into the conflict with all the confidence and enthusiasm of youth.

Greene did not know then that his Academy roommate was aboard the *Virginia*. Those last months at the Academy had been tense, as the Brigade of Midshipmen became split as the nation itself moved North and South. Song and chant contests were heard in the mess hall as popular sentiments were aired, and frequent squabbles had to be broken up. Perhaps, no where else in the country was the effect of dividing brother against brother felt more than at the Academies, as classmates and teammates suddenly became "enemies." The question of loyalty was particularly difficult for men from the border states. Midshipmen would gather in midnight "smokers," against regulations, to read the latest newspapers and discuss the events. It was a melancholy day when old friends parted knowing full well that they might meet in battle; as was the case on this fateful Sunday. No better account of the struggle has been found than that by Lt. Greene, who wrote immediately after the battle.

> Worden took his station in the pilot house, and by his side were Howard, the pilot, and Peter Williams, the quartermaster, who steered the vessel throughout the engagement. My place was in the turret, to work and fight the guns; with me were Stodder and Stimers and sixteen brawny men, eight to each gun. John Stocking, boatswain's mate, and Thomas Lockrane, seaman, were gun-captains. Newton and his assistants were in the engine and fire rooms, to manipulate the boilers and engine, and most admirably did they perform this important

An artist's depiction of the "Battle of the Ironclads." The Monitor *is in right foreground.*

service from the beginning to the close of the action. Weber had charge of the powder division on the berth-deck, and Joseph Crown, gunner's mate rendered valuable service in connection with this duty.

The physical condition of the officers and men of the two ships at this time was in striking contrast. The *Merrimac* had passed the night quietly near Sewell's Point, her people enjoying rest and sleep, elated by thoughts of the victory they had achieved that day, and cheered by the prospects of another easy victory on the morrow. The *Monitor* had barely escaped shipwreck twice within the last thirty-six hours, and since Friday morning, forty-eight hours before, few if any of those on board had closed their eyes in sleep or had anything to eat but hard bread, as cooking was impossible. She was surrounded by wrecks and disaster, and her efficiency in action had yet to be proved.

Worden lost no time in bringing it to the test. Getting his ship underway, he steered direct for the enemy's vessels, in order to meet and engage them as far as possible from the *Minnesota.*

The *Monitor* was between the *Minnesota* and the *Virginia* and as the fire became general, the Cheesebox-on-a-raft held her fire and steered even closer. Her turret recorded hits from the *Minnesota* and the *Virgina* as the common gunnery practice was to skim the ball over the surface of the water, attempting to strike the other vessel at the waterline. It is not quite sure when the Confederate flotilla recognized the peculiar "tin-can on a shingle" to be the *Monitor* or even as a foe as they couldn't see any guns but as the little warship continued her advance it became obvious that she was something the Virginia would have to deal with.

As we approached, the wood vessels quickly turned and left. Our captain, to the astonishment of Captain Van Brunt made straight for the *Merrimac,* which had already commenced firing; and when he came within short range, he changed his course so as to come along-

An artist's conception of the Battle of Hampton Roads, Sunday, 9 March 1862. The Monitor *is at middle, the* Virginia *at left.*

This engraving of the battle shows the close range at which the ships fought, and the superficial damage they inflicted on each other. ——*Courtesy U.S. National Archives.*

side of her, stopped the engine, and gave the order,

Commence firing!

I triced up the port, ran out the gun, and, taking deliberate aim, pulled the lockstring. The *Merrimac* was quick to reply, returning a rattling broadside (for she had ten guns to our two), and the battle fairly began. The turrets and other parts of the ship were heavily struck, but the shots did not penetrate; the tower was intact, and it continued to revolve. A look of confidence passed over the men's faces, and we believed the *Merrimac* would not repeat the work she had accomplished the day before.

The fight continued with the exchange of broadsides as fast as the guns could be served and at very short range, the distance between the vessels frequently being not more than a few yards. Worden skillfully manoeuvered his quick turning vessel, trying to find some vulnerable point in his adversary. Once he made a dash at her stern, hoping to disable her screw, which he thinks he missed by not more than two feet. Our shots ripped the iron of the *Merrimac*, while the reverberation of her shots against the tower caused anything but a pleasant sensation. While Stodder, who was stationed at the machine

which controlled the revolving motion of the turret, was uncautiously leaning against the side of the tower, a large shot struck in the vicinity and disabled him. [Another was thrown completely over the guns and down the hatch by the effects of the concusson.] He left the turret and went below, and Stimers, who had assisted him, continued to do the work.

The drawbacks to the position of the pilot-house were soon realized. We could not fire ahead or within several points of the bow, since the blast from our own guns would have injured the people in the pilot-house, only a few yards off. Keeler and Toffey passed the captain's orders and messages to me, and my inquiries and answers to him, the speaking-tube from the pilot-house to the turret having been broken early in the action. They performed their work with zeal and alacrity, but, both being landsmen, our technical communications sometimes miscarried. The situation was novel: a vessel of war engaged in desperate combat with a powerful foe; the captain, commanding and guiding, was enclosed in one place, and the executive officer, working and fighting the guns, was shut up in another, and communications between them was difficult and uncertain. It was this experience which caused Isaac Newton, immediately after the engagement, to suggest the clever plan of putting the pilot-house on top of the turret, and making it cylindrical instead of square; and his suggestions were subsequently adopted in this type of vessel.

As the engagement continued, the working of the turret was not altogether satisfactory. It was difficult to start it revolving, or, when

An artist's view of Hampton Roads, showing the fleet of foreign warships that witnessed the Monitor-Virginia *engagement.*

once started, to stop it, on account of the imperfections of the novel machinery, which was undergoing its first trial. Stimers was an active, muscular man, and did his utmost to control the motion of the turret; but, in spite of his efforts, it was difficult, if not impossible, to secure accurate firing. The conditions were very different from those of an ordinary broadside gun, under which we had been trained on wooden ships. My only view of the world outside of the tower was over the muzzles of the guns, which cleared the ports by only a few inches. When the guns were run in, the portholes were covered by heavy iron pendulums, pierced with small holes to allow the iron rammer and sponge handles to protrude while they were in use. To hoist these pendulums required the entire gun's crew and vastly increased the work inside the turret.

The effect upon one shut up in a revolving drum is perplexing, and it is not a simple matter to keep the bearings. White marks had been placed upon the stationary deck immediately below the turret to indicate the direction of the starboard and port sides, and the bow and stern; but these marks were obliterated early in the action. I would continually ask the captain,

How does the *Merrimac* bear?

He replied,

On the starboard-beam

or

On the port-quarter

as the case might be. Then the difficulty was to determine the direction of the starboard-beam, or port-quarter, or any other bearing. It finally resulted, that when a gun was ready for firing, the turret would be started on its revolving journey in search of the target, because the turret could not be accurately controlled. Once the *Merrimac* tried to ram us; but Worden avoided the direct impact by the skillful use of the helm, and she struck a glancing blow, which did no damage. At the instant of collision I planted a solid 180-pound shot fair and square upon the forward part of her casemate. Had the gun been loaded with thirty pounds of powder, which was the charge subsequently used with similar guns, it is probable that this shot would have penetrated her armor; but the charge being limited to fifteen pounds, in accordance with peremptory orders to that effect from the Navy Department, the shot rebounded without doing any more damage than possibly to start some of the beams of her armor-backing. [Washington was fearful of one of the two guns bursting, thereby

Photograph of the Monitor *in Hampton Roads after the battle. Note dents in turret, the newly installed sloping side to the pilot house, and the deck light cover laying on the deck. ——Courtesy U.S. Library of Congress.*

The "Monitor Boys" avoiding the oven-like temperatures below decks. Letters from home, out-dated newspapers, and comaraderie did little to dispell the boredom of blockade duty.

neutralizing the ship's only battery.]

The battle continued at close quarters without apparent damage to either side. After a time, the supply of shot in the turret being exhausted, Worden hauled off for about fifteen minutes to replenish. The serving of the cartridges, weighing but fifteen pounds, was a matter of no difficulty; but the hoisting of the heavy shot was a slow and tedious operation, it being necessary that the turret should remain stationary, in order that the two scuttles, one in the deck and the other in the floor of the turret, should be in line. Worden took advantage of the lull, and passed through the porthole upon the deck outside to get a better view of the situation. He soon renewed the attack, and the contest continued as before.

Two important points were constantly kept in mind: first, to prevent the enemy's projectiles from entering through the portholes, for the explosion of a shell inside, by disabling the men at the guns, would have ended the fight, as there was no relief gun's crew on board; second, not to fire into our own pilot-house. A careless or impatient hand, during the confusion arising from the whirligig motion of the tower, might let slip one of our big shot against the pilot-house. For this and other reasons I fired every gun while I remained in the turret.

Soon after noon a shell from the enemy's gun, the muzzle not ten yards distant, struck the forward side of the pilot-house directly in the sight-hole, or slit, and exploded, cracking the second iron log and partly lifting the top, leaving an opening. [The top of the pilot house was secured solely by its own weight to facilitate rapid escape in the event of mishap.] Worden was standing immediately behind this spot, and received in his face the force of the blow, which partly stunned him, and, filling his eyes with powder, utterly blinded him. The injury was known only to those in the pilot-house and its immediate vicinity. The flood of light rushing through the top of the pilot-house, now partly open, caused Worden, blind as he was, to believe that the pilot-house was seriously injured, if not destroyed; he therefore gave orders to put the helm to starboard and "sheer off." Thus the *Monitor* retired temporarily from the action, in order to ascertain the extent of the injuries she had received. At the same time Worden sent for me, and leaving Stimers the only officer in the turret, I went forward at once, and found him standing at the foot of the ladder leading to the pilot-house.

He was a ghastly sight, with his eyes closed and the blood apparently rushing from every pore in the upper part of his face. He

Meals were cooked on deck to escape the 150-degree temperature in the galley. The "Jack Tars" of the Navy of 1862 wore a motley assortment of uniforms.

The officers of the Monitor, *9 July 1862. Top row, left to right: Albert B. Campbell, 2nd Asst. Engineer; Mark Trueman Sunstrom, 3rd Asst. Engineer; William F. Keeler, Acting Asst. Paymaster; L. Howard Newman, Lieutenant, Executive Officer of the* Galena. *Middle row, left to right: Louis N. Stodder, Acting Master; George Frederickson, Master's Mate; William Flye, Acting Volunteer Lieutenant; Daniel C. Logue, Acting Asst. Surgeon; Samuel Dana Greene, Lieutenant. Bottom row, left to right: Robinson W. Hands, 3rd Asst. Engineer; E.V. Gager, Acting Master. —— Courtesy U.S. Library of Congress.*

told me that he was seriously wounded, and directed me to take command. I assisted in leading him to a sofa in his cabin, where he was tenderly cared for by Dr. Logue, and then I assumed command. Blind and suffering as he was, Worden's fortitude never forsook him; he frequently asked from his bed of pain of the progress of affairs, and when told that the *Minnesota* was saved, he said,

"Then I can die happy."

When I reached my station in the pilot-house, I found that the iron log was fractured and the top partly open; but the steering gear was still intact, and the pilot-house was not totally destroyed, as had been feared. In the confusion of the moment resulting from so serious an injury to the commanding officer, the *Monitor* had been moving without direction. Exactly how much time had elapsed from the moment that Worden was wounded until I had reached the pilot-house and completed the examination of the injury at that point, and determined what course to pursue in the damaged condition of the vessel, it is impossible to state; but it could hardly have exceeded twenty minutes at the utmost. During this time the *Merrimac*, which was leaking badly, had started in the direction of the Elizabeth River; and, on taking my station in the pilot-house, and turning the vessel's head in the direction

of the *Merrimac*, I saw that she was already in retreat. A few shots were fired at the retiring vessel, and she continued on to Norfolk. I returned with the *Monitor* to the side of the *Minnesota*, where preparations were being made to abandon the ship which was still aground. Shortly afterward Worden was transferred to a tug, and that night he was carried to Washington . . .

My men and myself were perfectly black with smoke and powder. All of my underclothes were perfectly black, and my person was in the same condition . . . I had been up so long, and had been under such a state of excitement, that my nervous system was completely run down . . . My nerves and muscles twitched as though electric shocks were continually passing through them . . . I lay down and tried to sleep—I might as well have tried to fly.

Thus ended the first engagement in history between ironclads. With both sides claiming victory, the battle has become the object of historical

Piece of the first Monitor,
removed after her battle with the
Rebel Steamer Merrimac in
Hampton Roads March 9th 1862
Presented to the
U.S. NAVAL ACADEMY
by G.V Fox Ass't Sec'ty of the
NAVY 1866

Section of damaged armor plate removed from the Monitor after the battle and presented to the U.S. Naval Academy. ——Courtesy U.S. Naval Academy Museum.

controversy. Typically the *New York Daily Tribune* headlined, "The Monitor Victorious, The Merrimac towed off in a sinking condition" and the *Raleigh Standard* maintained that *Merrimack* had rammed the *Monitor* which headed "instantly" homeward with "all hands at the pumps and in a sinking condition."

Stimers wrote to Ericsson and told him, "We were struck 22 times; pilot-house twice, turret nine times, side armor eight times, deck three times. The only vulnerable point was the pilot-house. The log is not quite in two, but is broken and pressed inward one and one-half inches." To the jubilant crew of the *Monitor,* the victory was theirs and they were ready to face the *Merrimack* if she would venture forth. But Washington did not hold the same confidence in the *Monitor.*

After Assistant Secretary Fox returned to the capitol and gave his full report of the battle the fact remained that the dreaded *Virginia* had not been destroyed nor was she seriously injured. The strategic planners in Washington believed another naval disaster had been staved off by the heroic efforts of the *Monitor* but the *Virginia* still lurked menacingly in Norfolk, still as much a threat as ever to the Peninsula campaign and the blockade. The North had only one warship that offered any threat to the *Virginia,* all wooden ships having been proven obsolescent in the battle. The skepticism of many naval officers concerning the capabilities of the *Monitor* had not been dispelled. When President Lincoln visited Lt. Worden at his bedside to thank him for his courage in the encounter, he was deeply disquieted to have Worden say that the *Monitor* could be "boarded and captured very easily." Whether it was apprehension because of the indecisive encounter or realization that the *Monitor* was the Union's sole weapon of defense, Lincoln moved with caution and he at once ordered the *Monitor* "be not too much exposed" and that she not go "skylarking" up to Norfolk unescorted.

On board the *Monitor,* Lt. Greene received this communication the day after the battle, 10 March 1862:

> My Dear Mr. Greene: Under the extraordinary circumstances of the contest of yesterday, and the responsibilities devolving upon me, and your extreme youth, I have suggested to Captain Marston to send on board the *Monitor,* as temporary commanding, Lieutenant Selfridge, until the arrival of Commodore Goldsborough, which will be in a few days. I appreciate your position, and you must appreciate mine, and serve with the same zeal and fidelity. With the kindest wishes for you all, most truly, G. V. Fox.

Lieutenant Selfridge remainded in command only a short while. As soon as it was determined that because of injuries, Worden would not be able to resume his command, Lt. William Jeffers was given the command. Worden had been only temporarily blinded, but the right side of his face would be permanently blackened due to the powder burns. While he was still in the hospital the *Monitor* crew wrote a letter praising his courage and their appreciation for his leadership. They signed the letter, "The Monitor Boys."

Back in Washington, the jubilation in the press over the battle was shifting to public clamor over the unpreparedness of the fleet. There were cries for Welles to resign due to "evidence of gross incompetency," if not the "blackest treachery." The situation climaxed when the U. S. Senate adopted a resolution offered by Senator Henry Wilson of Massachusetts to investigate the circumstances of Saturday's "deplorable calamity" and to determine responsibility for the tragic disaster. A vocal segment of the public had been convinced by the *New York Times* that the "long series of National disgraces" which the country had experienced, were not due to our Navy, but to the "administration of our Navy Department."

Consequently, Secretary of War Stanton became increasingly convinced that the crisis precipitated by the *Virginia* was too big a task for Welles and his Navy. In a novel situation, Stanton sent a telegram to Cornelius Vanderbilt of New York City, asking what sum he would contract for to destroy the *Virginia.*

Vanderbilt, an internationally famous shipping tycoon and a millionaire of tremendous power and influence, was not noted for his modesty or lack of confidence. He came immediately to Washington. In a conference with the President, to which Secretary Welles was not invited, Vanderbilt stated that he would do the job without compensation as a service to his country.

Vanderbilt's scheme was to use his ship, the *C. Vanderbilt,* "cover her machinery, etc. with 500 bales of cotton, raise the steam, and rush with overwhelming force on the iron-clad," sinking her before she could escape Norfolk. However, before undertaking this important mission, he wished it clearly understood that the *Monitor* had to be out of the way and he would not tolerate any interference from other naval vessels and he re-

fused to be subjected, in any way, to control from naval officers.

This unprecedented lack of confidence in our Navy on the part of the administration was largely due to growing concern on the part of port city governors about the *Monitor*'s ability to contain the *Virginia.* Lincoln, knowing that he could not politically survive another "Black Saturday," could take no chances.

Confidence on board the *Monitor* was not dampened by the whispers of doubt in the press. The crew, unaware of the Vanderbilt scheme, were national heroes and were sure they would settle the issue in the next battle. The pilot house was repaired and modified with sloping sides, 45° with the deck, "being solidly packed with oak and plated with two courses of iron." In a letter to Ericsson, Isaac Newton described how the second visit from the *Virginia* will "probably be her last appearance."

"I have succeeded in getting *both* guns out together at the depression of 1½°, this is a point of *vital* importance in fighting the *Merrimac* [apparently compensating for the *Virginia*'s sloping armor.]

"This is Jeffers opinion and he will fight her in that style—I think if both are fired nearly together it will carry in that portion of her side included between the axes of the two shot, or fire one gun first with a *shot,* the other immediately after with a *shell* which will give the hole made by shot."

Similarly, the Confederates had improved the *Virginia* by installing gun port covers, armor below the waterline and a ram specifically designed to reach the *Monitor*'s thin lower hull. The *Monitor*'s general dimensions having been published in the *Scientific American* by John Ericsson. The Confederate plan was to entice the *Monitor* into deep water where she could be readily boarded by 150 volunteers who would then throw combustibles down the ventilators, wedge the turret, and blind the helmsman by throwing canvas over the pilot house. The ship would then be in their hands.

As these new strategies evolved, it became apparent neither side wished to risk their only ironclads in combat again.

Lincoln visited the *Monitor* several times and stressed that she was to fall back if the *Virginia* appeared and to engage her "seriously" only when found in a position that would permit the *Vanderbilt* and other expendable ships to ram her. Several times the *Virginia* steamed cautiously from Norfolk, attempting to entice the *Monitor* into an exposed position. In the view of the press and the "Monitor boys" the final straw came on April 11, 1862 when the *Virginia* steamed out defiantly from Norfolk, captured three northern merchantmen as prizes, and fired a gun in challenge to the *Monitor* which stood off in shallow water in obeisance to orders, attempting to coax the *Virginia* further out into the Roads. The press called it "disgraceful." Paymaster Keeler of the *Monitor* wrote: "We are very *willing* and *anxious* for another interview. I believe the Department is going to build a big glass case to put us in for fear of harm coming to us."

The Monitor *as she appeared in the James River. Painting by Oscar Parks.*

Luckily for Secretary Welles, the problem was soon resolved; the Confederates were forced to scuttle the *Virginia* as they abandoned Norfolk. Due to her draft, they were unable to lighten her sufficiently to withdraw up the James River. At the turn of this century she was raised, and subsequently dismantled. Her armor and wood was made into souvenirs.

The *Virginia*'s crew withdrew with the Southern Army up the peninsula and took positions on Drury's Bluff. They would meet the *Monitor* one more time as she steamed up the James with other gunboats.

During the summer of 1862 the "Monitor Boys" were introduced to the drudgery of blockade duty—heat, boredom, the sudden excitement of skirmishes and news from the front. The *Monitor*'s ventilating system was found inadequate. By the end of August her machinery required overhaul. As much work as possible was carried on above deck; the log recorded temperatures of 150° in the galley, 125° in the berthdeck and 131° in the water closet *while at anchor with the steam plant secured*. Obviously life in the sun aboard this black iron box was not comfortable. As the weeks dragged on the crew yearned for action.

Several attempts were made to attack Southern batteries in company with the *Galena*. This was the other ironclad Bushnell had contracted to build, but these proved unsuccessful because the *Monitor* could not elevate her guns sufficiently and the *Galena* was easily penetrated by enemy shells. After a disappointing performance, but a welcome break in the routine, the *Monitor* returned to Hampton Roads. She stayed there until the fall when she was ordered to the Navy Yard in Washington for much needed repairs. Her bottom, it was found, was so badly fouled that she could barely make two or three knots.

John Ericsson was, in the interim, busily designing and constructing four more monitors of an "improved design." These were larger, they had a more conventional ships hull, and the pilot house on top of the turret. Eventually the Navy would commission thirty-three monitors of Ericsson's design, some having two turrets and over three times the displacement of the *Monitor*.

The original *Monitor* returned to Hampton Roads in November of 1862. Having secured the Chesapeake, perhaps by default, she would finally venture out into the Atlantic.

Away to the rescue! Crewman of the Rhode Island *attempting to save members of the* Monitor *crew. Some of the rescuers drowned in the attempt.*

5

THE LOSS OF U.S.S. MONITOR

In a communique dated 3 January 1863, Acting Rear Admiral S. P. Lee, Commander of the North Atlantic Blockading Squadron, informed Secretary of the Navy Gideon Welles, that the Union's most famous ironclad had foundered at sea. He stated in part, and with an error in the date:

> I have the painful duty to perform of reporting the loss of the *Monitor* at sea, south of Cape Hatteras, on Tuesday night, the 30th ultimo. . . . I left it to the discretion of their commanders to choose the weather and time of their departure.

The *Official Record* included the reports of the commanding officers which describe the circumstances that culminated in the catastrophe and the names of the sixteen officers and crewmen who were lost. A Congressional investigation was called for and contemporary newspapers and periodicals carried accounts by the survivors, but battles at Vicksburg and Fredericksburg soon drew public attention away from the loss of the ship.

Thus, the account of a great sea battle went untold except in private journals, personal letters, and at veterans' gatherings. The battle was not one of heavy shot versus iron plating, for the *Monitor* had already proven her ability to fight another ironclad, but the perennial struggle of man and ship against the sea. In such a conflict, the heavy iron armor of the *Monitor* was no defense.

During an active life of only nine months, the USS *Monitor* had highlighted the annals of naval history with accounts of its auspicious arrival at Hampton Roads on the evening of 8 March 1862 and the ensuing battle the next day. One little ship manned by forty-nine volunteers had turned a black day of defeat into victory.

But little was known of the other battle against the sea fought on the voyage down from New York, or the final, tragic struggle, less than a year later, when the *Monitor* left Hampton Roads for Beaufort, North Carolina. Histories tend to skip over the small, perhaps insignificant details, thus losing forever knowledge of the personal sacrifices and acts of heroism by common men. Fortunately, in the case of the *Monitor,* some of these details have been preserved.

The *Monitor* marks a great change in naval shipbuilding history, that of a switch from wood to iron. The old days of "iron men and wooden ships"

had passed. After her, warships were to be built of iron and a different kind of seaman had to be found to handle the new ships. Following the example of the *Monitor,* ships lost their graceful lines and white sails and became more complex with machinery; but there was not time to train seamen for new ships the likes of which no ordinary seamen had seen before. The men who answered the call for volunteers must have been an interesting lot, men like Samuel Lewis, alias Peter Truskitt, Quartermaster:

> We sailors generally shipped under some other name on account of danger running foul of bad captains or bad ships, when we might have to decamp at the first port, and were not particular about leaving any clews behind. That is why I called myself Truskit. I ain't much of a scholar, and can't put it as nicely as they do in the Century,* but I think I can tell a few facts about the fight that the magazine missed. I and my partner, Joe Crown, were in Bombay when the war broke out. We had both served in the Navy before, and were anxious to get into it again. I had medals for service on both British and Russian men-of-war, and the news that there was fighting over the water sort of fired men up. Well, the upshot of it was that Joe and I shipped for New York, and when we got there enlisted. We went on board the receiving ship *North Carolina* and had followed the dull daily routine for a week or so when Ericsson's *Monitor,* about which something had been whispered among the men, was completed, and a call was made for volunteers to go and man her. We understood that she was bound for Hampton Roads. . . .
>
> The next day we went on board. She was a little bit the strangest craft I had ever seen; nothing but a few inches of deck above the water line, her big, round tower in the center, and the pilot house at the end. . . .**
>
> We had confidence in her though, from the start, for the little ship looked somehow like she meant business, and it didn't take us long to learn the ropes. Joe was made gunner's mate of the first gun and I was loader.

---

* A contemporary magazine.

** The fact that both bow and stern were pointed obviously had this sailor confused.

If Peter Truskit was a novice before the *Monitor* left New York, he certainly knew as much as anyone on board about taking an ironclad to sea when they arrived at Hampton Roads. His recollections of the loss of the *Monitor,* along with those of others such as Paymaster William F. Keeler, Landsman Francis B. Butts, and Surgeon Grenville M. Weeks, has made it possible to piece together the events of the sinking, combining separate accounts and reports into a common narrative. The initial attempt at this was made by Captain Ernest W. Peterkin, USNR, in December, 1970, and after additional research, the narrative was refined with the objective of better estimating the last known position of the *Monitor,* thereby localizing the area to be searched, in an attempt to locate her hulk.

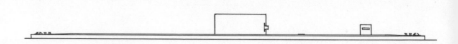

Battle trim, 9 April 1862.

November, 1862

The final episode in the short career of the *Monitor* began as she returned to Hampton Roads after spending two months in the Navy Yard at Washington for much needed repairs and overhaul of her machinery. While in the yards, many improvements and corrections were made. Acting Paymaster William F. Keeler in a letter dated 17 November 1862, to his wife describes them:

> Our vessel has undergone a variety of changes. A large telescopic smoke pipe capable of being run up some thirty feet, takes the place of the two low square box like things you see in the photograph. The fresh air funnels have been replaced by two much higher. Our old boats were all left behind and we were furnished with others better adapted to our wants and large iron cranes and davits to raise them out of the water and carry them on, instead of dragging them up to our decks to be in the way, or dragging them in the water after us.

> The ragged shot marks in our side have been covered with iron patches and the places marked "Merrimac," "Merrimac's Prow," "Minnesota," "Fort Darling," to indicate the source from whence the blow was received. New awnings have been furnished us, ventilators for our deck lights and many other little conveniences which would have added greatly to our comfort last summer could we have had them then.

Our guns have been engraved in large letters, on one of them

MONITOR AND MERRIMAC
WORDEN

and the other

MONITOR AND MERRIMAC
ERICSSON

Below, the Berth deck has been raised so that we can barely stand erect under the deck above, and the store rooms on each side thrown back some four feet. This arrangement makes the berth deck considerably wider but not as high, the width however is what we want. Below this deck I have two good store rooms for provisions and there is also a shell room. A large blower, driven by an engine attached, is placed partly above and partly below this deck, which draws the air down through the pilot house and through the deck lights

James River duty.

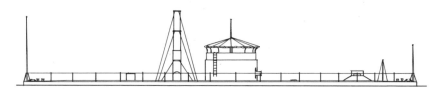

As rigged at time of sinking.

(when open) in the ward room and our state rooms and forces it into the engine room to aid the draft of the furnaces.

Three or four nice black walnut steps lead down from the berth deck to the Ward room. This room and our state rooms have been newly painted white and a new oil cloth put on the floors. With our bright lamps burning at night our Ward room looks as bright and cheerful as could be desired. When cool, steam is turned on the radiators and a very comfortable temperature maintained. . . .

While in Washington the men had received long overdue leave, many returning to their homes. They returned to find their ship the center of attention in Washington, the decks crowded with women and children to whom the officers were obliged to give tours of the famous warship.

But soon, with the repairs nearing completion and rumors of a second *Virginia,* the men of the *Monitor* had to return to the business of war. Supplies were taken on board and the *Monitor* got up steam once more for Hampton Roads. All were merry and jubilant as the *Monitor* cruised down the Chesapeake with the promise of new victories on the horizon. Having replenished their wardroom stores, Keeler reported, they ate well:

We breakfast at eight, lunch at twelve and dine at five. Our breakfast is usually fried oysters, beefsteak, fish balls, mutton chops, with an abundance of vegetables, sweet and common potatoes, etc. For lunch we usually have oysters or cold tongue, lobster (in cans), cold roast beef or corned beef, sometimes cold boiled ham, sardines, crackers, cheese, etc.

Dinner is *the* meal, soups, stewed oyster, boiled salmon, roast beef, mutton or turkey, boiled ham, and so on through a whole hotel bill of fare with all the sauces, condiments and fancy pickles. But our attempt at pie, pudding, etc. makes me wish for home made—we are well supplied with apples, nuts, raisins, and figs, etc. Don't imagine we are going to starve. . . .

The *Monitor* arrived at her old mooring off Newport News, Virginia at noon on Monday, 10 November 1862 to find that the war on the Peninsula had not progressed very far. For over a month the crew of the *Monitor* watched as troop transports unloaded their cargoes and eagerly waited for word from the front.

The days stretched out into weeks and still no orders for the anxious little warship. In one of his letters, Keeler relates the monotony of his daily routine:

The first thing I hear in the morning about day light is the Bo'sun's whistle and "all hands up hammocks." As "all hands" don't refer to me, I roll over and take another nap till my boy comes in to leave my boots and tell me " 'tis half past seven sir." He has previously taken the iron plug out of my deck light and let in a glimpse of day. "I dress and get ready and at just eight breakfast is ready. No one is in a hurry so that usually occupies an hour when all hands are mustered to quarters, that is each one takes the position assigned him in action and upon being questioned in turn relates the particular duty devolving upon him—then the turret division (those who fight the guns) are drilled for an hour or so.

The Surgeon and Paymaster, who are the drones, as we have no watch duties to perform pass our time as we see fit. I find considerable writing to do, and shall till I get fairly posted in all details of my work. The Dr., whose room joins mine, bores me to death by wanting to read me all his correspondence with his lady love and the newspapers in which of course I take no special interest, but he is a good, genial, warm hearted fellow and I humor him when I am not too busy.

Dinner at two, we have a regular course, soup, fish, meats, puddings, fruits and nuts, winding up with a cup of strong coffee. This takes an hour or an hour and a half, then those who choose take a cigar on deck.

Supper at six which is usually bread and butter, dried beef, cheese, crackers, coffee and tea.

At seven o'clock the bo'sun's whistle again and all hands down hammocks. In the evening all gather around the ward room table and "fight their battles o'er again" each one relating his individual experiences, stories are told and jokes cracked, till ten when all on board must be quiet and still. It is usual on men of war to have all lights extinguished at ten but this is not enforced in our case, we appear to be an exception to ordinary men of war. . . .

It was through the stories, the newspapers and acquaintances of fellow officers that the men of the *Monitor* learned the details of their engagement with the *Virginia.* Even though they had participated in the battle, few knew exactly what had happened, as they were all below the iron deck, fighting their ship. Visiting officers related their stories around the ward-room table at night and Keeler recorded:

> But of those noble fellows on board the *Cumberland,* too much cannot be said, they deserve much more credit than ourselves. Her 2nd Lieut. (Selfridge) was on board of us for a day or two after the fight as commanding officer & (it) would make your blood run cold to hear him describe some of the scenes he witnessed on board during that eventful day.

> A Capt. of one of the guns of which Lieut. S. had command, lost both legs at the knee by a shell which in exploding took off one of his arms at the shoulder. After he fell he contrived to get hold of the lockstring with his remaining hand & fired his gun—"Don't mind me boys, stand by your gun to the last," he said while the ship was rapidly sinking. Epaulettes & gold lace don't cover all the true brave hearts, nor do they conceal all the coward ones.

The monotony of daily routine was broken by frequent trips ashore for the officers and weekly inspections for the crew. On Sundays:

> The usual routine of daily work, of men drilling and at quarters, of painting and scraping and etc is not carried on. After breakfast every-thing is cleaned up nice and at ten o'clock the men are all "mustered for inspection."

> Each one is expected to be dressed in his Sunday best and at exactly four bells (10 o'clock) the bo'sun's call musters all hands for inspec-tion. The seamen and petty officers are drawn up on one side of the deck, the firemen and coal heavers on the other. Each man answers to his name as the Lieut. calls the roll.

> The Capt. is then informed that the men are ready for inspection. He passes slowly along in front of the lines of men looking closely at their dress, appearance and etc—"Jones why are your shoes not blacked?" Jones having no good excuse, the Paymaster's steward is ordered to stop his grog for a day or two.

> "Lieut. what is this man's name?"—"Smith sir."—"Well have his grog stopped for a week for coming to inspection without a cravat."

As the months dragged on there were a few changes in the ships company. Acting Lieutenant William Flye, Second Assistant Engineer George H. White and Doctor Logue were detached and several new officers came aboard to join the crew.

The new surgeon was Doctor Grenville M. Weeks whom Keeler thought was a little self conceited but felt that this would wear off in time as Weeks "found his level" and would have made "a companionable inhabi-tant" of their craft:

> Then in the place of Mr. White we have a Mr. (Third Assistant Engineer Samuel A.) Lewis* from Baltimore, a mere boy, nearly a cyphen in our little society. Mr. (George) Frederickson,* one of our Master's Mates, has been promoted to Ensign, which brings him to

our Ward room. Another Ensign has also been added, a Mr. (Norman) Atwater* (from New Haven of course as the name indicates) . . . These are all the changes in our little community.

The captain of the *Monitor* was Commander John Pine Bankhead who had relieved the well-liked Stevens on 11 September 1862. Stevens had commanded the *Monitor* for less than a month.

Operations were moving farther south and the officers of the *Monitor* discussed what would be most likely their next assignment. They had heard that the Monitor number two, the USS *Passaic,* had been launched under the command of Captain Percival Drayton and that the new warship had reached Hampton Roads on 30 November 1862 but was forced to pro-ceed immediately to Washington "to repair some defect in her boilers." The other ironclads, the *New Ironsides* (Captain Thomas Turner) and the *Galena* (Lieutenant Commander Leonard Paulding) were present at the Roads as were a number of wooden gunboats. Everyone expected the Navy's new ironclad fleet to receive orders for action as soon as the *Passaic* was able to join them. Perhaps even the new Monitor number three, the *Montauk,* (Captain John L. Worden of ex-*Monitor* fame) would arrive in time. Keeler expected Charleston, South Carolina, to be the next objec-tive but others thought that perhaps it would be Wilmington, North Caro-lina. Regardless, all were anxious to end the monotony; even another trip up the James would have satisfied them. Through the end of November and into December fresh rumors flourished daily about what the next move would be. During the interim mechanics were on board repairing the turret mechanism, and in early December a rifle shield or iron breast-work constructed of boiler iron was installed on top of the turret "of sufficient height and strength to protect those behind it from sharp shooters."

An injury befell the *Monitor* at this time, the consequence of which is difficult to assess.

The Second Assistant engineer, Mr. Albert B. Campbell,

> . . . was in the act of giving some final touches to the machinery, when his leg was caught between the piston-rod and frame of one of the oscillating engines, with such a force as to bend the rod, which was an inch and a quarter in diameter and about eight inches long, and broke its cast-iron frame, five eighths of an inch in thickness. The most remarkable fact in this case is, that the limb, though jammed and bruised, remained unbroken,—our men in this iron craft seeming themselves to be iron.

Mr. Campbell wanted to stay with his ship as he was one of the original crew members and the most experienced with her machinery and pumps, but it was felt wise to let his leg fully heal and he was transferred to a hospital.

* Lewis, Atwater, and Frederickson were among those lost at sea when the *Monitor* foundered.

Commander Stephen D. Trenchard, commanding officer of the U.S.S. Rhode Island. *——Courtesy U.S. National Archives.*

U.S.S. Rhode Island, *the steam packet ship that took the* Monitor *in tow for the passage to Beaufort, North Carolina.*

Finally orders were received and the captain had all hands busy preparing for sea. The *Atlantic Monthly* later described the activity:

> The turret and sightholes were caulked, and every possible entrance for water made secure, only the smallest openings being left in the turret top and the blower stacks through which the ship was ventilated.

Many of the same procedures of preparing the *Monitor* for sea were followed as on the first voyage from New York. The turret was wedged up from its center post and oakum was stuffed around the circumference of the turret to form a seal although this was contrary to the intentions of John Ericsson, the designer, who claimed that the machined brass ring placed in the deck was sufficient enough seal. In addition, oakum was prepared to be stuffed in the hawse pipe after the anchor was heaved in to seal that nine-inch diameter hole just five inches above the waterline.

The helm was moved from the pilot house to the top of the turret by a system of deck chains to make it less vulnerable to a raging sea as the forward section of the ship was continually awash when underway.

Complete stores, powder and shells were brought on board as there were no Union ports south of Norfolk. Most of this weight was placed well forward in the ship in the newly constructed store rooms under the berthing deck.

On 24 December 1862, Commander Stephen Decatur Trenchard commanding the paddle wheel steamer, *Rhode Island,* received these official orders to tow the *Monitor* to Beaufort, North Carolina:

24 Dec 1862

Confidential —
Sir: Proceed with the *Monitor* in tow to Beaufort, N.C. Avail yourself of the first favorable weather for making the passage. Return to this port.

Respectfully yours,
S. P. Lee
Acting Rear-Admiral,
Cmdg. North Atlantic
Blockading Squadron

Acknowledgment of Orders

25 Dec 1862

Sir: I have the honor to acknowledge receipt of your confidential communication of the 24th instant, and will proceed in conformity with your instructions as soon as the weather shall be favorable for the tow.

I am, very respectfully, your obedient servant,

Stephen D. Trenchard
Commander

Keeler wrote that the *Passaic* arrived on 27 December and that a

> . . . heavy storm is just coming on which when over is usually followed by several days of calm fine weather. We shall hold on here till the storm is over and take advantage of the calm that follows for our trip down the coast.

Having been cautioned about discussing future military operations in correspondence, Keeler on 28 December wrote:

> I wish I could whisper in your ear our destination and plans . . . You will have to nurse your curiosity and patience for a little while, when we hope again to make "the little *Monitor*" a household word.
>
> I am glad now that I wasn't detached and ordered to some other vessel as I desired to be. I wouldn't exchange our "iron box" for any vessel in the navy with our present prospects. . . .

At eight AM on 29 December the weather was crisp and clear, with the wind gently blowing from the south-southwest. Final preparations were underway as Keeler enjoyed himself on deck

> . . . listening to some very fine music from our English neighbor, the *Ariadne*—she carries a fine brass band. Every morning St. George's cross is hoisted to the tune "God Save the Queen" as I suppose they call it, we call it "America." After they are done saving the Queen they compliment us Yankees with the "Star Spangled Banner," "Hail Columbia," etc, etc which being well played are duly appreciated.

Later that morning the two boats on board the *Monitor* were transferred to the *Rhode Island*. Ensign Rodgers of the *Rhode Island* later wrote that this was a mistake as later in the war all the monitors carried their boats safely at their davits during the heaviest storms. The only boat left on board the *Monitor* was a collapsible one of black India rubber that had an iron frame. This boat could be stored below.

At nine the *Rhode Island* exercised her crew at her guns and completed coaling the ship. At ten the newly completed monitor *Montauk* arrived under tow of the *Connecticut* but due to engineering difficulties she had to return to the yard for repairs and so could not accompany the *Monitor* and *Passaic*.

Log of United States Steamer "Rhode Island" Commanded by Commander S. D. Trenchard.

REMARKS ON THIS 28th DAY OF December 1862
Sunday.

H.	Knots.	Fathoms.	Courses.	Wind. Direction.	Wind. Force.	Weather.	Temperature. Air.	Temperature. Water.	Barometer.
A.M. 1				N.N.E.	2	r	47		2977
2				"	"	"	46		"
3				"	"	"	45		"
4				"	"	"	44		2965
5				"	"	"	46		2979
6				"	"	"			
7				N.W.	"	b			2986
8				"	"	bc	"		
9				"	"	"			30'00
10				"	"	"			
11				"	"	"			
12				"	"	"			

Distance per Log
Latitude, D. R.
Longitude, D. R.
Latitude observed At anchor off Fortress Monroe
Longitude
Current
Variation

H.	Knots.	Fathoms.	Courses.	Wind. Direction.	Wind. Force.	Weather.	Temperature. Air.	Temperature. Water.	Barometer.
P.M. 1									
2									
3									
4									
5				N.N.W.	1	bc	53		30'02
6				"	"	"	"		
7				"	"	"	"		
8				"	"	"	"		3017
9				"	"	"	49		
10				"	"	"	48		
11				"	"	"	"		3017
12				"	"	"	"		

Midnight to 4 A.M.
Thies N. Meyer

4 to 8 A.M.
At 7.30 U.S. Transport "Hobby" passed bound out
Sam'l H. Field

8 A.M. to meridian
At 10 A.M. mustered all hands and held divine service.
Albert Taylor

Meridian to 4 P.M.
Thies N. Meyer

4 to 6 P.M.
Sam'l H. Field,

6 to 8 P.M.
Cleared battery for action.
Albert Taylor

8 P.M. to Midnight
Thies N. Meyer

Expended 260 Galls water
12 Sticks wood.

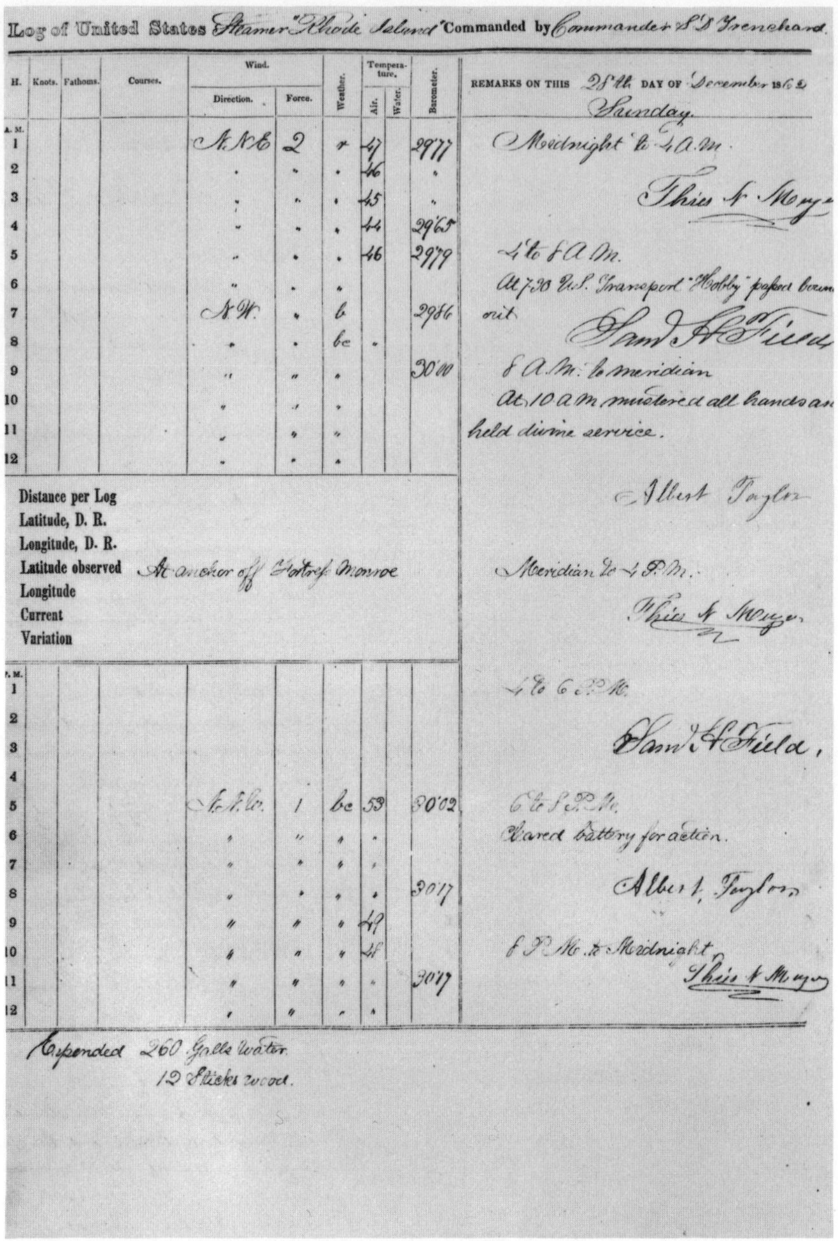

Log of U.S.S. Rhode Island, *28 December 1862.*

Log of U.S.S. Rhode Island, *29 December 1862.*

About midday preparations were being made to pass two hawsers (one 11-inch and one 15-inch circumference) from the *Rhode Island* to the *Monitor*. Boat crews passed the cumbersome hawsers between the two ships, until about 250-300 feet was let out. The two hawsers were made fast to the *Monitor*'s towing bit, leading them through the two chocks. Even when dry, the heavy hawsers tended to pull the bow of the little ironclad down, but in their strength lay her safety.

At 2:30 PM the *Rhode Island* heaved short on her anchor and let steam into her engine. As her paddle wheels churned the water, the engine on board the *Monitor* slowly turned the single screw propeller. The *Monitor* was finally underway with the bright prospects of future accomplishments on the horizon. The weather also held great promise. Trenchard recorded that the winds had calmed, ". . . being light from the southward and westward, with a smooth sea."

The Pilot, John H. Bean, guided the two warships down the harbor and past the protective guns of Fort Monroe, with Mr. Weeks especially enjoying the trip: "General joy was expressed at this relief from long inaction. The sick came upon deck, and in the clear sky, fresh air, and sense of motion, seemed to gain a new life."

Nothing was better for seamen than to be at sea. Many of the crew not on watch enjoyed the open deck and the gentle seascape with Hampton Roads fading in the distance. Mr. Weeks observed that "The *Rhode Island* left in her wake a rolling, foaming track of waves, which the *Monitor*, as she passed over it, seemed to smooth out like an immense flatiron."

As the afternoon lingered on, the sky gradually filled with small, puffy, white clouds, but none took alarm as the temperature was a pleasant 58° with the barometer holding steady at 30.1 inches of mercury. In the late afternoon the *State of Georgia* with the ironclad monitor *Passaic* in tow was sighted far ahead of the *Monitor*. At 4:45 PM the *Rhode Island* discharged the Pilot off Cape Henry. The shoal waters of the lower Chesapeake had been traversed safely. Now only the open ocean lay between the famous little warship and its next exploit. As they gradually passed out to sea, the wind freshened somewhat and Surgeon Weeks remembered the sunset with ". . . glorious clouds of purple and crimson. . . . a suitable farewell to the Virginia Capes."

At 5 PM the officers sat down to their usual meal and the joking was particularly intense as all were in good humor. The night was fair and calm but with all the deck lights (openings) secured for sea, it was not long before the air below decks lost its freshness. At 5:40 PM Cape Henry Light was sighted and found to bear to the west, distant four miles. The weather continued the same through the night and the *Monitor* "towed easily, making between five and six knots."

Commander Trenchard on board the *Rhode Island* issued the following night orders:

The officer of the deck is directed to have a very bright lookout kept off the bow and beam. He will sound at ten o'clock and inform

Track of Rhode Island, *standing out of Hampton Roads, as reproduced by E. W. Peterkin.*

me of the depth of water: also at four o'clock in the morning. The course will be S.S.E. as at present steered until course is changed. Keep a sharp lookout upon the *Monitor* astern, and should she signal *attend to it at once;* then report to me. Inform me of every change of wind and weather. The speed of the steamer should be regulated by the sea. If it increases, moderate the speed; if it smooth, increase it. Inform me when the steamer has made sixty miles from 10 P.M.

Sam H. Field, Officer-of-the-Deck on board the *Rhode Island,* recorded in the deck log the sighting of two sails ". . . one standing to the northward and eastward, the other standing to the westward."

Otherwise, the watch was uneventful as the night air was filled with the steady puffing and hissing of the steam engine and the sounds of the paddle wheels churning the water. On board the *Monitor,* Surgeon Weeks had difficulty sleeping, because of the stale air and remained awake in his bunk, listening to the steady thump of the *Monitor*'s engine.

At ten o'clock Mr. Field on board the *Rhode Island* took a sounding as directed and recorded twelve fathoms of water. The wind had increased to force two, but the barometer was still holding steady. Course was steady on south southeast with speed a constant six knots. The many stars visible seemed to foretell of a swift, pleasant journey.

Track of the Rhode Island, rounding Cape Henry, as reproduced by E. W. Peterkin.

Tuesday, December 30, 1862

The dawn brought continued good weather. The Surgeon and Paymaster were glad to stroll the open deck again, enjoying the fresh air after a somewhat uncomfortable night. With the deck lights closed, the new ventilator installed in Washington was of little help to draw in fresh air to the living spaces. Keeler thought to himself that he must compose a letter explaining the dilemma, so that in later ships it might be corrected.*

* In later monitors, fresh air was drawn through the turret and directed through the living spaces and then to the fires.

On board the *Rhode Island* the smell of breakfast from the galley permeated the ship. Commander Trenchard wrote in his journal: "The wind was light from the south and west; clear and pleasant. The *Monitor* is making a good headway in the good weather and is turning easily. Our speed averages five to six miles an hour."

At 5 AM Bankhead noted that they began ". . . to experience a swell from the southward, with a slight increase of the wind from the Southwest,

the sea breaking over the pilot-house forward and striking the base of the 'tower' . . ." forcing men to leave the deck for shelter on top of the turret. The helmsman at his station on the turret started to feel the force of a rising sea. The officers ate breakfast with a foaming sea washing over their heads as the *Monitor* gently rolled in the waves. Commander Bankhead, with the Acting Chief Engineer, Mr. Watters, inspected the sturdy little ship after breakfast and ". . . found the packing of oakum under and around the base of the tower had loosened somewhat from the working of the tower, as the vessel pitched and rolled."

Speed was about five knots. In the engine room the watch kept feeding the fires with coal. The engineer on duty was constantly alert to the sounds of an unoiled valve or squeaky rod and paid due attention to the disorder with his oil can. The bilge pumps kept the water that found its way into the interior of the ship at a low level, occasionally "sucking" air, making a gurgling sound as the *Monitor* rolled in the sea.

The swells continued from the south, as though indicating a storm in some part of the ocean but Mr. Weeks noted that the weather was still clear, ". . . the land only a blue line in the distance."

The watch on the turret reported to Commander Bankhead that the steady working of the ship had worn one of the hawsers at the chock and at 6:40 AM the order was given to signal to stop so that new chaffing gear could be parceled to the hawsers. The waves were now rolling constantly upon the deck of the ironclad and the men had to be very cautious as they worked. The wind had picked up a bit and the swells seemed to be increasing. At 7:30 AM the *Monitor* was once again ready to continue the journey. Again signals were passed between the two ships. The *Monitor*, not having a mast on which to hoist signal flags, used a chalk board and, when within distance, Commander Bankhead used his horn.

Speed was decreased to four knots as the wind continued from the south, southwest. Keeler wrote home that "Cloud banks were seen rising in the South and West and they gradually increased till the sun was obscured by their cold grey mantle."

Nothing but the cold looking sea could be seen on either horizon. The course was now due south and the next point of land was Cape Hatteras shoals.

Commander Trenchard of the *Rhode Island* had decided to take the sea route which closely followed the North Carolina coastline. Heading south, he had to hug the outer banks to avoid the strong, northerly heading Gulf Stream which skirted the coast. This would bring the two ships dangerously close to the shoals at Cape Hatteras. That area of the ocean had well earned all seamen's fear as the graveyard for many a merchantman who failed to keep constantly alert as to their position and the depth of water. There were no landmarks on the barren stretch of land between Cape Henry and Cape Hatteras and the outer banks were so low that an unalert lookout would not spot the breakers until the ship was dangerously close and at the mercy of strong currents and constantly shifting shoals. There was greater risk in this route, but the gain of a shortened voyage seemed to outweigh the risk of shipwreck on the shoals. The *State of Georgia* with the *Passaic* in tow had taken a route further out to sea. They would have to fight the two to three knot Gulf Stream on their voyage south. Nothing had been seen of them since passing Cape Henry the previous day.

At 9:30 the crew was mustered and exercised at quarters. Each man had his assigned station and duty to perform. In the next engagement, the *Monitor* would increase its rate of fire as the crew had become more efficient and familiar with the task of fighting the guns.

About midday, Paymaster Keeler joined some of the crew on top of the turret. The wind was gusty and he wore his new sea coat which his wife had made for him. He wrote later: "We amused ourselves for an hour or more by watching two or three large sharks who glided quietly along by our sides observing us apparently with a curious eye as if in anticipation of a feast."

Some of the men were just gaining their sea legs and most seemed to enjoy the steady surge of the ship through the waves. Some, including Weeks, ventured out on the deck as though in defiance of the sea. Being

Log of U.S.S. Rhode Island, *30 December 1862.*

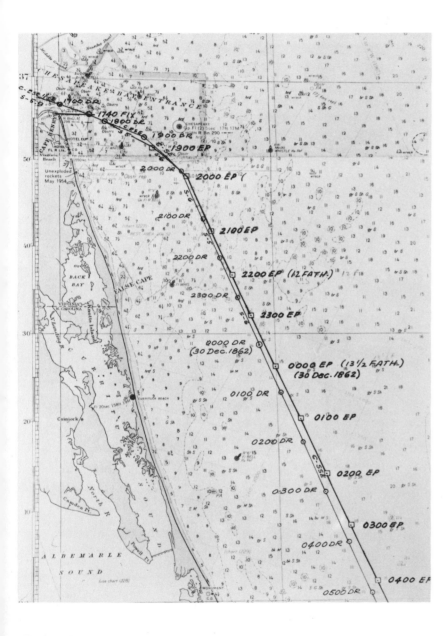

Track of the Rhode Island *during first night out of Hampton Roads, as reproduced by* E. W. Peterkin.

on the same level as the sea, ". . . with the spray dashing over us occasionally, amused ourselves with noting its shifting hues and forms, from the deep green of the first long roll to the foam-crest and prismatic tints of the falling wave."

At 11:20 the *Rhode Island* took a sounding of eighteen fathoms and at noon again sounded eighteen fathoms. At noon Albert Taylor on the *Rhode Island* recorded in the deck log the dead reckoning position of the two ships as being 35°-25′ latitude and 75°-16′ longitude. The distance from port as recorded by the sea log was 106 miles. On board the *Monitor,* landsman Francis B. Butts relieved the lee helmsman. It was his job to assist the helmsman in holding the wheel against the force of the sea and to relay the engine orders to the engine room.

At one o'clock the *Rhode Island* sighted the Cape Hatteras light bearing ". . . west by southwest fourteen miles distant."

Commander Trenchard recorded this in his journal and checked the charts to ascertain his position. The two warships were making good progress. Soon they would round treacherous Cape Hatteras and be heading for the next point of land, Cape Lookout and the conclusion of their journey.

Paymaster Keeler and Surgeon Weeks were again companions on top of the turret as the air was close below decks and the sight of water repeatedly filling the decklights was unnerving. Keeler wrote:

> The wind which in the morning was quite light continued to increase till the middle of the afternoon when it blew quite heavy, the sea rolling with violence across our deck rendering it impossible to remain on it without danger of being swept off.

And Surgeon Weeks remembered that:

> As the afternoon advanced, the freshening wind, the thickening clouds, and the increasing roll of the sea gave those most accustomed to ordinary ship-life some new experiences. The little vessel plunged through the rising waves, instead of riding them, and, as they increased in violence, lay, as it were, under their crests, which washed over her continually, so that, even when we considered ourselves safe, the appearance was of a vessel sinking.

There was a small huddle of other crew members on top of the turret. Some were off duty and could not sleep in the increasing violence of the sea, while others had been sent above by the Engineering Watch Officer from the suffocating heat of the fire room. "I'd rather go to sea in a diving bell!" Weeks heard one say, as the waves dashed over the pilot house, and the little craft seemed buried in water.

Another cried: "Give me an oyster-scow! — anything! — only let it be wood, and something that will float over, instead of under the water!"

The flat deck of the *Monitor* was continually awash now. The sea was pounding with great force upon the small pilot house in the bow. As the ship rose and fell in the sea, a great plume of water would gush out of the circular anchor well up forward like a geyser, making a terrific groaning sound as the little warship labored under the great weight of the water on her deck. It was an eerie sound but all had confidence that the *Monitor* would reappear after burying itself in successive waves.

The Chief Engineer kept Captain Bankhead constantly advised of the condition of the ship: "We made no water of consequence; a little trickled down about the pilot house and some began to find its way under the turret rendering it wet and cheerless below."

The storm showed no signs of increasing and the bilge pumps were able to control the little water that found its way below. The ship also had on board a Worthington displacement type pump and the Adam's pump of new design, a centrifugal type pump, capable of pumping 3,000 gallons per minute. Both were steam driven and worked independently of the main engine while the bilge pumps worked via an eccentric gear off the main engine.

At 4:30 PM Cape Hatteras bore northwest by west, distant sixteen miles. The lookouts on top of the turret reported a steamer with a ship in tow and also sighted the *State of Georgia* with the *Passaic* in tow on their port beam. The wind was holding steady at force two coming from the southwest by west. The weather was variable, with occasional squalls of wind and rain, with less swell in the afternoon.

As the sun set the swell somewhat decreased and the *Monitor* began to ride more easily. All on board were relieved; with continued good weather, the next day would end their sea voyage.

At 5 PM the officers sat down to dinner, everyone cheerful and happy, and though the sea was rolling and foaming over their heads, they laughed and jested freely. All were rejoicing that at last their monotonous, inactive life had ended and the "gallant little *Monitor*" would soon add fresh laurels to her name.

After eating, Keeler returned to the top of the turret. The night was dark. The *Monitor* was now directly off Cape Hatteras. The seas rolled high and pitched together in the peculiar manner only seen at Hatteras.

From a ship at sea it is impossible to see the low-lying outer banks until close in to the breakers. The only shore reference is the Cape Hatteras Light which has a visibility of twenty miles. On board the *Rhode Island* Commander Trenchard was constantly asking the Officer-of-the-Deck and the Quartermaster for soundings, and bearings on Cape Hatteras Light. With a single line of bearing and the depth of water, an approximate position could be judged. The range of the light was checked frequently by sending a seaman up the mast to measure the point when he first sighted the light so that through triangulation the distance could be checked. The depth alone could be misleading as the shifting bottom of Diamond Shoals could lead an unsuspecting ship into a shallow trap which she could not maneuver out of because of high winds or sea.

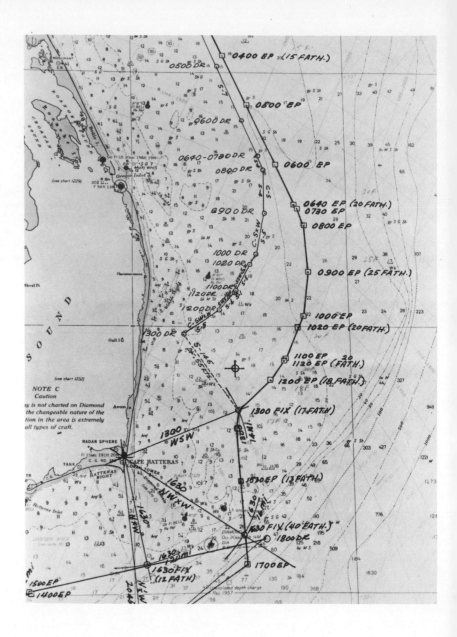

Track of the Rhode Island *rounding the Capes when the* Monitor *was lost, as reproduced by E. W. Peterkin.*

On board the *Rhode Island,* the officers were getting increasingly uneasy about their tow. Ensign Rodgers of the *Rhode Island* recalled:

> Dark clouds made their appearance to the southward, and a breeze sprang up from that quarter, which increased to quite a gale by sundown. The wind kicked up quite a sea into which the little *Monitor* pitched and rolled heavily.

Rodgers had the first dog-watch on deck, and when he went below at four bells, they were about twenty miles off Cape Hatteras. He turned into his berth that evening, little thinking what a few hours would bring forth.

At 6:30 PM Paymaster Keeler returned to the top of the turret just as darkness fell. He noticed in the water a change in color from cold gray to green-blue emerald. The air smelled different and warm. The ships had entered the Gulf Stream. The water temperature was recorded as being greater than the air temperature, both being in the balmy 70s. However, the wind had increased to force three, and Keeler described it

> . . . blowing violently; the heavy seas rolled over our bows dashing against the pilot house and surging aft, would strike the solid turret with a force to make it tremble, sending off on either side a boiling, foaming torrent of water.

The order was given for the *Monitor* to steam close to the *Rhode Island* so that signals could be exchanged. When off the quarter of the *Rhode Island,* Commander Bankhead used his horn to inform Commander Trenchard that if the *Monitor* needed assistance during the night, they would hoist a single red lantern on the signal mast as it was impossible for the watch to read the chalk board in the darkness and it was getting increasingly difficult to hail the watch using the horn. Agreeing on this signal, the *Monitor* fell in astern of the *Rhode Island.* They still were making six knots.

Francis Butts who had volunteered for duty on the *Monitor* in November while she was in the yard, was assisting on the helm. He later remembered:

> The vessel was making very heavy weather, riding one huge wave, plunging through the next as if shooting straight for the bottom of the ocean, and splashing down upon another with such force that her hull would tremble, and with a shock would sometimes take us off our feet, while a fourth would leap upon us and break far above the turret, so that if we had not been protected by a rifle-armor that was securely fastened and rose to the height of a man's chest, we should have been washed away.

Commander Trenchard noted in his journal at seven o'clock in the evening that "The wind commenced freshening and hauling more to the south."

As men on board the *Rhode Island* watched the little ironclad from the fantail, they feared for her safety. The *Monitor* would plunge from view behind a swell, being nearly submerged in foam. But each time she disappeared she reappeared, to the relief of those who watched.

Surgeon Weeks on board the *Monitor* recorded the concern of the crew in their desire to be first in everything:

> . . . we had rounded the point, and many on board expressed regret that the *Monitor* should not have been before the *Passaic* in doing so. Our spy-glasses were in constant use; we saw several vessels in the distance, and about seven P.M. discovered the *Passaic* four or five miles *astern* to the north of us, in tow of the steamer *State of Georgia.* A general hurrah went up—'Hurrah for the first iron-clad that ever rounded Cape Hatteras! Hurrah for the little boat that is first in everything.' The distance between ourselves and the *Passaic* widened, and we gradually lost sight of her.

The men were still in good spirits and full of confidence as the last hurrahs were muffled by the angry sea. In the engine room, Mr. Watters was preparing his machinery as best he could for the death struggle that was to follow. All bilge injection pumps were on line ready to be operated at the slightest indication of a leak. These could pump at a minimum of 2,000 gallons per minute. The computed position of the *Monitor* at this time was fifteen miles south of Cape Hatteras Shoals. All was going well, however, those with a knowledge of the sea were leery for the future.

Shortly after 7 PM the situation worsened. The smaller of the two hawsers (port side) parted. The chaffing gear had only slowed what was inevitable as the hawser had worn through at the chock. With only the starboard hawser left, the *Monitor* began to yaw and tow badly, as reported afterward by Admiral Lee: ". . . the vessel working and making more water. The increased motion caused more oakum to be knocked loose and consequently the *Monitor* was making more water around the base of the turret."

In the engine room, the heat was unbearable. The coal heavers had difficulty carrying the coal from the coal bunkers to the furnace doors, as the ship pitched in the raging sea. The men were stripped to their waists and as sweat mixed with the coal dust, they were covered with grime.

Mr. Watters watched the steam pressure gauge. The fate of the *Monitor* depended upon keeping the steam pressure up to eighty pounds and as the gauge fluctuated so did Mr. Watters' heartbeat. His trained ear heard a squeaking engine bearing and he sent a man to oil it. If the *Monitor* continued to take water at the same rate, her pumps could handle it if the steam pressure held. He silently prayed that Providence would smooth the seas for them, not testing his little ship so severely.

Topside, in the turret, Surgeon Weeks was watching the horizon which was barely visible in the moonlight:

> At half-past seven a heavy shower fell, lasting about twenty minutes. At this time the gale increased; black heavy clouds covered the

sky, through which the moon glimmered fitfully, allowing us to see in the distance a long line of white plunging foam, rushing towards us,—sure indication, to a sailor's eye, of a stormy time.

A gloom overhung everything; the banks of clouds seemed to settle around us; the moan of the ocean grew louder and more fearful. Still our little boat pushed doggedly on: victorious through all, we thought that here, too she would conquer; though the beating waves sent shudders through her whole frame. Bearing still the marks of one of the fiercest battles of the war, we had grown to think of her as invulnerable to any assault of man or element, and as she breasted these huge waves, plunging through one only to meet another more mighty, we thought,—"She is staunch! She will weather it!"

The wind had increased to force four and the barometer was dropping. Men on top of the turret watched each successive wave swallow their ship. The pilot house was being completely submerged; waves were hitting the turret with great force and gushing up the sides in a foamy torrent. The ship began taking water down the blower pipes and seepage was noticed in the coal bunkers. The forced ventilating system on which the fires depended for draft was operated by two steam engines driving large leather belts. If these got wet and stretched, the engineering spaces would be filled with toxic gases from the furnaces.

The events of the earlier struggle against the sea were vivid in Mr. Watters' mind. He watched the level of the water in the bilges. Rising water was a threat to his ship. He sent word to Commander Bankhead that the ordinary bilge injection pumps could not keep the water down. They were making more water than the pumps could throw out. Keeler remembered the report being given to the Captain and the ominous look on his weathered face. The engineers were ordered to ". . . have ready for use all pumps connected with the engineer's department."

The pace was increasing. Surgeon Weeks recorded:

> . . . the air below, which had all day been increasing in closeness, was now almost stifling, but our men lost no courage. Some sang as they worked, and the cadence of the voices, mingling with the roar of the waters, sounded like a defiance to the Ocean.

> Some stationed themselves on top of the turret, and a general enthusiasm filled all breasts, as huge waves, twenty feet high rose upon all sides, hung suspended for a moment like jaws open to devour, and then, breaking, gnashed over in foam from side to side.

> Those of us new to the sea, and not appreciating our peril, hurrahed for the largest wave; but the captain and one or two others, old sailors, knowing its power, grew momentarily more and more anxious, feeling, with a dread instinctive to the sailor, that, in case of extremity, no wreck yet known to the ocean could be so hopeless as this. Solid iron from keelson to turret-top, clinging to anything for safety, if the *Monitor* should go down, would only insure a share in her fate. No mast, no spar, no floating thing, to meet the outstretched hand in the last moment.

The sea, like the old-world giant, gathered force from each attack. Thick and fast come the blows on the iron mail of the *Monitor*, and still the brave little vessel held her own . . . !

Below decks, the air was hot and damp. Men not on watch tried to pass the time as best they could; some began securing equipment as the ship tossed in the sea. Topside, heavy swells were sweeping the deck; the great weight of water slowed the movements of the ship. After each successive swell, she would labor to bring her bow to the surface, lifting the water that was pushing her down. Her hull was built for strength, but men could not help glancing at her iron plates and rivets to see if there were signs of weakness. As the ship worked in the sea, she sounded as though she was in agony.

Seaman Butts was the first to recognize that the situation was worsening in the engine room. As he passed through the door in the engine room he met the acid smell of wet, burning coal and sweating men: "About eight o'clock, while I was taking a message from the Captain to the Engineer, I saw water pouring in through the coal-bunkers in sudden volumes as it swept over the deck."

Mr. Hands, the engineer on duty, was drenched in perspiration and his face was smeared with smudges of coal, but his complexion was pale, either from lack of oxygen or fright of a feeling of helplessness in the face of a steadily increasing danger.

Mr. Hands shouted over the din of the engine for Butts to immediately report to the captain that ". . . the coal was too wet to keep up steam which had run down from its usual pressure of eighty pounds to twenty."

Also, Butts was to find Mr. Watters and summon him to the engine room.

> I immediately went to the engine room, and found the bilge pump connected with the main engine in good condition, and working well, as it had been during the day. I had the discharge-pipe of the centrifugal pump connected to its proper place, and all ready for use, and before leaving the engine room I gave orders to Mr. Hands, the engineer then on duty, in case the water should increase to let me know, and at the same time to start the Worthington pump and use the bilge injection.

He then left to report to Commander Bankhead the seriousness of the situation. On his passage through the turret he noticed that with each swell water was pouring in where the oakum had been loosened.

> When she rose to the swell, the flat under surface of the projecting armor would come down with great force, causing a considerable shock to the vessel and turret, thereby loosening still more of the packing around its base.

When he reached the top of the turret he noticed that the wind had hauled more to the southward and had freshened with rainy and squally weather. Engineer Watters reported to the Captain the wet coal and dropping steam pressure and both parted with hopes that the storm would soon subside.

On board the *Rhode Island,* the watch was restless with anxiety for their tow. The *Monitor* seemed to be nearly swallowed up by the raging sea. Watson on board the *Rhode Island* later wrote:

> It was soon seen that the *Monitor* was making heavy weather of it and the engines were slowed down, but the course was still kept head into the wind and sea.
>
> This was a mistake, for experience later on in towing other vessels of her class proved that the safest way to handle them in heavy weather was to let them lie in a trough of the sea, when the waves would wash over their decks and the rolling would not be excessive.

Commander Bankhead ordered the engineer to put on the Worthington pump and to get the centrifugal pump ready, and to report back immediately if he perceived any increase of the water. The pumps kept the water down for a time. Paymaster Keeler vividly remembered the report from the engineer, in the howling wind on top of the turret.

A group of officers were huddled to the side as the engineer poked his head up through the hatch to say, "The water is gaining on us, sir."

When Mr. Watters returned to the engine room, he found the water about one inch deep on the engine room floor and he quickly looked around to confirm that the Worthington pump and bilge injection were in use and working properly.

On board the *Rhode Island,* the quartermaster at 8:45 PM made a line of sight with Cape Hatteras Light bearing "N ½ W distant 20 miles." Soon they would be clear of the "Cape Horn of the Atlantic," if the *Monitor* could just hold her own with the flooding water.

But on board the little ship, it soon became apparent that they were fighting a losing battle. In his report, Commander Bankhead stated; "I am of the firm opinion *Monitor* must have sprung a leak somewhere in the forward part where the hull joins on to the armor, and that it was caused by the heavy shocks received as she came down upon the sea."

Keeler later explained the critical situation in a letter:

> The opening through which the water was rushing was rapidly enlarged by the constant beating of the sea, which was now at times rolling over the top of the turret. Again came the report that the water was gaining and had risen above the engine room floor.
>
> In order to understand our situation and contrast it with our passage from New York to Hampton Roads last spring, it will be necessary to bear in mind that in the latter case, "the sea was on our beam" as sailors term it, that is, the wave would come up on our side, rolling onto us on one side and off on the other.

Now we were going "head on," or in other words were crossing them at right angles. Now her bow would rise on a huge billow and before she could sink into the intervening hollow, the succeeding wave would strike her under her heavy armor with a report like thunder and a violence that threatened to tear apart the thin sheet iron bottom and the heavy armor which it supported.

> Then she would slide down a watery mountain into a hollow beyond and plunging her bow into the black rolling billow would go down, down, down, under the surging wave till naught could be seen but the top of the black "cheese box" isolated in a sea of hissing, seething foam, extending as far as we could see around us.
>
> Then as she rose slowly and sullenly under the accumulated weight of the waters, the foam pouring in broad sheets off the iron deck, a wave would roll over the bow and strike the pilot house with a force that would send the water in torrents on to the top of the turret, where our little company were gathered.
>
> From behind the iron breastwork which surmounted the top of the turret, a circle of anxious faces were gazing over the expanse of angry waters, and awaiting with anxiety the report from the pumps.

Surgeon Weeks noted that the storm continued to increase in fury: ". . . the waves now dashing entirely over the turret, blinding the eyes and causing quick catching of the breath, as they swept against us."

Seaman Butts recalled the order to signal the *Rhode Island* at about half-past eight. At nine o'clock the *Rhode Island* recorded in her log that she acknowledged the signal and stopped her engines:

> At nine o'clock Captain Bankhead signaled us to stop the engines, and finding that the *Monitor* had fallen off into the trough of the sea, and that the waves were making a complete breach over her, we started the engines again.

Commander Bankhead in *Monitor;*

> Signaled several times to the *Rhode Island* to stop, in order that I might ascertain if, by so doing, she would ride easier, or decrease the influx of water, but could perceive no difference, the vessel falling off immediately into the trough of the sea and rolling heavily.
>
> I remained in the engine room and finding that the water did not decrease, I had the centrifugal pump started. It worked well and constant but still the water increased.

Up on the turret, Butts remembered the report from the engineer:

> The water in the vessel was gaining rapidly over the small pumps, and I heard the Captain order the chief engineer to start the main pump, a very powerful one of new invention. This was done and I saw a stream of water eight inches in diameter spouting up from beneath the waves.

Keeler related additional information about this pump:

> As a last resort the large centrifugal pump, of a capacity of three thousand gallons per minute, was started and once more the water

diminished, but it was of short duration.

From the *Rhode Island* the *Monitor* ". . . appeared to be lying in a trough of the sea, laboring heavily, the sea making a complete breach over her."

Commander Trenchard knew the *Monitor* was having trouble, but he didn't know how serious it really was. The little ship was immersed in a sea of foam, the waves breaking on top of the turret. They could see with the eye glass the small huddle of men on top of the turret and prayed for their safety.

On board the *Monitor* Commander Bankhead knew the situation was worsening as the ". . . engineer reported that the pumps were all working well, but produced no effect upon the water, which by this time had risen several inches above the level of the engine-room floor."

At 9:15 PM Trenchard ordered slow speed and a course change to try to keep the *Monitor* head into the wind and sea: "The steamer was then brought head to wind and sea, under easy steam, and the *Monitor* rode much easier, and made better weather."

At 9:30 PM ". . . it blew a gale, attended with rain and squally weather . . . the sea continued to rise, the vessel striking heavily forward."

The *Monitor* was then working heavily in the sea as she lifted great quantities of water on her deck each time her bow lifted to the surface.

At 10 PM the inevitable report came from below—the leak was gaining on the pumps.

The ships were barely making headway. The *Rhode Island* had reduced her speed to three knots and against such a wind and sea was scarcely able to keep way on. The wind was howling from southwest by south and had increased to force six. The heavy rain had reduced visibility considerably and was at times traveling horizontally with the surface of the sea. By that time, as later reported in *Harper's Weekly,*

> The storm was at its height, the waves striking and passing over the *Monitor,* burying her completely for the instant, while for a few seconds nothing could be seen of her from the *Rhode Island* but the upper part of her turret, surrounded by foam.
>
> This was caused as follows: a huge wave would lift her up, when, in descending to meet another, instead of riding it like other vessels, she plowed through, the projecting armor at her bow striking the water with such force that the spray and foam were thrown around her to the distance of forty feet.

In the engine room, Mr. Watters saw that flooding was gradually increasing, threatening the fires: "The ashpits at that time were more than half full of water, allowing but very little air to reach the fires."

He reported to Commander Bankhead that he would have to slow the main engines in order to save steam for the pumps. But still the steam pressure decreased and the amount of water in the ship increased. The forced draft blowers were throwing a great amount of water. The situation in the engine room was becoming critical; men were working at a feverish

pace but to no avail. They were splashing around in several inches of water as it rose towards the level of the fires. Mr. Weeks knew that:

> When the fires were reached, the vessel's doom was sealed; for with their extinction the pumps must cease, and all hope of keeping the *Monitor* above water more than an hour or two would expire.

The *Monitor* was now sluggishly moving through the sea, her decks continually awash, but she still continued to pound in the sea as she would ride up one swell and through the next: "This constantly striking the water with the force that it did, and the immense weight of ammunition in her hull, must of separated one (hull) from the other, . . ."

The storm showed no signs of decreasing and the barometer was still dropping. Soon it became obvious to all the officers huddled on top of the turret that the famous little warship was doomed by the storm. They had fought their ship against the iron shot of the enemy and had won, but the stormy waters off Cape Hatteras proved too great a foe. The end was near, wrote Weeks—it was only a matter of time:

> A consultation was held, and, not without a conflict of feeling, it was decided that signals of distress should be made. Ocean claimed our little vessel, and her trembling frame and failing fire proved she would soon answer his call; yet a pang went through us, as we thought of the first iron-clad lying alone at the bottom of this stormy sea, her guns silenced, herself a useless mass of metal. Each quiver of her strong frame seemed to plead with us not to abandon her. The work she had done, the work she was to do, rose before us; might there not be a possibility of saving her yet? her time could not have come so soon.
>
> We seemed to hear a voice from her saying,—"Save me, for once I have saved you! My frame is staunch still; my guns may again silence the roar of Rebel batteries. The night will pass, and calm come to us once more. Save me!" The roar of Ocean drowned her voice, and we who descended for a moment to the cabin knew, by the rising water through which we waded, that the end was near.

The report in *Harper's Weekly* stressed the urgency of the situation:

> She was now found to be fast sinking, and a consultation was held as to whether it was best to abandon her or not. The engineer, entering at this moment, reported that the water in the wardroom was waist deep; that it was still gaining rapidly, and that in less than two hours she must go down.

Commander Bankhead gave the order to raise the red lantern, the prearranged signal of distress. Keeler, Weeks, and Butts all described the following moments:

> Again and again it was repeated and signal after signal flashed out amid the storm. . . .
>
> The men were quiet and controlled, but all felt anxiety. Master's Mate Peter Williams suggested bailing in the faint hope that in this way the vessel might be kept longer above the water. . . .

Paymaster Keeler led the way, in company with Stocking, Williams, and one or two others, and though the water was waist deep, and they knew the vessel was liable to go down at any moment, they worked on nobly, throwing out a constant stream of water from the turret. . . .

Every pump was at work and gangs of men had been organized to bail, more however with the design of keeping them employed and preventing a panic than with the hope of any good result. The water was already a foot deep on the engine room floor and was fast deepening in the Ward Room. . . .

Words cannot depict the agony of those moments as our little company gathered on the top of the turret, stood with a mass of sinking iron beneath them gazing through the dim light, over the raging waters with an anxiety amounting almost to agony for some evidence of succor from the only source to which we could look for relief. Seconds lengthened into hours and minutes into years. . . .

From [the waters] rapid influx it was very evident that but a short time would elapse before it would reach the fires and then the iron heart of the *Monitor* would cease to beat. . . .

The Chief Engineer reported that the coal was so wet that he could not keep up steam, and I heard the Captain order him to slow down and pull all steam that could be spared upon the pumps. . . .

Our consort stopped and attempted to come alongside, but with the two vessels connected with the hawser it was found impossible. . . .

Commander Bankhead later wrote in his report:

Finding that the heavy stream-cable used to tow the *Monitor* rendered the vessel unmanageable while hanging slack to her bow, and being under the absolute necessity of working the engines to keep the pumps going, I ordered it to be cut. . . .

Captain Bankhead shouted, "Who'll cut the hawsers!" "I will," answered Mr. Stodder, the Master, and taking a hatchet, climbed down the turret and was followed by two others.

According to the account in *Harper's Weekly,*

Butts at the leehelm thought that there was "danger of being towed under" and watched the three volunteers "going cautiously forward holding on the life line, which was stretched around the deck." I saw James Fenwick, quarter-gunner, swept from the deck and carried by a heavy sea leeward and out of sight. . . . Our daring boatswain's mate, John Stocking, then succeeded in reaching the bows of the vessel, and I saw him swept by a heavy sea far away into the darkness.

Then Mr. Stodder, holding by one hand to the ropes while the waves were rolling high over his head, severed the towing hawser and safely returned to the turret.

Ensign Rodgers of the *Rhode Island* later criticized this action, but he was not one of the officers who stood on that iron turret knowing that his ship was doomed:

Every seafaring man knows that the safest place for the *Monitor* that night was astern of and under our lee, and there was not the least doubt in the minds of some of the officers of our ship, all of whom, except the Captain, were from the merchant marine service, that we could have easily held her there, in that position, head to the wind and sea with our ship under easy steam, had the *Monitor*'s people not cut the hawser and thereby cast themselves adrift.

Butts watched the *Rhode Island* "turn slowly ahead to keep from drifting upon us and to prevent the tow-lines from being caught in her wheels. At one time, when she drifted close alongside, our Captain shouted through his trumpet that we were sinking, and asking the steamer to send us her boats."

All Keeler heard was "A hoarse unintelligible reply . . . amid the roar of the elements. Again and again it was repeated and signal after signal flashed out amid the storm as we saw no sign of boats and the same unintelligible response induced us to believe that they understood neither our signals or our hail."

The minutes dragged like hours as men waited in terror for what was to come.

Every minute was that much nearer certain death to us, and when our signals were not responded to, the word was passed among the men that it was the intention to abandon us to our fate. This made them desperate, and the sailors insisted that we fire upon the vessel.

On board the *Rhode Island,* Ensign Rodgers remembered being awakened from an exhausted sleep.

It was nearly eleven o'clock when I was aroused by one of the messenger boys, who told me all the officers were wanted immediately. On arriving on deck, I first took a look at the weather. The night was dark, not even a star could be seen, but a little light from the moon occasionally struggled through the clouds. There was a stiff breeze blowing from the south, just about such a wind as would begin to make you think about putting some reefs into the topsails of a sailing ship close hauled. There was quite a sea running as you know there always is off Hatteras, even in a moderate gale.

All had to be confusion on board the *Rhode Island* as the watch woke the officers and crew, and sleepy men tried to orient themselves on a tossing ship.

Commander Trenchard ordered the *Rhode Island*'s engines stopped as the officers were hurriedly briefed on the situation and tasks assigned. In the excitement, the usual delay in lowering the boats was prolonged. Coxswains could not find their regular crews, and were forced to grab volunteers.

The ship's launch was hurriedly put over the side and lowered cautiously into the raging sea, the sailors nervously grasping the rat lines as each swell approached their small wooden craft, at the order of "away to the rescue."

In this interim, Butts noted that

> The *Monitor* forged ahead under the impetus of her headway, and came so close up under the steamer's stern, that there was great danger of her running into and cutting the steamer down. When the engines of the *Rhode Island* were started to go ahead to get out of the way it was discovered that the hawser had got afoul of the paddle wheel, and when they were put in motion, instead of getting clear of her, the rope wound upon the wheel and drew the vessels together.

Weeks was impressed by the boat launched from the *Rhode Island* manned by a crew of picked men:

> A more heroic impulse could not have accomplished this most noble need. For hours they had watched the raging sea. Their Captain and they knew the danger; every man who entered that boat did it at peril of his life, yet all were ready. . . .

On board the *Monitor* the situation was worsening. The water was now above the ashpits. Butts was ordered to leave the wheel and act as a messenger by the captain. At 11:30 PM with the engines working slowly and all the pumps at full speed, Bankhead ordered the engineer to stop the engines and to apply all remaining steam to the pumps. With no way on the *Monitor* was at the mercy of a raging sea and rolled in a trough, taking the full punishment of each wave. Bankhead wrote

> The engine being stopped, and no longer able to keep the vessel head to sea, she having fallen off into the trough and rolling so heavily as to render it impossible for boats to approach us, I ordered the anchor to be let go and all the chain given her, in hopes that it might bring her up.

Butts remembered one fact that was to be important a hundred years later, the anchor "was let go with all the cable, and struck bottom in about sixty fathoms of water."

Gradually, the chain took a strain and Butts saw the bow of the *Monitor* slowly swung around, "head into the wind." However, this was a small reprieve for the fast flooding ironclad.

> The fires could no longer be kept up with the wet coal. The small pumps were choked up with water, or as the engineer reported, were drowned, and the main pump had almost stopped working from lack of power.
>
> This was reported to the Captain, and he ordered me [Butts] to see if there was any water in the wardroom. This was the first time that I had been below the berth-deck. I went forward, and saw the water running in through the hawse pipe, an eight inch hole, in full force, as in dropping the anchor the cable had torn away the packing that had kept this place tight.

Butts reported this to the Captain and joined in the bailing, being handed the buckets on top of the turret to spill their contents into the sea.

> I kept employed most of the time, taking the buckets from through the hatchway on top of the turret. They seldom would have more than a pint of water in them, however, the remainder having been spilled in passing from one man to another.

Soon he was again summoned by Commander Bankhead

> I was again sent to examine the water in the wardroom, which I found to be more than two feet above the deck; and I think I was the last person who saw Engineer G. H. Lewis as he lay seasick in his bunk, apparently watching the water as it grew deeper and deeper, and aware what his fate must be.
>
> He called to me as I passed his door, and asked if the pumps were working. I replied that they were.
>
> "Is there any hope?" he asked.
>
> . . . feeling a little moved at the scene, and knowing certainly what must be his end, and the darkness that stared at us all, I replied.
>
> As long as there is life there is hope.
>
> "Hope and hang on when you are wrecked" is an old saying among sailors. I left the wardroom, and learned that the water had gained so as to choke up the main pump. As I was crossing the berth-deck I saw our ensign, Mr. Frederickson, hand a watch to Master's Mate Williams, saying, "Here this is yours; I may be lost"—which, in fact, was his fate. The watch and chain were both of unusual value. Williams received them into his hand, then with a hesitating glance at the time-piece said, "This thing may be the means of sinking me," and threw it upon the deck.

Men below decks were splashing through the water. Some were sorting through their personal gear, trying to decide what to save. The bucket line was breaking down as it was obvious to all it was useless and most were anxious to climb to the top of the turret to await the boats.

> There were three or four cabin-boys pale and prostrate with seasickness, and the cabin-cook, an old African negro, under great excitement, was scolding them most profanely.
>
> As I ascended the turret-ladder the sea broke over the ship, and came pouring down the hatchway with so much force that it took me off my feet; and at the same time the steam broke from the boiler-room, as the water had reached the fires, and for an instant I seemed to realize that we had gone down. Our fires were out and I heard the water blowing out of the boilers.

Keeler still standing close to his captain remembered the engine room report

> . . . that the water had reached the furnaces and the fires were being extinguished. Our Commander's orders were given calmly and coolly and met with a ready and cheerful response from officers and men; no one faltered in obedience, but a ready aye, aye sir, met every order. Some however, obeyed mechanically, while others worked coolly and

resolutely as if realizing that our safety depended upon the prompt and ready execution of every order.

About the time the launch and first cutter left, reported Butts,

> She drifted toward the *Monitor* and there was great danger of a collision before the hawser could be extricated. The launch was between the two steamers. . . .

On board the *Monitor,* the sight of the *Rhode Island* was comforting. Surgeon Weeks thought that she was coming to their assistance. But soon joy turned to terror as the *Rhode Island* came closer:

> . . . the big hawser, which was perhaps seventy-five fathoms long, and which as we afterwards learned, had been cut by the *Monitor*'s people got entangled in one of our side wheels, and we were for a time entirely helpless and in great peril.

Finally, according to Keeler: "After an hour that seemed an eternity to us, boats were seen approaching; what a load was taken from our anxious hearts—with what interest we watched as they toiled and struggled slowly over the heavy seas, now hidden from our sight in a watery hollow, then balanced on the foaming crest of a mountain wave."

Butts, just returning from below, reported to the captain and saw the launch coming alongside, tossing wildly in the sea with the *Rhode Island* not far behind.

> The Captain gave orders for the men to leave the ship, and fifteen, all of whom were seamen and men whom I had placed my confidence upon, were the ones who crowded the first boat to leave the ship. I saw three of these men swept from the deck and carried leeward on the swift current.

Things happed fast then. Butts wrote:

> . . . as we looked, the devoted boat was caught between the steamer and the ironclad,—a sharp sound of crushing wood was heard, thwarts, oars, splinters flew in the air—the boat's crew leaped to the *Monitor*'s deck.

and Keeler:

> Her launch was under her quarter and was crashing and grinding most fearfully between the two vessels; its crew had leaped upon our deck to escape being crushed with the boat, and for a time it seemed as if we had but received an addition to our imperilled number.

and Weeks:

> Death stared us in the face; our iron prow must go through the *Rhode Island*'s side, and then an end to all. One awful moment we held our breath. . . .

and later, *Harper's Weekly:*

> . . . the two vessels had approached so near each other that five or six of the crew of the *Monitor* seized the ropes hanging from the side of the *Rhode Island* and started to climb up her side, but only three reached there.

Ensign Rodgers observed that the *Rhode Island*

> . . . drifted down upon the *Monitor* and it seemed for a few minutes when she was right under our quarter, that she would sink us then and there. She was so close to us that the launch was crushed between the two vessels, and the men in her, together with some of the *Monitor*'s crew whom they had taken off, scrambled or were pulled aboard of the *Rhode Island* by means of some lines which we threw them.

From the turret of the *Monitor,* Surgeon Weeks watched helplessly as the seas picked up the immense steamer almost on top of them, exposing to view at times her garboard strake. The sounds of crushing wood and the sight of men being yanked up on ropes by the roll of the ship as they attempted to climb to safety left an unforgettable impression.

> It looked at one time as if she would strike the bow of the *Monitor,* but, fortunately, she just missed it, and scraping along her side, drifted off to leeward.
>
> . . . a ship's length lay between us, and then we breathed freely. But the boat—had she gone to the bottom, carrying brave souls with her? No, there she lay, beating against our sides, but still though bruised and broken, a life-boat to us.

The launch commanded by Acting Ensign A. O. Taylor had its starboard gunwale crushed, but kept afloat and brought off sixteen men, among them Surgeon Weeks, but not without great difficulty.

The *Monitor*'s action in cutting the towing hawser set off a calamitous chain of events described by Ensign Rodgers:

> . . . this unfortunate proceeding was the cause of an accident that placed the *Rhode Island* herself in the greatest peril. No allusion is made in either of the official reports, to the entanglement of the big tow line in one of our side wheels, neither is any good reason given for allowing the two vessels to approach each other so close as to crush a boat between them; nor to the brave conduct of the men from the engineer's department, who went into the paddle-box with their axes and cut the hawser.
>
> The mistake made in cutting the hawser was very unfortunate, but it was soon followed by another, which, I have no doubt, cost the lives of sixteen men and was the immediate, if not the principal cause of the sinking of the *Monitor*.
>
> . . . the *Monitor*'s people let go her anchor, with the hope and with the result, it appears from Captain Bankhead's report, of bringing their craft head to the wind and sea, a position which they had a short time before abandoned, when they cut themselves adrift from our ship, although when I was alongside of her about midnight, she lay in the trough of the sea with the waves beating across her decks.
>
> Letting go an anchor twenty miles at sea, with the hope of bringing his craft into a position he had just abandoned, was an expedient of doubtful value on the part of Captain Bankhead; but when this procedure must be accompanied by a catastrophe, that he should have known would sink his vessel in a short time, the question arises, but of course cannot be answered, would the *Monitor* have foundered that

night had her officers that confidence in their ship, that was gained by experience on board other iron-clads, of the monitor type, by other naval officers during the later years of the war.

It was my impression the night of the disaster, and it was the opinion of other officers of the *Rhode Island,* that all of the *Monitor*'s people, with good management, might have been saved.

Acting Ensign Taylor agreed with him:

The *Monitor* should not have been lost. She was going against a head-sea. Had she turned back before dark she would have had no difficulty. . . .

These were the opinions of those not aboard the foundering ironclad, months after the tragedy—how they would have acted under similar circumstances is an unanswerable question. The regret for actions during a critical situation has been the lament of many a sea captain, for in the end all responsibility rests with the captain. It was Acting Paymaster Keeler's opinion that

Every expedient which human ingenuity or skill could suggest had been tried in vain and all that remained was to save the lives of those on board.

Keeler had left the top of the turret to return to his state room upon seeing the launch approaching. On deck again, he was quite surprised to see the *Rhode Island* close aboard.

Hoping to be able to get off in one of the approaching boats and to take with me the books and accounts of the vessel, I started for my state room to gather them up.

I passed down the turret ladder, felt my way around the guns and making a misstep fell from the top of the berth deck ladder to the deck below.

A dim lantern swinging to and fro with the motion of the vessel, just served to make the nearest objects visible in the darkness, rendered more dense if possible by the steam, heat and gas which was finding its way in from the half extinguished fires of the engine room.

I passed across this deck, down into the Ward room where I found the water nearly to my waist and swashing from side to side with the roll of the ship, and groped my way through the narrow crooked passage to my state room. It was a darkness that could be felt. The hot, stifling, murky atmosphere pervaded every corner.

After groping about for a little time, I collected what books and papers I deemed it important to save, but found they made so large and unmanageable a mass that the attempt to save them would be utterly useless and would only endanger my life, as my whole physical energies would be required to get me safely over the wave washed deck and into the boats.

I took down my watch, which was hanging on a nail nearby and putting it into my pocket, took out my safe keys with the intention of saving the government "green backs." The safe was entirely submerged; in the thick darkness, below the water and from the peculiar form of the lock I was unable to insert the key. I desisted from the attempt and started to return.

My feeling at [that] time is impossible to describe, when I reflected that I was nearly at the farthest extremity of the vessel from its only outlet, and this outlet liable to be completely obstructed at any moment by a rush of panic stricken men, and the vessel itself momentarily expected to give the final plunge.

Everything was enveloped in a thick murky darkness, the waves dashing violently across the deck over my head; my retreat to be made through the narrow crooked passage leading to my room; through the Ward room where the chairs and tables were surging violently from side to side, threatening severe bruises if not broken limbs; then up a ladder to the berth deck; across that and up another ladder into the turret; around the guns and over gun tackle, shot, sponges, and rammers which had broken loose from their fastenings and up the last ladder to the top of the turret.

I reached the goal and found our consort close alongside, so near in fact, that I expected every instant to see her thrown against our iron side, and both vessels go down together.

In the interim, Francis Butts was assisting to the last possible moment, trying to save his ship. In the few short months that he had been aboard he had grown to respect the "tin can on a shingle" for what she had accomplished and for what she was capable. The men who had handled her machinery and her guns were now abandoning her. Slowly her boilers cooled and her machinery stopped as the water continued to rise. The worst fears of some of the old sailors when they first laid eyes on her were coming true—she would become an "iron coffin" for some of them.

Butts was still in the bucket line as a few devoted sailors were doing all that could be done until they were told it would be their turn to get in the boats.

I occupied the turret all alone, and passed buckets from the lower hatchway to the man on the top of the turret.

I took off my coat—one that I had received from home only a few days before (I could not feel that our noble little ship was yet lost)—and rolling it up with my boots, drew the tompion from one of the guns, placed them inside, and replaced the tompion.

A black cat was sitting on the breech of one of the guns, howling one of those hoarse and solemn tunes which no one can appreciate who is not filled with the superstitions which I had been taught by the sailors, who are always afraid to kill a cat. I would almost as soon have touched a ghost, but I caught her, and placing her in another gun, replaced the wad and tompion; but I could still hear that distressing howl.

Steam pressure in the boilers fell to five pounds per square inch, and Engineers Watters knew that his ship was doomed. He had done everything that he knew how to do. Whether it would have been different with Second Assistant Engineer Albert Campbell aboard was a haunting question. He had been most familiar with the engines.

The men on top of the turret were amazed that the launch was still afloat after the two ships separated. But she was made of wood, not of iron and she would float even in her crushed condition.

Meanwhile, on board the *Rhode Island,* Master's Mate Rodney Browne was "begging" Captain Trenchard to allow him to lower his boat (the first cutter).

The Captain said he thought it impossible for a boat to live in such a sea, as even the launch was crippled. I then told him that I was an old whale-man and if I could have a good crew and rig a steering oar, I fully believed I could reach the *Monitor.*

I called his attention to the fact that a rudder was but little use in such a sea, as, when it was most needed, it might be in the air instead of the water, while a steering oar could always be effective, not only to steer, but to pull a boat's head to a sea more quickly. He consented, and a crew was called to volunteer.

It was astonishing to see how many were eager to go. Fourteen were selected. I then rigged my steering oar and a lashing for my right foot, so the oar could not throw me overboard, and stationed a good man at each boat fall on board the *Rhode Island* and my crew and self took our places in the boat, the bow oarsman with a knife to cut the fall in case of failure to unhook the tackle. I was at the stern tackle myself.

I then had those on shipboard lower away slowly and watching my chance at the right moment ordered, "Let go all" and we went down on the run, successfully unhooked tackles and we were clear of the ship and our *first* great danger.

In some way I injured my wrist, but at the time did not realize to what extent. Now began our pull for the *Monitor* whose red light was plainly visible.

During the gale the wind had varied many points so that the seas were very irregular and we had often to throw the boat's head to the sea to take some larger wave, head and head, and then the value of a steering oar was very apparent.

As Browne and his crew were putting their backs into the oars, the launch was alongside the *Monitor.* Seeing that she still floated, sailors were preparing to abandon ship.

Commander Bankhead ordered Lieutenant Greene to load the boats with all the men they would safely carry.

Peter Truskit, one of those ordered to the top of the turret to get into one of the boats was ". . . on the companion ladder, just behind my messmate, Jack O'Brien, and we were both dodging the third waves, which are always the biggest. One had just passed, when he sprang for the boat, and missed it. I heard him shriek, "O, God!" and then he was swept away forever."

William Keeler watched the horrible scene; the men moved cautiously down the ladder as the two boats tossed wildly on the sea: "With the heavy sea running it was a difficult matter to go alongside of her, and the first boat to reach her was thrown by a wave upon the deck and a hole stove in her. The next wave washed the boat off. . . ."

Sensing that the boats might be destroyed and that the men were moving too slowly, Commander Bankhead ordered Keeler to lead them.

Already two or three of our number had been swept off and those who remained seemed to hang back fearing to make the effort.

Upon the order from Captain Bankhead to "lead the men to the boats," I divested myself of the greater portion of my clothing to afford me greater facilities for swimming in case of necessity and attempted to descend the ladder leading down the outside of the turret, but found it full of men hesitating but desiring to make the perilous passage of the deck.

I found a rope hanging from one of the awning stanchions over my head and slid down it to the deck. A huge wave passed over me tearing me from my footing and bearing me along with it rolling, tumbling, and tossing like the merest speck.

I was carried as near as I could judge ten or twelve yards from the vessel when I came to the surface and the back-set of the wave threw me against the vessel's side near one of the iron stanchions which supported the life line; this I grasped with all the energy of desperation and drawing myself on deck worked my way along the life line and was hauled into the boat, into which the men were jumping one by one as they could venture across the deck.

Truskit remembered his dash for life across the iron deck and the leap for the boat: "I caught the boat upon the gunwale, and managed to pull myself in, but it was a close call."

Keeler never forgot the scene as, bruised as he was, he tried to help his shipmates into the boat.

It was a scene well calculated to appall the boldest heart. Mountains of water were rushing cross our decks and foaming along our sides; the small boats were pitching against our sides, mere playthings on the billows; the howling of the tempest, the roar and dash of water; the hoarse orders through the speaking trumpets of the officers; the response of the men; the shouts of encouragement and words of caution

the bubbling cry of the strong swimmer in his agony

and the whole scene lit up by the ghastly glare of the blue lights burning on our consort, formed a panorama of horror which time can never efface from my memory.

Some of the sailors who had been ordered to the top of the turret to get in the boats clung in terror to the stanchions at the sight before them.

Below, Butts and the other men kept steadily bailing. They left, reported Weeks, only when the captain ordered them to save themselves.

They descended from the turret to the deck with mingled fear and hope, for the waves tore from side to side, and the coolest head and bravest heart could not guaranty safety. Some were washed over as they left the turret, and, with a vain clutch at the iron deck, a wild throwing up of the arms, went down, their death cry ringing in the ears of their companions.

The foundering of the Monitor, *as depicted in Harper's Weekly, 1863.*

The boat sometimes held her place by the *Monitor*, then was dashed hopelessly out of reach, rising and falling on the waves. A sailor would spring from the deck to reach her, be seen for a moment in mid-air, and then, as she rose, fall into her.

. . . she gradually filled; but some poor souls who sought to reach her failed even as they touched her receding sides, and went down.

Not all that sacrificed were of the *Monitor*. Some were of the *Rhode Island* who had answered the call of those in peril on the sea.

Trenchard later wrote:

Acting Master's Mate Stevens, who, when the launch was manning, went quietly into the boat, took one of the oars, and, while alongside the *Monitor*, on striving to save others, was himself washed from the boat.

There were instances where sailors gave their lives to help another. Weeks reported that

We had on board a little messenger-boy, the special charge of one of the sailors, and the pet of all; he must inevitably have been lost, but for the care of his adopted father, who, holding him firmly in his arms, escaped as by miracle, being washed overboard, and succeeded in placing him safely in the boat. [The man himself was swept from the deck by the next wave.]

The last one to make the desperate venture was the surgeon; he leaped from the deck, and at the very instant saw the boat being swept away by the merciless sea. Making one final effort, he threw his body forward as he fell, striking across the boat's side so violently, it was thought some of his ribs must be broken.

"Haul the Doctor in!" shouted Lieutenant Greene, perhaps remembering how, a little time back, he himself, almost gone down in the unknown sea, had been hauled in by a rope flung him by the doctor.

"Stout sailor-arms pulled him in, one more sprang to a place in her, and the boat, now full pushed off—in a sinking condition, it is true, but still bearing hope with her, for she was wood.

Paymaster Keeler was in the boat:

We were soon loaded and shoved off, but our dangers were not yet over. We were in a leaky overloaded boat, through whose crushed sides the water was rushing in streams and had nearly a half a mile to row over the storm tossed sea before we could reach the *Rhode Island*.

Over the waves we toiled slowly, pulling for life. The men stuffed peajackets into the holes in her side, and bailed incessantly.

The launch, returning from the *Monitor* after its near miss with disaster, was terribly over-laden with frightened exhausted sailors. The first cutter was just beginning its trip when again apparently unavoidable calamity struck. The description is from *Harper's Weekly:*

They approached each other, and there seemingly no chance of preventing a collision, when Dr. G. M. Weeks, of the *Monitor* and Ensign Taylor of the *Rhode Island* and one of the sailors, sprang to the side to part them. The force of the blow was thus broken and the boats saved from destruction. The right hand of Dr. Weeks was caught between the boats, crushing the bones of three of his fingers so seriously that amputation was afterward found necessary.

Ens. Taylor reported:

We neared the *Rhode Island* but now a new peril appeared. Right down upon our center, borne by the might of rushing water, came the whale-boat sent to rescue others from the iron-clad.

We barely floated; if she struck us with her bows full on, we must go to the bottom. One sprang, and, as she neared, with out-stretched arms, met and turned her course.

She passed against us, and his hand, caught between the two, was crushed, and the arm, wrenched from its socket, fell a helpless weight at his side; but life remained. We were saved, and an arm was a small price to pay for life.

About this time on board the *Rhode Island* the paddle wheel had been freed by a volunteer using an axe in the paddle box and she steamed ahead some distance.

Finally the launch approached to within hailing distance of the *Rhode Island* and she stopped her engines to recover the boat and the exhausted crews at approximately 12:15 AM.

Keeler recalled the rescue:

> . . . after a hard long struggle . . . we found ourselves under the weather quarter of our consort in imminent danger of being swamped as she sunk in the hollow of the sea. The ends of ropes, which the more active of our number seized and climbed up; others grasped them firmly and were thus drawn over the side.
>
> In my exhausted state and with my crippled hand I could do neither of these, but watching for my opportunity I saw a loop, or what a sailor would call a bight of rope, let down, I passed it under my arms and was drawn on board the *Rhode Island* to receive the congratulations and hospitalities of her officers, and I assure you they were not deficient in either.

Surgeon Weeks had a considerably more difficult time of it.

> We reached the *Rhode Island;* ropes were flung over her side, and caught with a death-grip. Some lost their hold, were washed away, and again dragged in by the boat's crew. What chance had one whose right arm hung a dead weight, when strong men with their two hands went down before him? He caught at a rope, found it impossible to save himself alone, and then for the first time said,—"I am injured; can anyone aid me?" Ensign Taylor, at the risk of his own life, brought the rope around his (the Surgeon's) shoulder in such a way it could not slip, and he was drawn up in safety.

Once aboard "the heartiest and most tender reception was made. Our drenched clothing was replaced by warm and dry garments, and all on board vied with each other in acts of kindness." All were rejoicing to be alive, but still concerned for their shipmates. Many watched from the rail as the red lantern swung drunkenly in the distance, disappearing a hundred times behind a wave, only to reappear again.

> The only one who had received any injury, Surgeon Weeks, was carefully attended to, the dislocated arm set, and the crushed fingers amputated by the gentlest and most considerate of surgeons, Dr. Weber of the *Rhode Island.*"

The *Monitor's* pumps had stopped. Now it would be only minutes before her final plunge into the depths. Then all would be over.

The engineers were still manning the engine room, incapable of any words. Their eyes told Mr. Watters that they were anxious for their own safety, and he "reported the circumstances to Captain Bankhead. A few minutes later I received an order to leave the engine room and proceed to get in the boats."

Watters was the last to leave. He checked to be sure the space was clear and before stepping through the engine room door turned to take one last look and glance at his watch. It was between 12 midnight and 1 AM. When Watters reached the top of the turret he saw the whale-boat approaching and for the first time the raging sea that had doomed his ship. He heard the captain say, "It is madness to remain here longer; let each man save himself."

Master's Mate Browne in the first cutter, later gave his account:

> After a severe pull, we neared the *Monitor* and then the danger of our boat being thrown upon her deck and stove, confronted us. But my men were cool and obeyed every order promptly.
>
> Once we did go over the *Monitor* bodily, and how we escaped wreck is more than I can tell. As the men came down from the *Monitor's* turret, holding by the life line, they were hauled into the boat. Some that were washed overboard from the deck of the *Monitor,* we picked up and some we were unable to save.
>
> It was a pitiable sight to see them vainly struggling amid the foam, and not be able to save them.
>
> One strange incident happened: We picked up near our boat, Master's Mate Stevens belonging to the *Rhode Island.* It was a great mystery to me how *he* could possibly have gotten there, but I learned later that he had volunteered to go in the Launch and pull an oar, and by some way had been washed overboard from her and thrown by the sea onto the deck of the *Monitor* and from her washed overboard again and almost miraculously picked up by one of my boat's crew. We got him down in the stern sheets of my boat. But he seemed dazed and I had to hold him down with my foot.

As soon as the boat was full, Browne shoved off for the *Rhode Island,* where Ensign Taylor was still struggling with the launch. But the best seaman could not have taken her back to the *Monitor* for she was too badly broken up, unmanageable, and half full of water.

They abandoned the attempt and Commander Trenchard put Ensign Rodgers in charge of a third boat, "to assist the others in getting the crew on board."

At this time Ensign Rodgers commenced his own personal adventures:

> The Launch had been crushed and the 1st Cutter had taken off safely one boat load, and was on its way back to the *Monitor* on her second trip, when I was ordered to take charge of another boat and started for the sinking vessel. She was not a large one like the cutter and launch, and pulled only four oars.
>
> I got clear of the ship, and started for the *Monitor,* which lay quite a distance to the windward of us. The sea was running quite high, and it seemed at times as if our boat would end over.

There were still about twenty-five or thirty men on board the *Monitor.* The vessel was filling rapidly. The final moments were near, Commander Bankhead ordered all hands into the approaching boats:

> By this time, finding the vessel filling rapidly, and the deck on a level with the water, I ordered all the men left on board to leave the turret and endeavor to get into the two boats which were approaching us.

Bankhead then left the top of the turret, Surgeon Weeks noted, to go to his cabin for the last time:

> For a moment he descended to the cabin for a coat, and his faithful

servant followed to secure a jewel-box, containing the accumulated treasure of years. A sad, sorry sight it was. In the heavy air the lamps burned dimly, and the water, waist-deep, splashed sullenly against the wardroom's sides. One lingering look, and he left the *Monitor*'s cabin forever.

Time was precious; he hastened to the deck, where in the midst of a terrible sea, Lieutenant Greene nobly held his post."

The first cutter was already alongside the sinking ironclad. Bankhead saw that ". . . the sea was breaking upon our now submerged deck with great violence, washing several men overboard. . . ."

Slowly, the boat approached with Ensign Rodgers at the helm:

As we neared the *Monitor* my attention was called by one of the men at the oars, to a cry which he said he heard at some distance and right abeam of us. I changed our course, but in so doing so got into the trough of the sea and came near getting swamped; soon however, I had the satisfaction of seeing a man's head on the crest of a wave. We pulled up and got him into the boat more dead than alive. He proved to be a Master's Mate Williams, and he had been washed overboard from the sinking vessel. As soon as we got him into the boat, I started again for the *Monitor*.

I pulled up under her lee but did not dare go close alongside. Had I done so we would have been swamped.

The appearance of the iron-clad at this time was truly appalling. She lay in the trough of the sea, and the waves were making a complete breach over her decks. She looked just like a half-tide ledge in rough water, and for the most of the time her turret only was visible. When the boats came alongside of the *Monitor*, her captain and executive officer went upon the deck and, clinging to the life-lines with the waves washing over them, called to the crew to come down from the turret and get into the boats, which they were reluctant to do at first.

The executive officer

. . . seized the rope from the whale-boat, wound it about an iron stanchion, and then his wrists, for days afterwards swollen and useless from the strain."

His body-servant stood near him.

"Can you swim, William?" he asked.

"No," replied the man.

"Then keep by me, and I'll save you."

Describing the scene later, Watson, of the *Rhode Island,* wrote:

Some were able to jump into the boats, and some landed in the water and were hauled in. Seeing an old quarter-master with a large bundle under his arm, the executive officer, thinking that it was his clothes-bag, told him that that was no time to be trying to save his effects. He sad nothing, but threw it into the boat. When the bundle was passed over the side of the *Rhode Island* it proved to be a little messenger-boy; probably the smallest and youngest one in the service.

Log of the Rhode Island, 31 December 1862.

Ensign Rodgers pushed off first, but took only seven men: "I was obliged to leave the others on the sinking craft to their fate, as there were now thirteen of us in my already overloaded boat."

Butts, still in the turret, was one of the last to abandon ship:

As I raised my last bucket to the upper hatchway no one was there to take it. I scrambled up the ladder and found that we below had been deserted. I shouted to those on the berth-deck, "Come up; the officers have left the ship, and a boat is alongside."

As I reached the top of the turret I saw a boat made fast on the weather quarter filled with men. Three others were standing on deck trying to get on board. One man was floating leeward, shouting in vain for help; another, who hurriedly passed me and jumped down from the turret, was swept off by a breaking wave and never rose.

I was then about twenty feet from the other men, whom I found to be the captain and one seaman; the other had been washed overboard and was now struggling in the water. The men in the boat were pushing back on their oars to keep the boat from being washed on to the *Monitor*'s deck, so that the boat had to be hauled in by the painter about ten or twelve feet.

I secured the painter of one of the boats, (which by use of the oars, was prevented from striking the side,) and made as many get into her as she would safely hold in the heavy sea that was running.

Browne recalled those last tense moments filled with anxiety because his boat was so overloaded that he was forced to leave the *Monitor* with some of her crew still on board.

We had now got in my boat all of the "Monitor's" crew that could be persuaded to come down from the turret for they had seen some of their shipmates (who had left the turret for the deck) washed overboard and sink in their sight.

Perhaps they felt that a like fate would be their own especially if they could not swim. The last to leave the "Monitor" was her noble Captain, J. P. Bankhead, Lieut. Green, and several other officers but the last to leave (although severely hurt) was the Captain.

But Bankhead left only after being told by Richard Anjier, quartermaster that he wasn't going to leave. "No, sir; not until you go."

Seeing the captain get in the boat, Butts made his dash for life, after Anjier, and followed by Joice.

Now or lost, and in less time than I can explain it, exerting my strength beyond imagination, I hauled in the boat, sprang, caught on the gunwale, was pulled into the boat with a boathook in the hands of one of the men, and took my seat with one of the oarsmen.

"The other man, named Thomas Joice, managed to get into the boat in some way, I cannot tell how, and he was the last man saved from that ill-fated ship.

Commander Bankhead later wrote how he felt about leaving some of the men behind.

Feeling that I had done everything in my power to save the vessel and crew, I jumped into the already deeply-laden boat and left the *Monitor*, whose heavy sluggish motion gave evidence that she could float but a short time longer.

Lee noted that some men left in the turret, terrified by the peril, declined to come down, and Weeks saw that

Two or three still remained clinging to the turret; the captain had begged them to come down, but, paralyzed with fear, they sat immovable, and the gallant Brown, promising to return for them, pushed off.

After taking all that would come, Browne, and the last boat to leave the *Monitor* started for the *Rhode Island*.

My boat was overloaded, for such a sea, but my noble crew were cool, steady and prompt to respond to every order and to them belongs the greater share of our success. I have never seen a worse sea for boats. As we neared the *Rhode Island* and as she rose to a sea, we could see her keel from her stem post to almost amidships.

Butts recalled this nightmare and his narrow escape with death.

After a fearful and dangerous passage over the frantic seas, we reached the *Rhode Island*, which had drifted two miles to leeward.

We came alongside under the lee bows, where the first boat, that had left the *Monitor* nearly an hour before, had just discharged its men; but we found that getting on board the *Rhode Island* was a harder task than getting from the *Monitor*.

We were carried by the sea from stem to stern, for to have made fast would have been fatal; the boat was bounding against the ship's sides; sometimes it was below the wheel, and then, on the summit of a huge wave, far above the decks; then the two boats would crash together.

Lines were thrown to us from the deck of the *Rhode Island*, which were of no assistance, for not one of us could climb a small rope; and besides, the men who threw them would immediately let go their holds, in their excitement, to throw another—which I found to be the case when I kept hauling in rope instead of climbing.

It must be remembered that two vessels lying side-by-side, when there it any motion to the sea, move alternately; or, in other words, one is constantly passing the other up or down.

At one time, when our boat was near the bows of the steamer, we would rise upon the sea until we could touch her rail; then in an instant, by a very rapid descent, we could touch her keel.

While we were thus rising and falling upon the sea, I caught a rope, and, rising with the boat, managed to reach within a foot or two of the rail, when a man, if there had been one, could easily have hauled me on board.

But they had all followed after the boat, which at that instant was washed astern, and I hung dangling in the air over the bow of the *Rhode Island,* with Ensign Norman Atwater hanging to the cat-head, three or four feet from me, like myself, with both hands clinching a rope and shouting for some one to save him.

Our hands grew painful and all the time weaker, until I saw his strength give way.

He slipped a foot, caught again, and with his last prayer, "O God!" I saw him fall and sink, to rise no more.

The ship rolled, and rose upon the sea, sometimes with her keel out of the water, so that I was hanging thirty feet above the sea, and with the fate in view that had befallen our much-beloved companion, which no one had witnessed but myself.

I still clung to the rope with aching hands, calling in vain for help. But I could not be heard, for the wind shrieked far above my voice. My heart here, for the only time in my life, gave up hope, and home and friends were most tenderly thought of.

While I was in this state, within a few seconds of giving up, the sea rolled forward, bringing with it the boat, and when I would have fallen into the sea, it was there.

I can only recollect hearing an old sailor say, as I fell into the bottom of the boat, "Where in —— did he come from?"

When I became aware of what was going on, no one had succeeded in getting out of the boat, which then lay just forward of the wheelhouse. Our captain ordered them to throw bow-lines, which was immediately done.

Butts was there to help: "The second one I caught, and, placing myself within the loop, was hauled on board. I assisted in helping the others out of the boat, when it again went back to the *Monitor.*"

Browne, after helping the injured Commander Bankhead to place a bowline over his head and seeing him safely pulled aboard, turned to discover that half of his crew had deserted him, having felt that they had given service enough on such a night.

But in the darkness, some of my boat's crew availed themselves of the "friendly bowlines," and I was left minus one half of my boat's crew (having only seven left) before I was aware of it (and my boat pulled fourteen oars). No doubt, they may have thought I did not intend to go again to the *Monitor* (whose red light was still visible). I asked those of my crew remaining if they would go back once more to the *Monitor?* and the brave fellows answered, "We will go if you do."

Browne and his remaining crew shoved off for a third trip to the *Monitor,* to fulfill his promise that he would return for those still clinging to the turret. He was hailed by Commander Trenchard to return so that he could be towed up to the *Monitor* as they were now almost two miles to leeward, but the hail was muffled and unintelligible over the sounds of the storm.

. . . Mr. Browne started on another trip and soon afterwards was hailed, and directed to lie on his oars, or drop astern and be towed up,

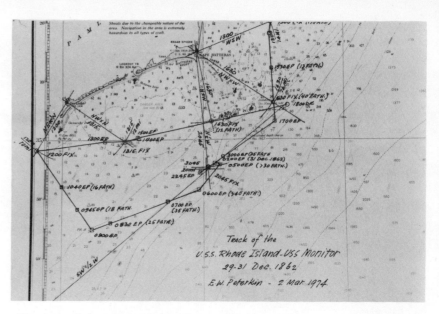

The track of the Rhode Island *after the* Monitor *sank, as reproduced by E. W. Peterkin.*

as the *Rhode Island* would steam for the *Monitor* as soon as the men could be got on board from the boats alongside, and the boats hoisted up.

Mr. Browne, perhaps not understanding the order, proceeded on in the direction of the *Monitor.* . . .

As the wind and sea were against him he made but little progress, yet he continued gaining until with a quarter of a mile to the *Monitor,* when the light became extinguished. . . .

Browne saw the red light on the *Monitor,* about a mile away, as they desperately pulled to reach her. With seven oars short, ". . . we made but slow progress and before we reached her, her light disappeared."

When he approached what he supposed to be position of the vessel, he saw nothing except an eddy, apparently produced as she went down.

The *Monitor* sank at approximately 0130, 31 December 1862. There was no great noise to signal the end of the struggle, no terrific explosions or final convulsions—just the sounds of the eternal sea. The *Monitor* had become history.

Browne stood by as long as he deemed prudent, in order to rescue any survivors, but found none: "We pulled around, as near as we could estimate, the place where we supposed she had sunk but no sign of any one could we find although one of my crew was positive he heard some one call."

Meanwhile, on board the *Rhode Island,* Weeks saw that the drenched sailors from the *Monitor* and *Rhode Island* alike were receiving warm care.

For an hour or more we watched from the deck of the *Rhode Island* the lonely light upon the *Monitor's* turret—a hundred times we thought it gone forever, a hundred times it reappeared.

Butts, too, had watched in vain:

All on board the steamer were anxiously watching the light in the turret and vainly peering into the darkness for a glimpse of the rescuing boat, the light suddenly disappeared and forever, for after watching for a long time to try and find it again, they were forced to the conclusion that the *Monitor* had gone to the bottom with all that remained on board.

Ensign Rodgers thought that Browne and his boat must have been lost, because they lost sight of the lights of the sinking ship and the first cutter, and it was feared that they had both gone down together.

Surgeon Weeks, too, was concerned with the fate of the first cutter.

We had looked, most anxiously, for the whale-boat which had last gone out, under the command of Master's Mate Brown, but saw no signs of it. We knew it had reached the *Monitor,* but whether swamped by the waves, or drawn in as the *Monitor* went down, we could not tell.

However, those in the first cutter knew they were still afloat and realized that even in their exhausted state, their survival depended upon the strength in their arms. To Browne it seeemed hopeless as the distance betweeen the steamer and the whale boat began to open:

. . . we started for the *Rhode Island,* but before long we found that she was steaming *away* from us, throwing up rockets and burning blue lights,—leaving us behind.

Apparently, the misfortune of the night before was still stalking the first cutter. The sea was waiting to claim still more victims.

It was a gloomy outlook and, exhausted as we were, we were compelled to give her up. And now, all that we could do was to keep our boat afloat all that weary night, hoping daylight would show us some hope of rescue.

Cold, wet, hungry, tired, lame and sore, the hands of my crew blistered and bleeding. My right foot being lashed to the floor of the boat, my leg had chafed against the seat until it had cut into the flesh deeply. I carry the scar to this day—it looks like a deep burn, larger than my hand.

My wrist cut, and bone displaced by accident in unhooking the boat's tackle was swollen and pained me intensely. The steering oar which I carried under my left arm hugged close to my body, had rasped up and down so that I was bruised and bleeding from my hip to my arm pit and a large gland in the latter place was so swollen that after our rescue it had to be lanced. Yet not a word of complaint or fear was heard from my noble boys, but a look of brave determination was on every face.

We knew we were drifting to sea, several knots an hour. We had no sail, compass, or provisions and could only judge by the drift in what

direction we were going. It was the longest night I ever passed.

There was no rest, for the seas were so irregular and tumbling in from every direction, a constant watch had to be kept and oars ready to meet some ugly sea, head and head. . . .

The *Rhode Island* hoisted boats and proceeded to windward in search of the first cutter and the *Monitor* for the rest of the night, burning Coston's night signals at intervals.

The weather showed little promise of moderating. The wind was still howling out of the southwest and was now force seven, approximately 30 knots. The rain had stopped and dark luminous storm clouds raced through the sky. The sea was scattered with white caps and wind-blown foam still restricted visibility. All eyes strained, in hopes of seeing some sign of the lost boat and her little crew.

It was an eerie scene, with the blue light of the rockets breaking the gloom every half hour. But there was no sign of the whale-boat. Commander Trenchard gave orders to keep as "near the position as possible until daylight" in hopes of finding the first cutter.

Browne, in the first cutter, saw the second and third rockets from the *Rhode Island,* but the distance was opening. Finally they lost sight of the lights as the Gulf Stream swept them further out to sea. Browne knew that though his men were exhausted, with hands blistered and bleeding, they must fight the current to survive. If they were swept out beyond the sea lanes, they would have little chance of rescue. Browne knew what Commander Trenchard would decide and while his crew kept watch for the signals from the *Rhode Island,* he kept them pulling into the current.

He made a drag of the boat's mast, by which he kept her head to sea, and the crew on the lookout for signals. As no more could be seen he then pulled for the northward and eastward, finding the sea to be too rough to pull directly to the west, hoping to fall in with some of the numerous coasting vessels.

He kept the crew pulling all night in order to overcome the great strength of the northeast current; considering that if they did not exert themselves to do so they would be out of the track of all vessels.

Slowly, the hours passed and the sky began to get light, and with the light came renewed hope.

Commander Trenchard wrote in his report

After daylight, not seeing anything of the missing boat, I decided to cruise between the position she had separated from us and Cape Hatteras and the extremity of its shoals with the hope of falling in with her.

According to Weeks:

Captain Trenchard would not leave the spot, but sailed about, looking in vain for the missing boat, till late Wednesday afternoon, when it would have been given up as hopelessly lost, except for the captain's dependence on the coolness and skill of its tired officer.

The survivors. Master's Mate Browne and his men, cold, wet, and hungry, were adrift without compass or water. The first ship they sighted was a blockade runner, decks loaded with cotton, that left them to their fate.

In the early dawn, Browne spotted a "small black boat some distance off, with two or three men in her; seeing her as she rose three times upon the waves, and then disappearing." Perhaps this was the India rubber life boat* from the *Monitor,* or perhaps a boat from another unrecorded sinking.

Soon afterward Browne sighted a full rigged ship approaching: but two officers on her deck merely examined the lifeboat and her crew, and sailed on. The full account of this experience is best related in a long narrative of the experience, which accompanied a letter Browne addressed to President Taft. Found in the *Monitor* folder of the ZC file, Division of Naval History, it carried this note by Browne: This letter was written *solely for my children to be given them at my death. They have as yet not seen it.*

* This India rubber life boat was mentioned in the original specifications of the *Monitor* dated September 16, 1861:

"As it is incompatible with the service for which the battery is designed to carry boats, none will be permanently carried. . . . A skeleton frame of metal will be furnished by the contractor with an India rubber covering which may be put together in case of need, suitable light seats and oars to be furnished."

Oakland, Calif., November 29, 1909

Pres. Wm. Taft
Washington, D. C.

Honorable Sir:—

The enclosed is a copy of "(Sequel)" to the story of the loss of the "Monitor" which Col. Roosevelt, while President, asked me to write for him as it gives details additional to those contained in the Official Records of the Navy, Series 1, Vol. 8, (Page 356).

Yours respectfully,
D. Rodney Browne,
(Signed)   Formerly Act'g Master, U.S.N.

About 7 AM we made a full rigged ship and knew she would pass near us if she held her present course. She came nearer and I could plainly see the officer on her quarter-deck smoking a cigar. He went to the cabin companionway and another officer came on deck. He leveled his spy glass at us, looked aloft and went below leaving us to our fate.

She was running the blockade, carrying all the sail she could stand, with preventers back stays leading abaft. Her decks were piled with bales of cotton. She *knew* that a boat in that place must be in distress but cotton was of more value than human lives.

I knew we were out of the usual track of vessels but hoped for the best. Several hours after this, we made a schooner to the leeward, and saw we had some chance to cut her off.

We found several overcoats in our boat (left there by some of the officers we had rescued on our previous trips).

We stranded our boat's painter, tied the coats together at the button holes with rope yarns and made quite a sail. Then we took an oar for a mast, one strand of the painter for a backstay. We then run the oar through the armholes of the coats. The other two strands of the painter we used as braces.

As my wrist was by this time so swollen and painful we rigged an oar on each quarter of the boat and two of my crew did the steering. So with the wind free and plenty of it we went booming on our course to cut off the schooner.

One of my crew had taken his black silk neck handkerchief and tied it to a boat stretcher and fastened it to our mast head for a flag.

I felt assured if we did not get on board this vessel, we might stand a poor chance for our lives.

I told my crew what I believed to be the fact: that we were at least fifty miles from land with no water or provisions, a gale of wind, a heavy sea, and a strong current against us and this schooner, perhaps our last show.

One of my crew said, "Well, if they won't take us, we will take them, or try for it." So on we stood for her.

On nearer approach we made out the Captain on the quarter deck with a musket and on nearer view we saw her crew (five men) armed with bricks, (of which her cargo was composed).

When we got within hail, down went the gun and bricks and they stood ready to assist us. It was our black flag and uniform that had aroused their belligerent attitude. For our flag was the 'Pirates flag.'

We had to board her on the weather side and as we swung alongside, while on the top of a wave, we jumped from the boat on to her deck and the next sea threw our boat (which you will remember was fourteen oared) over the schooner's rail and across her main hatches, staving in our ship's bottom.

But we were on deck and glad enough to be there. She proved to be the schooner, "A. Colby" of Bucksport, Me., loaded with brick for the U. S. Government and bound for Fernandina, Fla.

I briefly told the Captain our experiences and how Cape Hatteras light bore according to my judgement, (in which he placed but little faith), he seemed to think he was farther South, but I told him that with close reefed sails and a strong current on his starboard bow, he had made almost as much Easting as Southing.

He said, "I am chartered by the Government and as you are a Navy Officer I will shape my course for Hatteras if you so order me."

Later we made Cape Hatteras lighthouse, as I expected we would, but Captain insisted it must be Cape Lookout and stood in nearer to the land and went below to look at his chart.

All at once we struck a shoal, I ordered the helm hard a starboard and jumped into the main rigging so as to look down on the water and saw by its greenness that we were on a small shoal.

We struck three times, answered the helm, went off or over it, and cleared another shoal that had still less water on it. We then sounded the pumps and found we were making water very fast and at once shaped our course for Hatteras Inlet.

All hands at the pumps. The Captain had some Cherry brandy on board and he served it out to the men when they went to the pumps, and it served to stimulate them and had no ill effects.

My crew would not let me help at the pumps as my wrist was so swollen although their hands were sore and bleeding. So I bathed my wrist in the brandy and Captain Harriman swathed it up.

We feared that the wind might fall and leave us on a lee shore and with a cargo of brick, a bad leak, (and we knew not *how* bad) it was not a very cheerful situation.

I shall never forget his words at the time: "Mr. Browne," said he, "I own the most of this vessel and it is all I have got in the world, but even in our present situation, I do not regret having picked you up, for human life is worth more than money." He was a different man than the Captain of the blockade runner,—*he* thought his cotton of more value.

When we got nearer to the land, we discovered a vessel laying inside the bar. We came to an anchor and lowered the schooner's boat and I and her crew pulled in.

We found it was the U. S. Str. "Miami," Capt. Townsend. He sent off a boat and fifteen men to keep us afloat as we knew not the extent of our damage.

We passed a very comfortable night, as the "Miami's" crew would not let us do any work, so we went below for the sleep we so much needed. The next day the "Miami" came out and towed us to Beaufort.

The sea began to moderate and with this extra help of fresh men we had but little difficulty in keeping the leak under.

> NOTE: *This version of the same events is found in the* Official Records *as part of the report submitted by Commander Trenchard of the Rhode Island and is inserted at this time for a comparison.*

1030 (after making schooner)

He got up the crew's coats for sails and peaking his oars to assist, ran down for her.

1100 (after rigging sail)

and about eleven o'clock managed to get alongside. The schooner proved to be the *A. Colby,* commanded by H. D. Harriman of Bucksport, Me. bound for Fernandina, with bricks for government use. Mr. Browne and his crew were received with every kindness and attention and the boat taken on board.

1100 (after coming alongside)

The cutter was taken aboard the schooner, and Mr. Harriman was requested to change course so far as to land the officer and men at Beaufort, N. C.

This he consented to do.

1100 (after changing course for Beaufort)

but in running in for the coast, with a view of ascertaining more correctly his position

having been without an observation for several days his schooner struck on Diamond Shoals off Cape Hatteras.

1100 (after striking Diamond Shoals)

Being laden with brick which strained the vessel dangerously every time she struck bottom,

it was feared that the *A. Colby* would soon go to pieces. As it was, she began to leak dangerously.

1100 (after she began leaking)

Mr. Harriman managed to get her afloat.

1100 (after getting afloat off Diamond Shoals)

and, continuing on his course for Beaufort.

Upon arriving at Beaufort, I took the schooner's boat and went on board the flag ship. I was shown into the Commanding Officer's cabin and found him engaged with some Army Officers.

After a time he looked up and seeing me said, "Well, what can I do for you, Young Man?" I replied, "I am the officer in command of the boat lost from the Str. Rhode Island, off Hatteras and have the honor to report to you for orders, and to turn over my boat's crew."

Log of the Rhode Island, *2 January 1863.*

Log of the Rhode Island, *3 January 1863.*

He jumped up and taking me by both hands (I wish he had let the lame one alone) shook them until I thought he would shake them off."

Turning to the other officers, introduced me, saying, "Gentlemen, this is good news, I have three Steamers out looking for this officer and crew."

He refused to take my boat's crew and said, "Go aboard any vessel here and get any thing you need. You need not be afraid of your men leaving you after what they have been through with you."

He sent for my boat, and had it repaired and a sail and a mast fitted. He then said, "Go ashore and have a good time until the Rhode Island comes in."

My crew did have a good time, fishing, hunting, etc. and after I had my hand attended to and the gland under my arm lanced, I enjoyed it also.

And now for Captain Harriman. At Beaufort his vessel was temporarily repaired and sent to Fernandina with her cargo of brick.
She was then ordered to Philadelphia for repairs. There, they put her in complete repair, even to coppering her (she had never been coppered before).

Gave her new sails and rigging (gave the old sails and rigging to Capt. Harriman as a present), and he got a charter from the Government as long as the war lasted, so he was much better off than if he had not rescued us.

The *Rhode Island,* the morning after the *Monitor* sank, was still steaming to the south of Cape Hatteras Shoals. The quartermaster recorded in the log at 9 AM 31 December, that the wind shifted around to the north-northwest and had decreased to force six with the sky still overcast. At 9:45, Commander Trenchard "mustered the crew saved from the *Monitor* in all 47 men and officers."

On mustering the officers and crew, four officers and twelve of the men were missing. Those who escaped did so without receiving any serious injury with the exception of our surgeon, whose fingers on one hand were so badly mashed by being caught between the boats as to render partial amputation necessary.

At 1 PM the *Rhode Island* hailed the steamer *Kennebec,* carrying troops from Hampton Roads, but got no word of her boats. An hour later she signaled the *Columbia,* whose captain boarded the *Rhode Island* and reported his ship had also experienced a heavy southwest gale. The *Rhode Island* then continued her search for the remainder of the day.

On 1 January, 1863 the *Rhode Island* questioned the schooners *J. D. McCarthy* and *Shark,* both of New York but neither had sighted the lost boat. That afternoon, the *Rhode Island* abandoned the search and steamed for Beaufort to deliver some dispatches and to report the loss of the *Monitor.*

Upon her arrival, Captain Trenchard learned that Browne and his men had been rescued. Browne later described the reunion with his Captain.

Several days later the Steamer "Rhode Island" was signaled (outside the bar), I manned my boat and sailed out to her. As we neared her, glasses were leveled on us and when they made out who we were, everybody was on deck and as we came alongside we were received with hearty cheers.

Capt. Trenchard met me at the gangway and throwing his arms around me gave me a good hug. This was the *only time,* during the time I served under his command, that he ever forgot his dignity. They all thought we were in Davy Jones' locker.

I found our Paymaster had sent my accounts to Washington, as discharged by death, and it was some time before I was reinstated again and then I was *promoted for gallantry.*

With the dispatches delivered and her lost crewmen finally aboard, with the other survivors of the *Monitor,* the *Rhode Island* set course for Fort Monroe at Hampton Roads, Virginia. Weeks described their arrival:

Two day's sail brought us to the fort, whence we had started on Monday with so many glowing hopes, and alas! with some who were never to return. The same kindness met us here as on the *Rhode Island*; loans of money, clothing, and other necessaries, were offered us. It was almost well to have suffered, so much of a beautiful feeling did it bring out.

Once in port Commander Bankhead and Commander Trenchard ate dinner with Acting Rear-Admiral S. P. Lee, commander of the Blockading Squadron after having sent this telegram to the Secretary of the Navy:

TELEGRAM — Hampton Roads, Jan. 3, 1863 — 9 PM.
Received at Washington 9:30 PM.

The *Monitor* in tow of the *Rhode Island,* passed Hatteras Shoals Tuesday afternoon, the weather fine and promising; about 9 PM, squally weather, and about half past 10 it blew hard, and at 1:30 AM on Wednesday 31st, the *Monitor,* having sprung a leak, went down.

The survivors of the *Monitor* were back where they started, but a nightmare experience had filled the few hours between 29 December 1862 and 1 January 1863 for them. Eventually they received assignments to new ships, but they all remembered their service on the famous little "cheesebox on a raft" that had so helped the Union cause. They were proud to have served in her, and proudly called themselves "The Monitor Boys."

Their last days together were best described by Surgeon Weeks:

A day or two at the fort, waiting for official permission to return to our homes, and we were on our way,—the week seeming, as we looked back upon it, like some wild dream.

One thing only appeared real: our little vessel was lost, and we, who in months gone by, had learned to love her, felt a strange pang go through us as we remembered that never more might we tread her deck, or gather in her little cabin at evening.

We had left her behind us, one more treasure added to the priceless store which the Ocean so jealously hides.

The *Cumberland* and *Congress* went first; the little boat that avenged their loss has followed; in both noble souls have gone down.

Their names are for history; and so long as we remain a people, so long will the work of the *Monitor* be remembered, and her story told to our children's children.

Her work is now over. She lies a hundred fathoms deep under the stormy waters off Cape Hatteras. But 'the little cheesebox on a raft' has made herself a name which will not soon be forgotten by the American people.

With a last word by Paymaster Keeler:

The *Monitor* is no more.

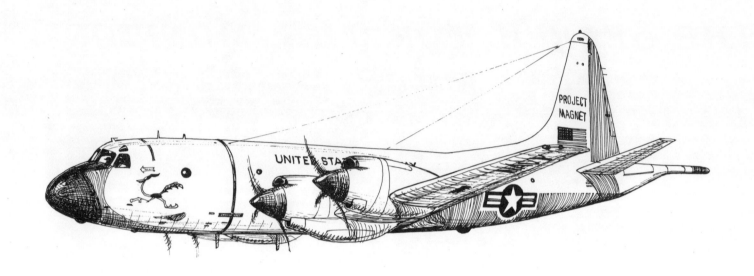

Lockheed RP-3D Orion assigned to Squadron VXN-8 for surveying the earth's magnetic field.

6

THE SEARCH FOR THE MONITOR

The USS *Monitor* sank in a wild storm off Cape Hatteras on New Year's Eve, 1862. For more than a century historians and would-be salvors puzzled over the mystery of where, exactly, the ship went down. The wreck of the ship was often claimed to have been sighted, but she was never positively identified until 1973. This is the story of the search for the *Monitor*.

The name of Cape Hatteras, being synonymous with stormy weather, meets with deep respect among seagoing people, even in this modern world of advanced navigational systems. For three centuries Cape Hatteras has produced stories of shipwreck in the treacherous seas off the Outer Banks of North Carolina. Its notoriety as the "Graveyard of the Atlantic" is well deserved—more than a thousand ships have been wrecked there since the early seventeenth century.

The unpredictable and sometimes savage sea characteristics that exist at Cape Hatteras are the result of two vast ocean currents, the warm northerly-flowing Gulf Stream and the colder southward-moving Labrador Current. These currents collide off Cape Hatteras. The early Spanish navigators learned to use the 4.5 knot current of the Gulf Stream to speed their passage to Europe. The Labrador Current, running south inshore of the Gulf Stream, presented an exacting test of navigation for ships headed south past Hatteras. A few miles too far east and they would be bucking the Gulf Stream; a few miles too far west and they would be on dangerous shoals.

Precise navigation depended heavily on visual sightings of landmarks, of which the Outer Banks offered very few. They are barren strips of sand lying well off the actual coast line, and ships had to travel close inshore to get dependable sightings. The first navigational aid at Cape Hatteras was a lighthouse erected in 1802. In 1854 the light was raised to a height of 150 feet, making it visible some 20 miles to sea. That beacon was the last point of reference used by the *Monitor* before she went down, and its exact location played a critical role in the search for the ship.

The storm that sent the *Monitor* to the bottom of the sea left no trace of the ship. No wreckage ever washed ashore. Reportedly, the bodies of five crew members were found on the beach and buried by Union troops.

The commanding officers of the *Monitor* and the *Rhode Island* submitted official reports on the disaster. A few of the crew recorded their versions in letters, news accounts, magazines, and later, at veterans' gatherings. A study of these accounts results in three conclusions: The first is that no single account tells the full story—events happened in quick succession and were observed from different viewpoints by men struggling for survival. The second was that no one was absolutely sure whether or not the *Monitor* had experienced any structural fatigue or whether she sank because of progressive flooding. Ericsson, to his dying day, claimed that no separation was possible between the upper raft and lower hull, while Commander Bankhead (later supported by Engineer Stimers) stated that there could have been a break because of shrinking green timbers. Of interest here was the fact that, although the ship carried a full load of ordnance material stowed well forward, no attempt was made to lighten the burden on the heavily pounding bow.

This last point was in contrast to the situation on the USS *Passaic,* which survived the same storm. That ship, monitor no. 2, represented a new generation of monitor design. She had a more conventional ship's hull with a reduced overhang between the raft and lower hull. Additionally, the pilot house had been placed on top of the turret and was circular in shape. While the *Monitor* was being towed head-on into the wind and sea, the *Passaic* reversed course, putting her stern into the sea, and thereby reduced the tremendous pressures on the hull. At the same time, the ship was lightened by throwing overboard the ammunition stowed forward under the berth deck. After the storm subsided, the *Passaic* and her towing ship, the *State of Georgia,* again resumed course and reached Beaufort safely, there to learn of the disaster that had befallen the *Monitor* and the *Rhode Island*.

A third and most important conclusion derived from all accounts of the loss of the *Monitor* was that the exact spot where she went down was unknown. This was partially due to the sketchy navigation preceding her loss, and the stormy seas, but mostly due to the sudden confusion of abandoning ship during the night. From various reports, statements were collected and evaluated for accuracy and reliability. The most accurate

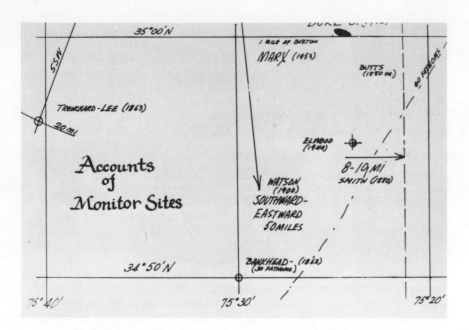

From the historical accounts and modern claims of discovery the search area covered approximately 500 square miles.

accounts were those written immediately after the sinking; other accounts written months and sometimes years afterwards, held important clues that helped fill the gaps in the chain of events that ended when the *Monitor* sank.

The search for the *Monitor* began in the Official Records of the Union Navy in the Civil War, where the reports of the sinking are printed, and in the National Archives where the smooth log of the *Rhode Island* is held. Additional research uncovered several more accounts by crew members of both ships. Analysis of the accounts, and their assimilation into a common narrative, indicated that the minimum possible area in which to search for the *Monitor* covered approximately 500 square miles. This extended from a mile north of the Hatteras lighthouse to 50 miles south of it. The next step was to interpret accounts of the sinking as best as possible, making calculated estimates of the set and drift experienced by the two ships to determine the approximate position at which the *Monitor* went down.

In the Official Records, Commander Trenchard of the *Rhode Island* and Commander Bankhead of the *Monitor* reported that the *Monitor* sank approximately 20 miles SSW of Cape Hatteras. However, in a letter dated 27 January 1863, to the Secretary of the Navy, Commander Bankhead refined the position by stating "As near as I could judge, making allowances for current, drift and sea, we were about 25 miles south of Cape Hatteras, say in latitude 34° 50′ North, longitude 75° 30′ West, depth of water 30 fathoms."

Francis Butts, a *Monitor* survivor, stated in his account that the anchor struck in 60 fathoms of water. Watson, on board the *Rhode Island,* claimed that the *Monitor* sank "southward and eastward fifty miles" off Cape Hatteras. While William F. Keeler, the paymaster of the *Monitor,* said in his letter that at the time the ship sank the *Rhode Island* was eight to ten miles east of the shoals. The last navigational fix on board the *Rhode Island* before the sinking was made at 2045. Her log from then on is incomplete, giving little if any information about how much headway they were making and how much drift they were experiencing until the *Monitor* sank at 0130.

The log of the *Monitor* was lost, and much interpretation was required to piece the fragmented accounts together to determine a search area. Each investigating group had to consider the same inconsistencies and gaps in the records to develop their theories of the sinking and search plan. These searches were carried out over a period of 26 years in what Captain W. F. Searle, the Navy Supervisor of Salvage, termed the "Great Monitor Sweepstakes." Until 1974, no attempt met with complete success and all of them experienced the frustration and defeat which the incomplete historical records and the unfavorable environment of Cape Hatteras combined to produce.

The first recorded search for the *Monitor* took place shortly after World War II ended. In August of 1949 the Navy began testing a newly developed Underwater Object Locator (UOL) Mark IV. The tests were conducted in an area south of the lighthouse, approximately where the *Monitor* was supposed to have sunk, with Mr. Jim Elwood and Lieutenant Commander Charles Landahl making observations. Only one large object was detected on the bottom, at 34° 55.5′ North and 75° 24.5′ West, in 310 feet of water; it was approximately 140 feet long and from 25 to 40 feet wide.

An attempt was made to put divers down on the wreck, but they were "strung out like kites on a string" in the swift current. The UOL report created no immediate interest in the Navy, but it did open the "Monitor file" in the Office of Naval History, and in the office of the Supervisor of Salvage.

Shortly afterwards a group of laymen headed by Raynor T. McMullen, a retired postal clerk from Dundee, Michigan, organized the U.S. Monitor Foundation of Washington, D.C., and offered a reward of $1,000 to anyone who could find and salvage the *Monitor*. Additionally several groups in Norfolk became interested in recovering the *Monitor* for historical display.

Sensing that the stakes were getting higher, and wishing to extract the Navy from a deluge of "requests for assistance," while at the same time disengaging it from any claim of responsibility, it was recommended that the Navy abandon the wreck and allow private enterprise to salvage it—if it was ever found.

This was officially done by the Secretary of the Navy on 30 September 1953. Then, under the laws of salvage, any would-be salvor who discovered the wreck and could commence salvage operations could legally claim possession.

Suddenly interest grew into intrigue as a result of *Monitor*'s change in status to a salvage prize. Different groups conducted secretive searches, plotting supposed wreck positions with Xs on the charts as if they were treasure maps. Few such searchers possessed any archeological or oceanographic background, nor did they have any sophisticated underwater search equipment at their disposal. Most of them expected to find the *Monitor* in an undeteriorated state of preservation with her hull structure intact, as it was when she went down, making salvage possible by conventional methods.

One of the most interesting and best described accounts of a search, and the first public claim of discovery, was produced in 1955 by Robert Marx, a Marine corporal then stationed at Camp LeJeune, North Carolina. Marx originated the "shallow water" theory that centered search operations in the area north of the lighthouse. In his book, *Always Another Adventure,* he related that his interest was stimulated by a Marine officer in the summer of 1954. He started his search by reading accounts in the Official Records and at the National Archives. Then he drove along the Outer Banks, inquiring among local fishermen for the location of wrecks and rumors of the *Monitor*. There he met a retired sea captain named Gray who showed him a family ledger in which was recorded that in January of 1865 the family had seen, while on a picnic, the "Yankee Cheesebox on a Raft" in the surf just off the lighthouse.

Marx believed that this was a firm lead to the location of the *Monitor*. With this information he initiated a search, using scuba divers from the Marine Corps Base, working just off the beach close to the lighthouse. The search was unsuccessful. Shortly afterwards, additional research revealed that the lighthouse was not the one that existed in 1863, and that the shoreline had eroded considerably. This led Marx to surmise that the suspected position of the *Monitor* was more than a mile off-shore and approximately a mile north of the existing lighthouse.

While investigating the story that five bodies from the *Monitor* had washed ashore in January of 1863, Marx met Mr. Ben Dixon MacNeil. MacNeil, a journalist and amateur historian at Cape Hatteras reportedly discovered their graves near the old lighthouse and had recovered buckles and buttons as evidence. A chart owned by MacNeil, showed all the reported sinking positions; about a mile off the present-day lighthouse was a large red X with the words "Here is where I found her." Marx was convinced that the tip he had found in the Gray family ledger was confirmed by Mr. MacNeil's chart. Their theory was that after the last boat trip from the sinking ship, she still had enough steam for the men remaining on board to attempt to run her onto the shoals and beach her. This explained the five bodies washed up on the beach, probably drowned trying to get through the surf. If the men had been lost twenty miles at sea their bodies would have been widely disbursed by the storm.

Marx used the same search technique that MacNeil had tried—observing from a plane flying low over the water when the wind was out of the northwest and the sea was calm. These conditions were rare, but they cleared the usually turbulent waters and Marx could see wrecks all over the bottom "like toys in a bathtub." He claimed to have spotted the *Monitor*, and talked *Life* Magazine into backing his next expedition to dive on the wreck. The Coast and Geodetic Survey made two ships available to pinpoint the location of the contact with sonar, and buoys were placed over the site.

Marx went down to the wreck in forty five feet of water and claimed to have found the gun turret. He also claimed to have written his name on a piece of paper and tucked it inside a coke bottle which he left on the wreck. But mishap hit the expedition when Marx was overcome by impure air in a scuba bottle and a storm destroyed their markers. A second expedition failed to locate any wreck in the area. Marx noticed that the depth readings were different and re-checked his bearings. They were on the right spot, but apparently the storm had shifted the bottom sand sufficiently to cover the wreck and prevent further exploration.

Thus it was thought that the elusive *Monitor* was buried in the shifting sands and only time was needed to bring another storm that would uncover her again. The publicity of the discovery, and the arguments by those who doubted Marx's claim placed the *Monitor* once more in the headlines. Many an amateur treasure hunter and scuba diver dreamed of being the first person to stand on the *Monitor*'s deck.

Marx, having convinced himself that he had found the *Monitor,* went on to other projects and never attempted again to confirm his claim. His story served only to intensify the efforts of others to locate the wreck.

In 1967 the State of North Carolina moved to protect the great number of historically valuable wrecks off the Outer Banks. It enacted legislation that required a permit from the state to conduct searches or salvage in waters within the jurisdiction of the state. In compliance with this legislation, the North Carolina Tidewater Services, Inc., was given a permit to search the area of the Marx claim in an attempt to verify it. A magnetometer was used, and searchers claimed to have located a large target, but again bad weather and shifting bottom sands prevented confirmation before they ran out of money.

During the search, Lieutenant Commander Lendahl informed Mr. Samuel P. Townsend, of the North Carolina Department of Archives and History, of the 1949 findings by the Navy's UOL. This information must have only confused the shallow-water theorists, because the UOL position was over twenty miles at sea, south of the lighthouse. To this day, the wreck in the shallow waters north of the lighthouse has not been identified.

Contemporary with the early searches, Captain Ernest W. Peterkin of the Naval Research Laboratory in Washington, D.C., commenced the most thorough and fully documented study of the navigational track of the *Rhode Island* ever made. What started as a casual interest developed into

The flight crew of the Project Magnet aircraft "Roadrunner" and participants of Project Cheesebox.

a major contribution to the final search for and confirmed identification of the *Monitor*.

In December of 1970 the Research Laboratory began tests of a new underwater strobe and camera system under the direction of Chester Buchanan. Captain Peterkin, knowing that the tests were to be conducted in the Cape Hatteras area, suggested that the USNS *Mizar*, the research vessel that photographed the sunken submarines *Scorpion* and *Thresher*, conduct a limited search on the basis of his research. Disappointingly, the position he recommended was found to be in the main shipping channel, where it would be too dangerous to deploy the equipment. Peterkin however would continue to refine his navigational track, using every possible variable; and an actual search based on his work would have to wait until 1973.

Meanwhile another research organization sprung up. This was the U.S. Monitor Foundation, under the direction of Mr. Michael O'Leary, and in cooperation with yet another group, the Underwater Archeological Associates, some detailed research was done. Both groups were attempting to confirm the claim by Marx that the *Monitor* lay in the shallow waters north of the lighthouse. In May of 1973 they claimed to have located the turret by sonar, and stated that a diver's marker had actually been placed on the wreck. However, as reported in the *News American*, ". . . the reluctance of the Civil War battleship to leave its subaqueous anonymity has again

been made apparent. A passing ship destroyed the marker and the search must begin again." Headlines such as "Monitor Lost, Found Again" and "Famed Monitor is Found Again" became part of the legend of the elusive ship. But so far most of the searches had been conducted in the shallow water area, mostly because of the claims of Robert Marx.

In early August of 1973, Peterkin read newspaper accounts of a June search (by O'Leary) in the shallow water area, containing implications that the searchers might request Navy assistance. Peterkin believed that the shallow water area seemed highly unlikely as a wreck site. He based his belief on the study he had made, and wanted to make his research available before the Navy obligated any equipment or funds in a shallow water search. He contacted the Assistant Secretary of the Navy for Research and Development, and was then invited to the Pentagon to compare his findings with those of a group wishing to borrow some underwater TV equipment.

At that meeting, Roland Wommack, representing the Trident Foundation, outlined the Monitor Project. Wommack had established the Trident Foundation to assist in various underwater archeological projects, and had become interested in the *Monitor* through association with Jim Elwood, who took part in the Navy's 1949 UOL evaluation. Their view was that the *Monitor* was not in the shallow water area, but more than 20 miles SSE of the lighthouse, and this view seemed historically defensible.

Mr. Wommack, convinced that they had located the wreck of the *Monitor,* was depending heavily on past Navy associations to borrow surplus equipment to make a search. They envisioned using underwater TV to confirm the identity of the wreck and to assist in planning diving operations which were to be recorded on film. The film would concentrate on the ". . . powerful human drama behind the three year effort of Roland Wommack and his colleagues to convince the skeptics that he had found the exact spot where the *Monitor* lies on the ocean floor."

However, they seemed to overlook the fact that they had not positively identified the wreck and lacked the equipment to do so; neither did they have funds for such a project. Peterkin was asked to participate, but any further Navy participation or assistance was precluded when Wommack more or less jumped the gun. Feeling pressed by other search efforts, he put to sea, planning to send a diver down in 300 feet of water, using only standard scuba equipment and without any decompression facilities. Luckily he was unable to investigate the position due to equipment failure and the wreck there is still unidentified.

In the spring of 1973, yet another search project was formed at the U.S. Naval Academy. Midshipman First Class Michael Ellison wanted to do some wreck diving, and asked an underclassman who had read the Marx account and had followed the newspaper stories, if he knew of any good wrecks in the area. My reply, half serious, was "Why don't you go dive on the *Monitor*?" Soon casual interest grew into intense concentration on plans for an expedition to Cape Hatteras. Professor Harry H. Keith, Ellison's academic advisor, contacted William J. Andahazy of the

Naval Research and Development Center (NSRDC) in Annapolis, and together we developed a search theory, based on Andahazy's specialty in magnetics. It was believed that magnetic detection offered the best method to look for a ferro-magnetic target that, from all reports, was buried in the sand.

Mr. Andahazy threw his full support behind the project with great enthusiasm, and in cooperation with Mr. Darrel Nixon and others assigned to the Magnetics Branch, developed a search plan and a computer model of the *Monitor* which would indicate what the parameters of the magnetic signal or signature were in different orientations relative to the earth's magnetic field.

This is how *Project Cheesebox* began. With Midshipman Ellison, we rounded up diving gear and additional midshipmen. Through Professor William M. Darden of the History Department we obtained the use of a government vehicle to transport the "expedition" to Cape Hatteras. Professor Darden, a native of North Carolina, became our "resident expert" on the Cape because of experience gained while fishing there. Working on weekends and after study hours, as the midshipmen had to carry a full academic schedule, all hands prepared for the expedition under the guidance of Mr. Andahazy. This trip had to wait for a free period between the final exams, and June Week, when Ellison was to graduate.

Arrangements were made to coordinate the surface search with an air search flown by a naval reserve crew in a P-3 anti-submarine aircraft, and the group was joined by Mike LaMott and Bruce Fadden from the local dive shop and by Midshipman Fred Christensen. But on arrival in North Carolina, we were stopped by the weather that has made Cape Hatteras legendary. Our tent was blown flat in squalls, surf conditions were terrific, and the weather prevented any low level flights by the P-3. All hands were happy to get back to Annapolis with the borrowed gear.

Defeated, but not undaunted, Andahazy kept the project alive. Ellison graduated from the Naval Academy and could no longer take part. I began talking to Professor Darden about a special project to investigate the historical records and document the search methodology in a systematic effort to solve the mystery of the *Monitor*. Obviously, more preparation was needed, and advanced technology would have to be involved.

Next, Mr. Andahazy arranged through Mr. Ron Lorentzen of the Naval Oceanographic Office for an airborne magnetic survey of search area "A," the shallow water area one mile north of the Hatteras lighthouse. By then two areas had been designated as a result of recent claims and historical investigation. One was the shallow water area where Marx claimed to have found the *Monitor*; the other was based on the navigational track of the *Rhode Island* and was located more than fifteen miles at sea. Both areas were to be searched systematically with the highly sensitive airborne magnetometer mounted in the RP-3D aircraft, an experimental type which conducted worldwide surveys under the Navy's Project Magnet.

A first flight was made on 17 July 1973; four hours were spent on a low altitude survey near the lighthouse. The entire survey was taped for later

The research vessel Eastward *operated by Duke University and home ported at Beaufort, North Carolina.*

analysis. A preliminary report was assembled and taken to the Supervisor of Salvage where we discussed the results of the search and the new Project Cheesebox with Commander Robert Moss, Commander James Coleman, and Mr. Ed Wardwell of Seaward, Inc. We also learned at that time that the National Geographic Society was supporting a *Monitor* search expedition aboard the vessel *Eastward* belonging to Duke University.

That expedition put to sea in August under the direction of John Newton of Duke University and with an impressive array of scientific equipment. Members included Dr. Harold E. Edgerton of the Massachusetts Institute of Technology and Mr. Gordon Watts of the North Carolina Division of Archives and History. Dr. Edgerton is an expert in underwater search and photographic operations using his side-scan sonar and deep sea cameras. Mr. Watts is an expert in historical research and archeology. Also aboard the *Eastward* were Dr. Robert Sheridan of the University of Delaware and Miss Dorothy Nicholson who represented the National Geographic Society. There were two objectives: first was a geologic study of the continental shelf off Cape Hatteras, primarily by Dr. Sheridan; second was a search for the *Monitor* based on a reproduction of the *Rhode Island's* track chart and subsequent designation of a search area by Gordon Watts and Dorothy Nicholson.

The *Eastward* spent two weeks at sea during exceptionally good weather in an almost flat calm. The search was assisted by auxiliary

Dr. Harold E. Edgerton explaining a side scan sonar trace to members of the Eastward *expedition. —— Courtesy D. Nicholson.*

vessels of the Army Reserve. But despite ideal weather conditions, continuous equipment malfunctions hampered the work. In the expedition report, Mr. Newton stated: "Buoys floated grandly for a period of minutes, then vanished beneath the sea, reception of the signals from the transponders of the navigational system was inexplicably nil and the identification of sonar and magnetometer targets was more difficult than had been anticipated."

Dr. Edgerton worked day and night making on-site repairs to his side-scan sonar and improvisation became a constant necessity. Search plans called for utilization of multiple sensors by simultaneously towing the side-scan sonar, the magnetometer, and operating the vertical sonar in an overlapping pattern oriented to the contours of the sea floor.

A search of the southern sector revealed twenty one sonar or magnetometer contacts. Only one of them seemed promising; it was located within eight miles of the spot where Commander Bankhead estimated the *Monitor* went down and was in 300 feet of water. Three days and nights were spent photographing and video-taping with underwater TV cameras before it became evident that the target was a modern fishing trawler with semi-circular pilot house first thought to be the *Monitor*'s turret. A deck windlass and several large deck hatches proved the ship not to be the *Monitor*.

After such discouragement, and with the complete failure of the magnetometer due to cable fatigue the expedition almost came to an end. But on the last day of the planned search a long amorphous echo appeared on the side-scan sonar while the *Eastward* was steaming northeast along the 200-foot contour. The echo would have been missed but for the fact that Fred Kelly, who was stowing fishing gear, happened to glance at the recorder and decided it warranted a second look.

Three more days were then spent collecting additional data as the

Eastward swung back and forth across the wreck. The TV cameras went out of focus repeatedly as they dangled over the wreck, and much of the data was blurred, but even so many encouraging details were recorded: "a flat, unobstructed surface" structure that looked like iron plate, and a circular protrusion that could possibly be the turret.

Then Dr. Edgerton's camera was snagged on the wreck; the cable parted and the camera was lost. Besides the loss of $5,000 worth of scientific equipment and several hundred feet of coaxial cable, any chance of bringing back definitive photographs of the wreck had been lost. There was no need to continue work, as the expedition had already extended its ship time, so the *Eastward* returned to Morehead City with reels of video tape and pieces of coal, clinkers, and wood fragments that had been dredged from the sea floor.

Back at his laboratory, Gordon Watts commenced an intensive five-month study of the video tapes. They were shown to an audience at National Geographic Society headquarters, and at the Naval Academy, in hopes that others interested in the *Monitor* might help in the identification, but in final analysis it was Gordon Watts whose interpretation of the tapes, at the 11 March 1974 Seaprobe meeting at the Naval Research Laboratory in Washington, presented a fairly strong argument that the *Monitor* had at last been found.

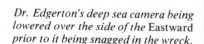

Dr. Edgerton's deep sea camera being lowered over the side of the Eastward *prior to it being snagged in the wreck.*

But before that meeting, many other factors came into focus to encourage the search and result in final positive identification of the *Monitor*.

In September 1974, the midshipmen working on the *Monitor* project were, with the support of the Academic Dean, Bruce M. Davidson, and the Director of Research, Dr. Richard Matthieu, formally organized into "Project Cheesebox," and a research design was outlined. I was then in my last year at the Academy, and because of prior college experience, was able to work out a special seminar under the guidance of Professor Darden. During the fall semester I divided my time between my regular studies, my duties as company commander, and trips to the various historical depositories in the Washington area, planning for a full investigation of the *Monitor*'s history and the determination of where she sank.

It was decided that the greatest obstacle to be faced, other than the unfavorable environment at Cape Hatteras and the lack of complete historical records, was the lack of documentation of search techniques and location theories which prevented any cumulative deductions. Where previous search attempts had been made and failed, there had been no record of the research methods or subject areas investigated. Therefore, "Project Cheesebox" was envisioned as a survey of all available historical records and search accounts so that the information could be gathered and evaluated in one document. Hopefully this would develop a sound search technique, supported by documented historical research.

John Newton and Gordon Watts, aboard the Eastward, *examining material dredged up from the vicinity of the wreck of the* Monitor.

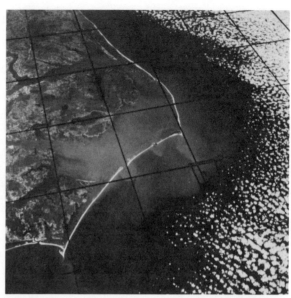

In January 1974 a second air survey was run based on the historical track of the Rhode Island. *The search area, within the rectangular box, was the same area searched by the* Eastward. —— *Courtesy NASA from outer space.*

In addition, engineering studies of the *Monitor's* structure would be conducted to assist in evaluating any wreck data. Towing tank tests of the *Monitor's* hull would add new data for comparison with modern design evaluation techniques and give empiracal data on the actual sea performance of the ship. This would perhaps shed new light on the circumstances of her sinking.

Consequently, "Project Cheesebox" evolved as a multi-disciplined project involving eight midshipmen working in different academic majors, each contributing to the study according to his capabilities; their specialties were history, engineering, oceanography, ocean engineering, and international relations.

In October of 1973, a meeting was held with Commander Don Walsh and Commander Jack McNish in the Office of the Assistant Secretary of the Navy for Research and Development to discuss the results of the first survey and the research then in progress. At that time Mr. E. W. Peterkin of the Naval Research Laboratory was introduced to the project members, thus commencing a relationship that added to the scope and success of the project.

The results of the engineering analysis and towing tank tests were significant. Examination of the *Monitor* design made it seem reasonable to expect the ship to have a large metacentric height with the result that she would be very quick-rolling and uncomfortable to ride. The tests proved otherwise. Linear tests in the Naval Academy towing tank showed that the hull form was a very stable platform, giving credence to the remark by Engineer Stimers, over a century earlier, that a wine glass stood undisturbed on the wardroom table during the stormy trip from New York to Hampton Roads in 1862.

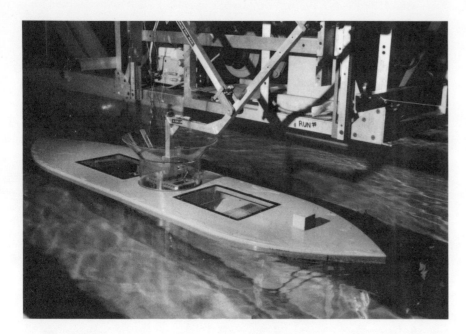

Tow tank test of the Monitor *were conducted at the U.S. Naval Academy by Midshipmen Hribar and Rau to determine the seakeeping qualities of the original vessel.*

In tests, the two tank model performed the same as the original Monitor *according to historical accounts; going through waves instead of over them.*

In the first series of tests the model was stationary and experienced wave heights equivalent to actual sea conditions of from 1.2 to 6 feet. Eighteen runs were made and the model's response in pitch and heave decreased with increased wave height. This type of response would not be expected from a modern vessel. Usually a vessel's pitching and heaving motions vary directly with wave height, meaning the higher the wave height, the more severe the vessels' motions. The *Monitor* acted very differently because of the large amount of water awash on her deck. Each time the bow submerged, a significant amount of water was picked up and acted as a damper to the ship's motion. This additional weight caused the bow to plow through a wave rather than over it. The linear tests showed that the *Monitor* was remarkably stable in even rough seas, behaving more like a semi-submersible than a surface craft. Though designed for smooth waters, with a low freeboard, the upper raft portion of the hull acted as a scoop when the seas increased, supplying the additional mass which dampened out the oscillating motion. The ride aboard the *Monitor* may have been wet, but it was relatively smooth.

In order to test the ships towing response, the model was taken to the David Taylor Model Basin (NSRDC) in Carderock, Maryland. Desiring to duplicate a confused condition of sea state seven, as had been reported when the *Monitor* sank, it was necessary to use a larger tank with more

sophisticated equipment. The David Taylor Model Basin is 15 feet deep and nearly a mile long. At that time the Navy's newest submarine hull form, the *Trident* submarine, was being tested, presenting a unique historical contrast with the *Monitor*.

For the tests a low sea state seven was generated and the model was towed with two hawsers scaled to those used the night the original *Monitor* sank. Eight runs at varying speeds were filmed as instruments recorded the ship's motion. The significant wave height during the tests was seventeen feet with a maximum of twenty feet. The film dramatically recorded the action of the *Monitor* at sea during a storm, making possible full understanding of how she reacted before she sank.

At zero speed in sea state seven it was observed that the deck was awash almost constantly. The low freeboard caused water to be taken on deck, both fore and aft, with each pitching motion. This water flowed along the deck until it crashed into various topside structures, causing large impact loads. Both the bow and stern emerged from the water in almost every pitching cycle, but no slamming of the bow was recorded. The pilot house, turret and smokestack were subjected to sizable impact loads from water washing across the decks. It was very evident that the oakum packing was washed out from these structures by the great force of the water that pounded against their sides.

At towing speeds ranging from 1.5 to 5.9 knots, the response of the model was very similar to the static test, with one significant difference—the large amounts of water on the flat deck tended to dampen the motions of the ship even more severely, causing the response to approach that of a critically damped sinusoid. This resulted in the hull form plowing through the waves and developing a tendency to nose under as a flat board would do when being towed. A further consequence of the added water was the much increased impact loads on the pilot house and turret. The pilot house was totally submerged on the downward motion of the bow which would have caused a considerable amount of water to enter the vessel through the viewing slits. The turret caused large amounts of water to spray over its top and enter through the iron grating roof.

The slamming of the flat under-body of the raft did not appear to be critical at any speed up to six knots. However, there were two instances when slams did occur which would have put a severe strain on the junction between the two bodies. The "shudder" referred to in several accounts of the sinking was probably caused by slugs of sea water crashing into the turret rather than by the slamming of the raft portion of the hull.

Another observation during this phase of the testing was that great resistance was created by the large amounts of water dampening the ship's motion which severely burdened the hull structure by creating very large bending moments amidships. This was thought to be significant because the *Monitor* was constructed with no longitudinal structural members other than the hull stringer to which the armor belt of wood was attached. In fact, her amidship hull cross-section resembled the trestle structure used in bridge construction. This could very possibly explain why crewmen aboard the *Monitor* first reported leaks in the coal bunkers located in the approximate position where maximum bending moment would occur. The hull plates were secured by rivets only and were sealed with oakum. As the hull worked while hogging and sagging in a seaway, the hull plating and rivets could have experienced structural fatigue, opening up the hull. The film proved that the model behaved in a fashion similar to that reported for the *Monitor* before she sank, and this gave validity to the evaluation of the *Monitor's* seakeeping ability as prepared by the midshipmen in "Project Cheesebox."

In November 1973, the interest generated in the search for the *Monitor* by the numerous news items, the video tapes from the *Eastward* expedition and the research being conducted by *Project Cheesebox,* focused in a memorandum to Admiral Isaac C. Kidd, Jr., Chief of Navy Materiel. The memo summarized previous search attempts, noting that the *Eastward* expedition had returned with the most promising evidence to date and the likelihood that the research conducted by the various groups might be mutually supportive. Since the Navy had been either directly involved or indirectly approached by the various groups representing both public and private interests, the memorandum recommended that a single office within the Navy be given cognizance over future Navy participa-

The Alcoa Sea Probe *is the largest all aluminum vessel afloat. It is equipped with twin cycloidal propellers enabling it to pivot 360°, spinning around on the axis of the ship.* ——*Courtesy Alcoa Marine.*

tion and assistance to avoid criticism from any of the groups that did not receive Navy support. This became particularly important with the suggested utilization of the Navy's forthcoming at-sea evaluation of the 243 foot Research Vessel Alcoa *Sea Probe.*

The prospect of utilizing the *Sea Probe* was exciting. The *Sea Probe* is an ultra-sophisticated research vessel designed to recover 200-ton payloads from 6,000 foot depths and to search, core, drill and sample mineral deposits in waters as deep as 18,000 feet. In conducting pinpoint search and recovery operations, the vessel acts as a dynamically positioned working platform able to "hover" over a site on the ocean floor without the use of any ground tackle. The ship is capable of this because of it's unique propulsion system; twin cycloidal propellers, one forward and one aft, which can direct their thrust 360° making it as simple to move sideways as forward or backward. Coupled with precision navigational instruments and it's oil-rig type derrick that lowers a semi-rigid drill string through the centerwell in the hull, the *Sea Probe* can thread a cable through a six-inch eye lying 900 feet below.

In the search mode, an instrument "pod" carries side looking sonar for search, forward looking sonar for obstacle avoidance, television cameras with flood lights for real-time inspection of any targets and two deep-sea 35mm cameras with strobe lights for detailed recording of any

The Sea Probe *lowering a semi-rigid drill string with the instrument "pod" or other tool to the seafloor. The ship can recover 200 tons from 6,000 feet and thread a cable through a 6 inch eye lying 900 feet below.*

targets. Additionally, it carries a droppable acoustic beacon for marking locations and for referencing precise shipboard control of the "pod" through a "thruster" system at the working end of the pipe.

Dr. Edgerton had suggested to the Navy that the *Monitor* be used as a target of opportunity to test the *Sea Probe*'s advanced search and inspection capabilities during the evaluation scheduled in the spring of 1974. To further the effort, the National Geographic Society had agreed to help support the expedition with additional funding. As a result, Commander Collin M. Jones, Officer-in-Charge of the Navy Experimental Diving Unit in Washington, D.C. was designated as the officer responsible for conducting the evaluation, which also meant refereeing what was to be the final heat of the "Great *Monitor* Sweepstakes."

In order to collate all the available data and to coordinate an effective search, Commander Jones convened a meeting on 11 March 1974 of all interested historians and search groups at the Naval Research Laboratory (NRL) in Washington, D.C. The purpose of the meeting was to allow individuals to present their research and exploration results so that a best estimate of the *Montor*'s location could be determined and maximum benefit derived from the limited search time available. The meeting attracted immense public interest when it was preceeded on 8 March 1974 by the public announcement by Mr. Newton and Mr. Watts that they had sufficient evidence that they had found the *Monitor*. This resulted in nation-wide news coverage and considerable interest in the *Sea Probe* expedition.

The meeting at NRL was singularly unique in the history of the quarter-century search for the *Monitor* because it was the first time different organizations and search efforts joined forces in a cooperative effort to solve this mystery of Cape Hatteras. The meeting was attended by members of the press, representatives of the Navy's Supervisor of Salvage and Oceanographic Offices, the National Geographic Society, the Smithsonian Institution and many other interested scientists and historians.

Commander Jones delivered the introductory remarks, stating the meeting's purpose and reaffirmed that any position data given to him for the purpose of the search would be held in confidence. Mr. Peterkin, the first speaker, reported on his study of the track of the *Rhode Island* from the existing log and various accounts of the survivors. He outlined what he believed to be the most probable search area based on the historical records and designated a position considered to be the best approximation of the ironclad's location. Then I followed with a description of the research in progress at the Naval Academy which included, in addition to the engineering studies, a detailed investigation of the records, complementing Mr. Peterkin's research, and the magnetic surveys conducted under the direction of Mr. Andahazy.

Next Mr. Andahazy summarized the theory and methodology behind the airborne surveys and the results of the analysis of the data. Eleven uncharted anomalies were determined worthwhile to investigate and of these eleven possibles, three matched the criteria set by the mathematical analysis, one of which coincided with the wreck site explored by the *Eastward* expedition.

The Trident Foundation was represented by Mr. Roland Wommack who related the information contained in the 1949 UOL report and his search attempts in cooperation with Mr. Jim Elwood. Next Mr. Michael O'Leary representing the Monitor Foundation stated that he was convinced that the *Monitor* did *not* lie north of the lighthouse as Bob Marx had claimed.

The meeting reached a high point of interest when Mr. John Newton dramatically stated his belief that the *Monitor* had been found and then turned the podium over to Mr. Gordon Watts who interpreted the data obtained on the *Eastward* expedition. The video tapes had originally faded in and out of focus as the camera swung by the wreck from the anchored research ship, however, now they obviously had suffered greatly from the constant re-runs. Nevertheless, they revealed very promising characteristics and this wreck would definitely be one of the first to be looked at by the *Sea Probe*. Participants refrained from hasty conclusions in view of the past history of erroneous claims, desiring more irrefutable evidence, but all were excited about what conclusive evidence the *Sea Probe* could produce.

Commander Jones closed the meeting with a statement of his gratitude to the participants and that the limited berthing aboard the *Sea Probe* would be assigned to those experts he felt necessary to evaluate the wreck-sites investigated. Additionally, every consideration would be given to the preservation of the wreck, if in fact it was the *Monitor,* so not to disturb it's archeological value.

On 15 March 1974, Commander Jones, Mr. Peterkin and Mr. Buchanan met to make the difficult selection of a sequence of sites to be looked at and to select the scientific party. Eleven contacts were selected on the basis of the magnetic data and the *Eastward* survey. Each was assigned a corresponding number of priority; the first site to be looked at would be the Duke position.

By far the hardest decision was the selection of the scientific party. It included Commander C. M. Jones; Mr. Ernest W. Peterkin; Mr. William J. Andahazy; Mr. Chester Buchanan (who was to coordinate the mosaic having experience from the previous deep-sea searches for the nuclear submarines *Scorpion* and *Thresher* and the A-bomb lost off Spain); Dr. Andreas Rechnitzer from the office of the Oceanographer of the Navy (who had been the officer-in-charge for the record depth setting dives of the submersible *Trieste*); Mr. Gordon Watts; Mr. John Newton; Dr. Harold Edgerton; Miss Dorothy Nicholson representing the National Geographic Magazine; JOC Archie Galloway from the Office of Chief of Naval Information; Mr. Nathan Benn, a photographer for the National Geographic Magazine; Sandra Belock, an artist from North Carolina and myself.

The *Sea Probe* departed Moorehead City, North Carolina on the evening of 31 March 1974. The same Army Reserve LCU that accompanied

Dr. Kent Schneider, Bill Andahazy, Chester Buchanan, John Newton, and CDR Collin Jones discussing the project while transiting to the wreck site.

the *Eastward* the previous summer was to be on station to assist in locating the wreck. Dr. Edgerton rode the LCU so he could operate his side-scan sonar. Dr. Kent Schneider, an archeologist for the State of North Carolina joined the scientific party aboard the *Sea Probe*.

At 0800 on 1 April the *Sea Probe* was in the area to be investigated. Mr. Newton was in radio communication with Dr. Edgerton on the LCU who had the wreck on sonar. At 0842 the *Sea Probe* recorded a fathometer contact with a bottom relief of 18 feet. All eyes were affixed to the video monitors to catch the first glimpses of the wreck as the instrument "pod" was lowered on the drill string. Even with her sophisticated search equipment it was 1605 before the *Sea Probe* was oriented so that the wreck became visible on the TV monitors. As the details of the wreck were being studied by the scientific party, the 35mm cameras began recording the site with photographs once every eight seconds. This would allow photographic experts to assemble a mosaic of the entire site, hopefully presenting irrefutable proof of the wreck's identity and completely documenting its condition.

Almost immediately those watching the wreck on the TV monitors became aware of the extremely fragile condition of the wreck. Long submersion in salt water had severely eroded the iron plates and portions of the hull had completely collapsed. What was left was the skeletal remains of a ship, it's identity shrouded beneath the encrustations and marine growth of over a century. The question was "Is this the *Monitor,* or is it the old Staten Island ferry rumored to have sunk in the area?"

Once in the search area, the control of the ship's movement shifted from the pilot house to search central where the fathometer, side-scan sonar recorder, and under-water T.V. video searched for the wreck.

The control console in search central. The thrust of the propellers is controlled by the "joy stick" in the center of the panel. As the ship's operator views the wreck on the video screen, he guides the cameras along the wreck by pushing the stick in the desired direction.

Captain Scotty Crechton, commanding officer of the Sea Probe, inspects the instrument pod which carries the deep sea cameras, strobes, under-water T.V. cameras, flood lights, and side-scan sonar.

Research teams worked in shifts around the clock recording the sequence of photos and studying the minute details of individual photos. Interest was intense for in each photograph might lie some proof of the wreck's identity. Positive identification was not left until the mosaic was completed nearly four months later, although that certainly was the final proof, but rather was found in the specific details which were indentified in these individual photos. Gradually, the evidence became undeniable that the *Monitor* had been found.

Looking at the finished mosaic, the most difficult orientation to make is that the ship is resting upside down on top of the displaced turret. Once this is realized the pieces of the puzzle begin to fit together. The most distinguishing characteristic of the *Monitor* is her turret. All historical sources agree on it's general size, dimensions and construction details. Additionally, original drawings of the entire turret assembly in the C. W. McCord Collection of Ericsson drawings at Stevens Institute of Technology aided in positively identifying the ship. The turret has been displaced astern and slightly outboard from its original amidships position and the entire hull has come to rest on top of it. Due to the heavy weight of the turret (over 200 tons) and the topside armor, the ship probably lost stability and rolled over as she sank. The fact that a later monitor, the USS *Tecumseh,* which sank in Mobile Bay also turned "turtle" after striking a mine gives added credence to this theory.

Using the results from the tow tank tests and analyzing metal samples from the *Tecumseh,* Midshipmen Hribar and Rau were able to develop a sinking theory explaining the present orientation of the wreck. After turning over, the hull would probably sink stern first due to the weight of her machinery and as it accelerated to the bottom, the impact was calculated to be sufficient to shear the turret's center shaft and cause structural damage to the stern section of the raft. It was fortunate that the

Sandra Belock, CAPT Peterkin, and the author cataloging frames as they were developed and attempting to piece the photos together into a coherent picture of the wreck.

Dorothy Nicholson of the National Geographic Society studying the more than 1,200 photographs that were taken of the wreck.

CAPT Peterkin and Bill Andahazy discussing a sketch of the wreck made from the pieced together photographs.

One of the photos clearly shows the turret of the Monitor protruding from under the armor belt. The wreck was severely fouled with marine growth and some of the frames of the lower hull were visible.

The finished overall photo-mosaic is shown above. The scalloped effect is from the piecing together of the individual photographs. The arrow points to the displaced turret. The drawing below, by Steve Daniels, is a graphic interpretation of the photo-

mosaic. The photos on the opposite page are some of the individual shots which made up the mosaic and they are keyed to the overlaid grid.

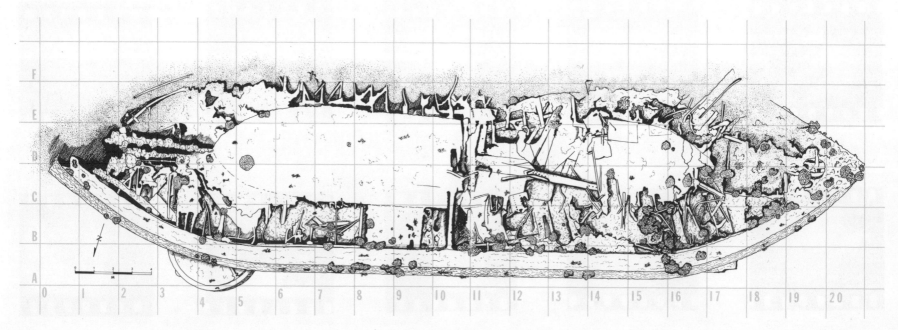

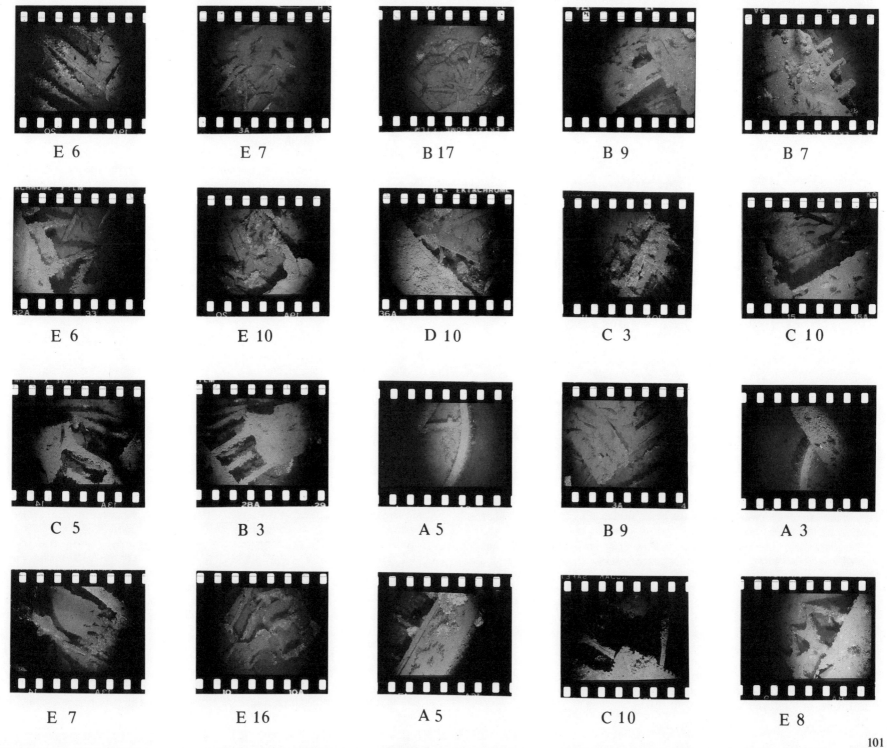

E 6   E 7   B 17   B 9   B 7

E 6   E 10   D 10   C 3   C 10

C 5   B 3   A 5   B 9   A 3

E 7   E 16   A 5   C 10   E 8

101

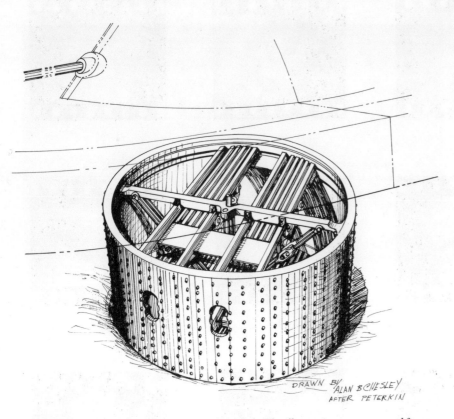

The turret in its present orientation in the wreck. The illustration was prepared from a sketch by CAPT Peterkin.

Examining the base of the turret, which due to it's inverted position is now visible to the camera, the most distinctive feature is the bisecting cross member that supported the weight of the entire turret and to which the central shaft was connected. Scrutiny of this beam close to the rim of the turret reveals two large protrusions on the side surfaces and a slight indentation on the top surface where the beam joins the rim. These protrusions correlate directly with the large hexagonal nuts used to secure the diagonal trusses from the roof of the turret to the base. (*See Peterkin drawing*).

The entire port side of the ironclad is propped up on the turret. With the exception of the extensive damage to the stern and starboard quarter, the armor belt is intact and is in seemingly good condition. The fact that a great proportion of the weight of the hull is still being supported by the armor belt testifies to the integral strength of this structure even after 112 years of submersion.

Photogrametric dimensioning showed the horizontal width of the armor belt to be 30 inches, with a vertical height of approximately five feet, both comparing favorably with the original specifications. In this same area the angle iron frames to which the armor belt was attached can be seen in addition to some of the sloping angle iron frames of the lower hull.

Again, what was learned from the study of the *Tecumseh* is applicable. Metallurgical analysis of that ship's iron plate revealed the poor quality, by modern standards, of her iron. As the molten iron was rolled out into plates, layers of slag remained in the metal. It was discovered that this imperfect process of a by-gone era has acted as a natural preservative for the iron. The iron plate corroded only as far as the first layer of slag with any further corrosion being prevented by the layers of impurities in the metal. But because the rivets were butted, their exposed ends did not have the same protection and in many cases the rivets have completely corroded away, allowing many of the hull plates to fall into the interior of the wreck.

In the lower hull, the stern section is still intact up to the main athwartships bulkhead. Forward of this, in the vicinity of the crews' berthing, the hull has completely collapsed. This can be explained because of the reinforced floors (vertical members of ships bottom framing) and reinforced framing that supported the machinery foundations in the after part of the lower hull. The bow section of the lower hull in the vicinity of the captain's stateroom, anchor windlass room and the chain locker is also still standing. A theory of possible depth charging of the wreck during World War II has been offered as an explanation for the collapse of the center section, but further careful on-site study will be needed to verify this.

Another detail that is visible and characteristic of the *Monitor* is the circular anchor well in the flat section of the bow. The diameter matches the original specifications and several of the photographs show an unusual line of encrustations which might possibly prove to be the anchor chain. In

turret was displaced slightly outboard, exposing to the *Sea Probe*'s cameras details that otherwise might have been hidden thus making the identification of the wreck more difficult and less convincing.

Photogrametic dimensioning makes it possible to determine the linear size of any object photographed. This process made it possible to measure the thickness of the turret's armor as eight inches and using geometry to determine the diameter of the turret as twenty-two feet. All of these measurements agree closely with the original specifications. The height of the turret was judged to be approximately seven feet and this inconsistency with the original specifications of nine feet can be explained due to a probable accumulation of sand around the turret on the sea floor.

Several of the photographs showed an oblong indentation which is in the correct alignment for one of the gun ports. The distinctive exterior rivet pattern has been obscured by concretions and the growth of fouling organisms on the turret's exterior.

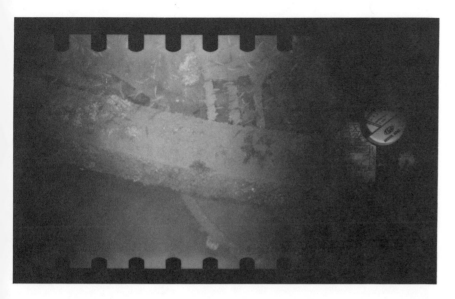

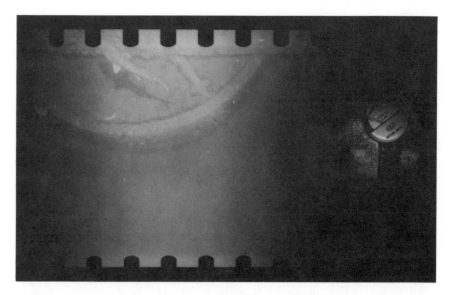

The armor belt, being propped up on the turret, is suspended over the sea floor apparently still maintaining much of its original strength after 112 years under water.

The base of the turret revealing the distinctive iron beam and the large hexagonal bolts and nuts. Note one of the 8 foot sharks that were frequent visitors to the wreck site.

the damaged stern section the distinctive extended propeller shaft and supporting skeg, heavily fouled with marine growth can be seen. The rudder is not visible and apparently has fallen away to the sea floor.

On the third day over the site, a press boat arranged by Duke University, arrived at the site to tape interviews. Little additional investigation was accomplished during the press visit and the announcement was made that all the evidence to date indicated that the *Monitor* had been located.

Mr. John Newton left the *Sea Probe* after the press interviews to coordinate the dredging in the close proximity of the wreck from the LCU. Mr. John Broadwater and Mr. Ed Jackel joined the *Sea Probe* expedition to assist in the further cataloging and evaluation of the photographs.

While nearly 1200 photographs were being processed and studied by the teams of researchers, the *Sea Probe* left the *Monitor* site to investigate other magnetic contacts from the air survey to better evaluate the ship's capability of deep-sea search. The *Sea Probe* returned to the site on the afternoon of the fourth day to tend to an LCU crew member with a large fishhook in his hand. The seas at this time began to build as the weather took a turn for the worse, making personnel transfer very hazardous and preventing any further photography of the *Monitor*. Additionally, the weather prevented the recovery of any artifacts and the retrieval of the Duke University camera. However, these were not considered essential as the *Sea Probe* had collected all the photographic data necessary to prove the wreck's identity. The archeologists aboard deemed the risk

of damaging the site too great and felt that little scientific data would be obtained from any recovery. It was felt prudent to conclude the operation and return to port as the contracted time had expired.

On the return voyage, the members of the expedition discussed the disposition of the data and the coordination necessary to follow through on the assembly of the mosaic. It was at this time that we were struck by the full impact of our accomplishment.

Years of search had located and photographed one of the most significant shipwrecks in our naval history. The efforts of many people and the development of modern technology had made it possible. After the elation of discovery and final confirmation had calmed, the responsibility for the discovery settled upon the group. The wreck had been lost and hidden in the stormy waters of Cape Hatteras for 112 years, a perfect time capsule. Now, through our efforts and those who had preceded us, it's natural protection was destroyed. Had we, by locating and identifying this historic vessel, also planted the seeds for the eventual complete destruction of the ship and any valuable data through mis-conceived salvage ventures and uncoordinated research attempts? Would the *Monitor* be allowed to be "raped" by irresponsibility as so many other historically significant shipwrecks? What of the hazards of diving in 210 feet of water?

Immediately upon docking in Moorehead City, Gordon Watts went to work, investigating means of protecting the site from disjointed recovery attempts. It must be left undisturbed until the necessary resources and technology could be gathered to study the site properly. Through his efforts initially and those of others later, the site was nominated and placed on the National Register of Historic Places and on the 113th anniversary of the vessel's launching the *Monitor* was declared the first Marine Sanctuary. On 30 January 1975 Secretary of Commerce, Frederick B. Dent established the sanctuary to "preserve the vessel's unique historic and cultural value." An intricate system of research proposal review was initiated that represents an unusual degree of cooperation between federal, and state agencies and individuals who are recognized experts in their field. Each proposal is sent to the Office of Ocean Management of the National Oceanic and Atmospheric Administration (NOAA), the cognizant federal agency for marine sanctuaries, who in turn sends the proposal to the Division of Archives and History of the State of North Carolina who distributes it to more than thirty recognized professionals in the fields of archeology, oceanography, history and other related disciplines for critique and comment. The State of North Carolina collects the reviews and forwards the proposal to interested federal agencies such as the Smithsonian Institution and the Naval Historical Center for further review. After the review on this level, NOAA collates all the comments and either grants or denies a permit. This review process is lengthy but is controlled by a strict adherence to time limitations and assures that any research conducted on the site is in the best interests of the purpose of the Sanctuary.

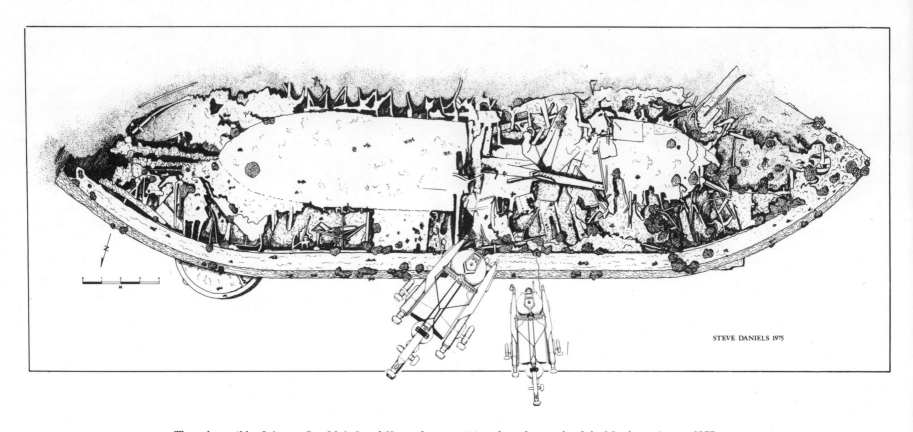

The submersibles Johnson-Sea-Link *I and II are shown positioned on the wreck of the* Monitor, *August 1977.*

STEVE DANIELS 1975

EPILOGUE

The history of the *Monitor* did not end with it's long awaited discovery. In fact, the story is just beginning as professional archeologists, historians, and oceanographers plan to study the wreck further and to determine the feasibility of any recovery. The scope of the project is staggering both in terms of the amount of research required and the expenditure necessary to properly study and excavate the site.

The first step is the development of a master plan that assures a logical sequence of research and establishes goals. Preliminary to the development of a master plan it is necessary to accurately document the *Monitor* site in its "as discovered" condition. Once this baseline is established, a comparison can be made with the ship's in-service condition and then archeologists can make an assessment on the feasibility of excavating the site and any recovery of artifacts. The project rquires a multi-disciplined approach that fosters cooperation between the various disciplines involved. The historical studies, especially those involving the ship's construction and engineering are prerequisite to any on-site excavation and hold the key to many crucial questions involving the other disciplines.

Oceanography plays an early and important role as the hazardous environment of Cape Hatteras has to be studied and it's impact on the feasibility of further on-site research evaluated. Ocean engineering and the state-of-the-art of deep sea recovery will have to be balanced with the dictates of archeological research. A compromise will have to be made between the limits of present day technology for studying and possibly recovering artifacts from deep-water sites and the level of destruction of data that is acceptable. Even under the most controlled conditions, as soon as an artifact is disturbed, some data is being destroyed while, hopefully, something siginficant is being recovered.

A project of this scope cannot be of short duration and represents a tremendous challenge to men of science. Advanced engineering will have to be employed and the new technology of the future will undoubtedly play a major role. Sophisticated research ships and submersibles will operate around the *Monitor* and divers using the advanced techniques of saturation diving will study the ship, excurting from submersibles or even living and studying in an underwater habitat beside the wreck on the sea floor.

In pursuance of the research design for the *Monitor* Marine Sanctuary, the Office of Coastal Zone Management (NOAA) sponsored in August of 1977 a photogrametric survey of the site in cooperation with Harbor Branch Foundation, Incorporated of Fort Pierce, Florida. The Foundation supports research in the marine sciences and operates an impressive array of underwater vehicles.

Supported from *Sea Guardian,* the Cabled Observation Rescue Device (CORD), made an underwater reconnaissance of the site and recorded the appearance of the wreck very clearly on video tape. Following the reconnaissance, the research submersibles *Johnson-Sea-Link* I and II supported from R.V.'s *Johnson* and *Sea Diver* surveyed the wreck site using stereographic cameras. The completed photogrametric survey will permit the assembly of additional mosaics in three dimensional relief, enabling scientists to accurately measure the juxtaposition of artifacts down to one-quarter of an inch or finer.

Divers also probed the wreck with hand-held cameras, which showed the location of the gun ports, the anchor chain running out of the anchor well and location of the hull plate resting on top of the Edgerton camera. This assisted in preparation for the plate's retrieval for metallurgical analysis. While operating close aboard the wreck, one of the submersible

The research vessel Johnson, *above left, preparing to launch the research submersible* Johnson-Sea-Link *to conduct a photogrametric survey of the* Monitor *wreck site, August 1977. Above right, the* Sea-Link *is water borne ready to dive.*

The red lantern recovered from the Monitor *wreck site 2 August 1977. ——Courtesy U.S. Naval Research Laboratory.*

A piece of armor plate, badly deteriorated, as recovered from the wreck of the Monitor, *August 1977. —— Courtesy U.S. Naval Research Laboratory.*

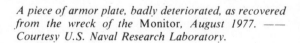

operators spotted an object half-buried in the sand. Gordon Watts who was aboard as an observer, identified the object as a ship's lantern, very possibly the red lantern that was raised as the distress signal aboard the *Monitor* when she sank.

The lantern was approximately 30 feet from the wreck. Because of the his risk of damaging it during the submersible operations, its location and condition were recorded and the lantern was recovered along with the hull plate and the Edgerton camera. Examination showed the lantern to be made of brass with a red lens completely intact. The lantern is the most exciting find since the discovery of the wreck and will undoubtedly be followed by a whole list of priceless artifacts to be recovered from the site.

When all the data from the latest expedition and all previous expeditions is reduced, collated and analyzed, scientists will have enough information to determine the feasibility of any further recovery and excavation at the site. The expense of further working the site will have to be balanced against the available technology and the desired results. Realistic goals will have to be established and a suitable master plan developed. Many experts feel that the complete recovery of the *Monitor* is the most desirable. Whether or not this is possible and feasible is yet to be determined. Recovery is only the first of many problems. Once that is accomplished, the immense task of preservation will just begin. The story of this project is yet to be written, as is the history of the United States' first Marine Sanctuary and the ultimate disposition of the famous ironclad that marked a turning point in naval technology.

The great sustaining force throughout the search and hopefully for the project of the future has been the stirring history of the little ship. Nowhere else in our history has a ship with such a short career been so celebrated as the *Monitor*. The story behind *Monitor* and her role at a crucial juncture of our history will continue to intrigue and inspire all who are familiar with it. There was only one original USS *Monitor* and there will never be another. Perhaps someday, the *Monitor* will once again stand porter at the entrance of the Chesapeake, not as a defense against Rebel guns, but as a reminder of that black Sunday in 1862 when the resolve of a few who called themselves the "Monitor Boys" became a triumph for a new technology, for a man who believed in himself and for a nation torn apart by civil war; a story that is so much a part of our naval heritage.

> *Their names are for history; and so long as we remain a people, so long will the work of the* Monitor *be remembered, and her story told to our children's children.*
>
> *Her work is now over. She lies deep under the stormy waters off Cape Hatteras. But "the little cheesebox on a raft" has made herself a name which will not soon be forgotten by the American people.*

The Edgerton camera that was recovered from within the wreck of the Monitor, *August 1977. Robert N. Bolster of the Chemistry Division is cleaning the framework at the Naval Research Laboratory. ——Courtesy U.S. Naval Research Laboratory.*

Postscript

Subsequent to the writing of the epilogue, the first national conference entitled, "The *Monitor,* Its Meaning and Future," was held in Raleigh, North Carolina. Recognized authorities in the fields of archaeology, history, conservation, maritime law, ocean engineering, and salvage gathered to assess the feasibility of raising the *Monitor*. The overwhelming complexity and cost of such a venture with no reasonable assurance of obtaining the objective, forced the realization that the *Monitor* would not be raised in the near future. Dr. Tise, Director of Archives and History, North Carolina, noted in his summary remarks that in every example of attempted shipwreck recovery projects in this country, there have been good intentions, but little commitment to total recovery and preservation. This commitment entails not just the physical raising of the ship, but also the lengthy and expensive conservation of the wreck and its proper display. The recovery costs for the *Monitor* were estimated at 10-20 million dollars and approximately eleven times that for the preservation of the hull once it leaves its sub-oceanic environment.

The conference endorsed the development of a master plan by the State of North Carolina to properly coordinate any further research concerning disposition of the *Monitor*. Only through detailed study and coordinated planning can this irreplaceable national artifact be properly and fully utilized. Through continued interest, this will not be the end of the *Monitor* story, but only a new beginning.

Appendix

Officers and crew of the USS *Monitor* during the engagement
with the CSS *Virginia*, 9 March 1862

Lieut. John L. Worden, U.S.N., Commanding
Lieut. Samuel D. Greene, U.S.N., Executive Officer
Louis N. Stodder, Master
John J. N. Webber, Master
Daniel C. Logue, Assistant Surgeon
W. F. Keeler, Paymaster
Isaac Newton, First Assistant Engineer
Albert B. Campbell, Second Assistant Engineer
R. W. Hands, Third Assistant Engineer
M. T. Sunstrum, Third Assistant Engineer
Daniel Toffey, Captain's Clerk
Geo. Frederickson, Acting Master's Mate
Jesse M. Jones, Hospital Steward
R. R. Hubbell, Paymaster's Steward
Richard Anjier, Quarter-Master
Peter Williams, Quarter-Master
Moses M. Stearns, Quarter-Master
Derick Brinkman, Carpenter's Mate
Robert Williams, First Class Fireman
John Driscoll, First Class Fireman
Abram Fester, First Class Fireman
Wm. Richardson, First Class Fireman
George S. Geer, First Class Fireman
Patrick Hannan, First Class Fireman
Mathew Leonard, First Class Fireman
Thomas Joyce, First Class Fireman
John Garrety, First Class Fireman
Edmund Brown, First Class Fireman
Joseph Crown, Gunner's Mate
John Rooney, Master at Arms

Thomas Carroll, 1st, Captain of Hold
john P. Conkin, Quarter Gunner
John P. Conkin, Quarter Gunner
John Stocking, Boatswain's Mate
Lawrence Murray, Landsman
Wm. H. Nichols, Landsman
William Bryan, Yeoman
David Cuddebuck, Officers' Steward
Edward Moore, Officers' Cook
Thomas Longhran, Ship's Cook
Thomas Carroll, 2nd, First Class Boy
Charles F. Sylvester, Seaman
Charles Peterson, Seaman
Anton Basting, Seaman
Hans Anderson, Seaman
Peter Truskitt, Seaman
Thomas B. Vial, Seaman
William Marion, Seaman
Anthony Connoly, Seaman
James Fenwick, Seaman (Quarter Gunner)
Daniel Welch, Seaman
Michael Mooney, Coal Heaver
Ellis Roberts, Coal Heaver
William Durst, Coat Heaver
James Seery, Coal Heaver
Robert Quinn, Coal Heaver
John Mason, Coal Heaver
Christy Price, Coal Heaver
R. K. Hubbell, Ship's Steward
A. C. Stimers, Chief Engineer, passenger, and volunteer officer.

Officers and crew of the USS *Monitor,* 31 December 1862

Cdr. John Pine Bankhead, U.S.N., Commanding
*Lieut. Samuel D. Greene, U.S.N., Executive Officer
*Louis N. Stodder, Master
*John J. N. Webber, Master
Grenville M. Weeks, Assistant Surgeon
*W. F. Keeler, Paymaster
*W. F. Watters, First Assistant Engineer
R. W. Hands, *Lost* Third Assistant Engineer
*Daniel Toffey, Captain's Clerk
*Geo. Frederickson, *Lost* Acting Ensign
Jesse M. Jones, Hospital Steward
R. R. Hubbell, Paymaster's Steward
*Richard Anjier, Quater-Master
*Peter Williams, Quarter-Master
*Moses M. Stearns, Quarter-Master
*Derick Brinkman, Carpenter's Mate
*Robert Williams, *Lost* First Class Fireman
*John Driscoll, First Class Fireman
*Abram Fester, First Class Fireman
*Wm. Richardson, First Class Fireman
*George S. Geer, First Class Fireman
*Patrick Hannan, First Class Fireman
*Mathew Leonard, First Class Fireman
*Thomas Joyce, *Lost* First Class Fireman
*John Garrety, First Class Fireman
*Edmund Brown, First Class Fireman
*Joseph Crown, Gunner's Mate
*John Rooney, Master at Arms
*Thomas Carroll, 1st, Captain of Hold
*John P. Conkin, Quarter Gunner
*John Stocking, *Lost* Boatswain's Mate

William Allen, *Lost* Landsman
William Eagan, *Lost* Landsman
*William Bryan, *Lost* Yeoman
*Thomas Longhran, Ship's Cook
*Thomas Carroll, 2nd, First Class Boy
*Charles F. Sylvester, Seaman
*Charles Peterson, Seaman
*Anton Basting, Seaman
*Hans Anderson, Seaman
*Peter Truskitt, Seaman
*Thomas B. Vial, Seaman
*William Marion, Seaman
*Anthony Connoly, Seaman
*James Fenwick, *Lost* Seaman (Quarter Gunner)
*Daniel Welch, Seaman
*Michael Mooney, Coal Heaver
Norman Atwater, *Lost* Acting Ensign
Samuel A. Lewis, *Lost* Third Assistant Engineer
Daniel Moore, *Lost* Officers' Steward
Robert Howard, *Lost* Officers' Cook
Jacob Nickles, *Lost* Ordinary Seaman
*Ellis Roberts, Coal Heaver
*William Durst, Coal Heaver
*James Seery, Coal Heaver
*Robert Quinn, Coal Heaver
*John Mason, Coal Heaver
*Christy Price, Coal Heaver
*R. K. Hubbell, Ship's Steward
Robert Cook, *Lost* First Cabin Boy
George Littlefield, *Lost* Coal Heaver
Francis B. Butts, Seaman

*Men so marked were aboard during the Battle of Hampton Roads.

Bibliography

BOOKS AND PAMPHLETS

Abbot, Willis J. "The Duel Between the *Monitor* and the *Merrimac*" in *Stories of the Republic*. New York: Putnam, 1912. Pp. 260–293.

An Account of the Reception Given by the Citizens of New York to the Survivors of the Officers and Crews of the United States Frigates Cumberland and Congress at the Academy of Music, April 10, 1862. New York: J. A. Gray and Green, Printers. 1862.

Adts, Nicholas Joseph. *Le Monitor et le Merrimac; Système de projectile se forçant dans l'ame au moyen d'un sabot.* Paris: Tanera, 1862.

Alund, O. W. *John Ericsson; Nagra Minnesblad.* (Ur Det Moderna Samhällslifvet, 13.) Stockholm: Albert Bonnier, 1890.

The American Annual Cyclopedia and Register of Important Events of the Year 1861. New York: Appleton, 1863.

Anderson, Bern. "*Monitor* and *Merrimack*," in his *By Sea and by River; the Naval History of the Civil War.* New York: Knopf, 1962.

Barnes, James. "The Birth of the Ironclads" and "The Most Famous American Naval Battle," in Francis Trevelyan Miller, ed., *The Photographic History of the Civil War.* New York: Review of Reviews, 1911.

Barthell, Edward E., comp. *The Mystery of the Merrimack.* Muskegon, Mich.: Dana Printing Co., (1959).

Bathe, Greville. *Ship of Destiny; a Record of the U.S. Steam Frigate Merrimac, 1855–1862; With an Appendix on the Development of the United States Naval Cannon from 1812–1865.* St. Augustine, Fla.: 1951.

Baxter, James Phinney. *The Introduction of the Ironclad Warship.* Cambridge: Harvard University Press, 1933.

Bennett, Frank Marion. *The Monitor and the Navy Under Steam.* Boston: Houghton Mifflin, 1900.

Besse, Sumner Bradford. *C. S. Ironclad Virginia; with Data and References for a Scale Model.* (Museum Publication, no. 4.) Newport News, Va.: Mariners' Museum, 1937.

————— *U. S. Ironclad Monitor; with Data and References for a Scale Model.* (Museum Publication no. 2.) Newport News, Va.: Mariners' Museum, 1936.

Blair, Clay. *Diving for Pleasure and Treasure.* Cleveland: World Publishing Co., 1960.

Boynton, Charles Brandon. *A History of the Navy During the Rebellion.* New York: Appleton, 1867.

Brooke, John Mercer. "The Plan and Construction of the *Merrimac*," in *Battles and Leaders of the Civil War.* New York: Century, 1887.

Burnett, Constance (Buel). *Captain John Ericsson: Father of the Monitor.* New York: Vanguard, (ca. 1960).

Bushnell, Samuel Clarke. *The Story of the Monitor and the Merrimac.* New Haven, Conn. (1924).

Butts, Francis Banister. *The "Monitor" and the "Merrimac."* (Rhode Island Soldiers' and Sailors' Historical Society. Personal Narratives of Events in the War of the Rebellion, Being Papers Read before the Rhode Island Soldiers' and Sailors' Historical Society, 4th ser., no. 6.) Providence: The Society, 1890.

————— *My First Cruise at Sea and the Loss of the Ironclad Monitor.* (Rhode Island Soldiers' and Sailors' Historical Society. Personal Narratives of the Battles of the Rebellion, Being Papers Read before the Rhode Island Soldiers' and Sailors' Historical Society, 1st ser., no. 4.) Providence: Sidney S. Rider, 1878.

Cannon, Le Grand Bouton. "The *Monitor* and *Merrimack*," in his *Personal Reminiscences of the Rebellion 1861–1866.* New York: (Burr Printing House), 1895.

————— *Recollections of the Iron Clads, Monitor and Merrimack, and Incidents of the Fights.* Burlington, Vt.: Free Press Steam Book and Job Printing House, 1875.

Carrison, Daniel J. "The *Monitor* and the *Merrimac*," in his *The Navy from Wood to Steel 1860–1890.* New York: Franklin Watts, (ca. 1965).

Chittenden, Lucius Eugene. "The Battle of the *Monitor* and the *Merrimac:* The Battle Described by Captain Worden and Lieut. Greene of the *Monitor*," in Riply Hitchcock, ed., *Decisive Battles of America.* New York: Harper, 1909.

Church, William Conant. *The Life of John Ericsson.* New York: Scribner, 1890. 2 vols. Later editions in 1906 and 1911.

Collum, Richard Strader. . . . *The Description of the Fight Between the Monitor and Merrimac on the 9th of March 1862. Given by Major R. S. Collum, U.S.M.C., and the Copy of the Letter Written by Lieutenant S. Dana Greene, the Executive Offier of the Monitor, to His Father and Mother.* (Philadelphia): Published by order of the Pennsylvania Commandery, Naval Order of the United States, 1898.

A Comprehensive Sketch of the Merrimac and Monitor Naval Battle, Giving an Accurate Account of the Most Important Naval Battle in the Annals of War. New York: New York Panorama Corp., 1886.

Cras, Hervé (Jacques Mordal, pseud.). "Corsaires et monitors américains de la Guerre de Secession," in his *Vingt-cinq siècles de guerre sur mer.* Paris: Robert Laffont, 1959. Also published in English: *Twenty-Five Centuries of Sea Warfare.* New York: C. M. Potter, 1965.

Curtis, Richard. *History of the Famous Battle Between the Iron-Clad Merrimac, C.S.N., and the Iron-Clad Monitor and the Cumberland and Congress of the U.S. Navy, March 8th and 9th, 1862, as Seen by a Man at the Gun.* (Norfolk, Va.: S. B. Turner & Son, 1907.) Reprinted: (Hampton, Va.: Houston Printing and Publishing House, 1957.)

Daly, Robert Welter. *How the Merrimac Won; the Strategic Story of the C.S.S. Virginia.* New York: Crowell, 1957. Bibliography.

Donovan, Frank Robert. *The Ironclads*. Illus. by Frank Kramer. (A Wonderful World Book.) New York: Barnes, 1961.

———— *Ironclads of the Civil War*. By the editors of *American Heritage*. (American Heritage Junior Library.) New York: American Heritage Pub. Co., 1964.

Dorr, Ebenezer Pearson. *A Brief Sketch of the First Monitor and Its Inventor*. A Paper Read before the Buffalo Historical Society, January 5, 1874. Buffalo: Matthews and Warren, 1874.

Eliot, George Fielding. *Daring Sea Warrior, Franklin Buchanan*. New York: Messner, 1962.

Ellet, Charles, Jr. *Military Incapacity and What It Costs the Country*. New York: Ross and Tousey; Philadelphia: J. R. Callender, 1862.

Ericsson, John. *Contributions to the Centennial Exhibition*. New York: Printed for the author at "The Nation" Press, 1876.

Fiveash, Joseph Gardner. *Virginia-(Merrimac) Monitor Engagement, and a Complete History of the Operations of These Two Historic Vessels in Hampton Roads and Adjacent Waters, C.S.S. Virginia, March 8–May 11, 1862, U.S.S. Monitor, March 9 (1862)-January 2d, 1863*. Norfolk, Va.: Fiveash Publishing Corp., (ca. 1907).

Flake, Elijah Wilson. *Battle Between the Merrimac and the Monitor, March 9, 1862*. Polkton, N.C.: The Author, 1914.

Fuller, Richard F. "Fortress Incidents: Including the Contest Between the *Merrimac* and *Monitor*," in his *Chaplain Fuller: Being a Life Sketch of a New England Clergyman and Army Chaplain*. Boston: Walker, Wise, 1863.

Geoffroy, William. *Facts Connected with the Cruise of the United States Steam Frigate Merrimac, Commanded by R. B. Hitchcock, Commander, late the Flagship of the Pacific Squadron, During the Years 1857, 1858, 1859, and 1860*. Baltimore: Kelly, Hedrier and Piet, 1860.

Georgiady, Nicholas Peter, and Louis G. Romano. *The Ironclads (the Monitor and the Merrimac)*. Illus. by Buford Nixon. (Events in American History.) Milwaukee: Independents Pub. Co., ca. 1966.

Guernsey, Alfred H., and Henry M. Alden. "The Virginia and the Monitor," in their *Harper's Pictorial History of the Great Rebellion*. Chicago: McDonnell Bros., 1866.

Hale, John Richard. "The Fight in Hampton Roads, March, 1862," in his *Famous Sea Fights from Salamis to Tsushima*. London: Methuen, 1911.

Hammar, Hugo. *John Ericssons Monitor och Drabbningen pa Hampton Roads*. Göteberg: Göteberg Handelstidnings Aktiebolags Tryckeri, 1925.

Headley, Phineas Camp. *The Miner Boy and His Monitor; or, the Career and Achievements of John Ericsson, the Engineer*. New York: Appleton, 1865.

Hill, Frederic Stanhope. "The Duel Between the *Monitor* and the *Merrimac*," in his *Romance of the American Navy*. New York: Putnam, 1910.

———— *Twenty-Six Historic Ships; the Story of Certain Famous Vessels of War and of Their Successors in the Navies of the United States and of the Confederate States of America from 1775 to 1902*. New York: Putnam, 1903.

Hopkins, Garland Evans. *First Battle of Modern Naval History*. Richmond, Va.: House of Dietz, 1943.

Hosmer, James Kendall. "The Battle of the *Monitor* and the *Merrimac:* A Prelude to the Peninsular Campaign of April to June 1862," in Ripley Hitckcock, ed., *Decisive Battles of America*. New York: Harper, 1909.

Iles, George. "John Ericsson," in his *Leading American Inventors*. New York: Holt, 1912.

Jones, Virgil Carrington. "An Ironclad for Davy Jones," in his *The Civil War at Sea*, Vol. II: *March 1862–July 1863; the River War*. New York: Holt, Rinehart & Winston, (ca. 1961).

Keeler, William Frederick. *Aboard the USS Monitor; 1862; the Letters of Acting Paymaster William Frederick Keeler, U.S. Navy, to His Wife, Anna*. Edited by Robert W. Daly. Annapolis, Md.: U.S. Naval Institute, 1964.

Kelland, Clarence Budington. *The Monitor Affair; a Novel of the Civil War*. New York: Dodd, Mead, 1960.

Kline, P. W., and E. J. Beale. *With Flash of Steel Amid Hearts of Oak; a Description of the First Battle Between Modern Iron Clads; the Memorable Battles of the Confederate Ram Virginia, Otherwise Known as the Merrimac, and the Federal Fleet, Including the Monitor in Hampton Roads, Virginia, March 8th and 9th, 1862*. Newport News, Va.: (ca. 1904).

Latham, Jean Lee. *Man of the Monitor; the Story of John Ericsson*. Pictures by Leonard Everett Fisher. New York: Harper, 1962.

Lauer, Conrad Newton. *John Ericsson, Engineer, 1803–1889*. (Glenoch, Pa.): A Newcomen publication, 1939.

Lewis, Charles Lee. *Admiral Franklin Buchanan; Fearless Man of Action*. Baltimore: Norman, Remington, 1929.

Lewis, Samuel (Peter Truskit, pseud.) "Life on the *Monitor;* a Seaman's Story of the Fight with the *Merrimac;* in William C. King and W. P. Derby, comp., *Camp-Fire Sketches and Battlefield Echoes of 61–65*. Springfield, Mass.: King, Richardson, 1888.

Littlepage, H.B. "*Merrimac* vs. *Monitor*, a Midshipman's Account of the Battle with the 'Cheese Box,' " in William C. King and W. P. Derby, comp., *Campfire Sketches and Battlefield Echoes of 61–65*. Springfield, Mass.: King, Richardson, 1888.

Littleton, William Graham. *The Cumberland, the Monitor, and the Virginia (Popularly Called the Merrimac)*. Philadelphia: 1933.

Luce, Stephen Bleecker. "The Story of the *Monitor*," in Military Historical Society of Massachusetts, *Naval Actions and History, 1799–1898*. (Papers of the Military Historical Society of Massachusetts, vol. XII.) Boston: Published for the Society by Griffith-Stillings Press, 1902.

Macartney, Clarence Edward Noble. "Worden," in his *Mr. Lincoln's Admirals*. New York: Funk & Wagnall, 1956.

MacBride, Robert. *Civil War Ironclads; the Dawn of Naval Armor*. Philadelphia: Chilton Books, (ca. 1962).

McCordock, Robert Stanley. *The Yankee Cheese Box*. Philadelphia: Dorrance, (ca. 1938).

Maclay, Edgar Stanton. *Reminiscences of the Old Navy*. New York: Putnam, 1898.

(Mariner, pseud.) *The Great Naval Battle as I Saw It, and Remarks Upon American Genius*. (Washington: 1872?). Proudfit Collection, New York Public Library.

Martin, Charles. *Personal Reminiscences of the Monitor and the Merrimac Engagement, and the Destruction of the Congress and the Cumberland.* New York: Macgowan and Slipper, 1886.

Melton, Maurice. *The Confederate Ironclads.* New York: Thomas Yoseloff, (ca. 1968).

The Monitor and the Merrimac. (Old South Leaflets, Annual Series, vol. 3, no. 3.) Boston: 1903.

The Monitor Iron Clads. Boston: J. H. Eastburn, 1864.

Moore, Frank, ed. *The Rebellion Record: A Diary of American Events.* New York: Putnam, 1861–1868.

Nicolay, John George, and John Hay. "*Monitor* and *Merrimac,*" in their *Abraham Lincoln: A History.* New York: Century, 1890.

(Norris, William.) *The Story of the Confederate States' Ship "Virginia." (Once Merrimac.) Her Victory Over the Monitor, Born March 7th. Died May 10, 1862.* (Baltimore, 1879?). Printed in *Southern Historical Society Papers,* n.s., IV (October, 1917).

Osbon, Bradley Sillick, comp. *Handbook of the United States Navy: Being a Compilation of All the Principal Events in the History of Every Vessel of the United States Navy, from April, 1861 to May, 1864.* New York: Van Nostrand, 1864.

Die Panzerschiffe Merrimac und Monitor und das Seegefecht in den Hampton Roads am 8 und 9 Marz, 1862. Darmstadt, Germany: Gustav Georg Lange, 1862.

Parker, William Harwar. "Battle of Hampton Roads" and "Battle of the *Merrimac* and the *Monitor,*" in Clement Anselm Evans, ed., *Confederate Military History.* Atlanta: Confederate Publishing Co., 1899.

——— *Recollections of a Naval Officer, 1841–1865.* New York: Scribner, 1883.

Patriotic League of the Revolution. *Memorial to the Fifty-Seventh Congress of the United States, for the Recognition of Services Rendered by Theodore R. Timby, the Inventor of the Revolving Turret as Used on the Monitor and All Battle-Ships from the Civil War to the Present Time.* Brooklyn: Eagle Press, 1902.

Patterson, H.K.W. *War Memories of Fort Monroe and Vicinity. Containing an Account of the Memorable Battle Between the "Merrimac" and "Monitor," the Incarceration of Jefferson Davis, and Other Topics.* Fort Monroe, Va.: Pool & Deuschle, 1885.

Porter, David Dixon. "Fight Between the *Merrimac* and *Monitor,* March 8, 1862," in his *The Naval History of the Civil War.* New York: Sherman Publishing Co., 1886.

Porter, John Luke. "Plan and Construction of the Merrimac," in *Battles and Leaders of the Civil War.* New York: Century, 1887.

Porter, John W.H. "The First Iron-Clad, the *Virginia*" and "The Battle in Hampton Roads," in his *A Record of Events in Norfolk County, Virginia from April 19th, 1861 to May 10, 1862, with a History of the Soldiers and Sailors of Norfolk County, Norfolk City, and Portsmouth, Who Served in the Confederate States Army or Navy.* Portsmouth, Va.: W.A. Fiske, 1892.

Pratt, Fletcher. *The Monitor and the Merrimac.* Illus. by John O'Hara Cosgrove II. (Landmark Books, 16.) New York: Random House, 1951.

Rawson, Edward Kirk. "*Monitor* and *Merrimac,*" in his *Twenty Famous Naval Battles; Salamis to Santiago.* New York: Crowell, (ca. 1899).

Reaney, Henry. "How the Gunboat *Zouave* Aided the *Congress,*" in *Battles and Leaders of the Civil War.* New York: Century, 1887.

Roe, Louis A. *The Battle of the Ironclads, America's Most Memorable Naval Battle.* New York: Cupples & Leon, 1942.

Rogers, William. "The Loss of the *Monitor,*" in Military Order of the Loyal Legion of the United States, Maine Commandery, *War Papers Read Before the Commandery of the State of Maine.* Portland: Lafavor-Tower Co., 1902.

Rogers, William Edgar. *The First Battle of the Ironclads as Seen by an Eye Witness; Printed from a Talk by Col. W. E. Rogers to the Mount Pleasant Citizen's Association, Washington, D.C., October, 1923.* Washington: Hayworth Printing Co., 1923.

Scharf, John Thomas. *History of the Confederate States Navy, from Its Organization to the Surrender of Its Last Vessel.* New York: Rogers & Sherwood, 1887.

Der Seekampf zwischen den Panzerschiffen Merrimac und Monitor auf der Rhede von Hampton am 8 und 9 Marz, 1862. Leipzig: G. Peonicke, 1862.

Selfridge, Thomas Oliver, Jr., *Memoirs of Thomas O. Selfridge, Jr. Rear Admiral U.S.N.* New York: Putnam, 1924.

——— "The Story of the *Cumberland,*" in Military Historical Society of Massachusetts, *Naval Actions and History, 1799–1898.* (Papers of the Military Historical Society of Massachusetts, vol. XII.) Boston: Published for the Society by Griffith-Stillings Press, 1902.

Shippen, Edward. *Thirty Years at Sea; the Story of a Sailor's Life.* Philadelphia: Lippincott, 1879.

Shirreffs, Gordon D. *Powder Boy of the Monitor.* Illus. by James Heugh. Philadelphia: Westminster Press, 1961.

Sloan, Benjamin. *The Merrimac and the Monitor.* (Bulletin of the University of South Carolina, no. 189.) Columbia: Bureau of Publications, University of South Carolina, 1926.

Soley, James Russell. *The Blockade and the Cruisers.* New York: Scribner, 1883.

Stern, Philip Van Doren. "CSS *Virginia,*" in his *The Confederate Navy: A Pictorial History.* Garden City, N.Y.: Doubleday, 1962.

Stiles, Israel N. "The *Merrimac* and the *Monitor,*" in Military Order of the Loyal Legion of the United States, Illinois Commandery, *Military Essays and Recollections.* Chicago: A. C. McClurg, 1891.

Stimers, Alban C. *The Monitor and Alban C. Stimers.* Published by Julia Stimers Durbrow. Orlando, Fla.: Ferris Printing Co., 1936.

Stuyvesant, Moses S. "How the *Cumberland* Went Down," in Military Order of the Loyal Legion of the United States, Missouri Commandery, *War Papers and Personal Reminiscences 1861–1865.* St. Louis: Becktold, 1892.

Suarce, Colonel Baron de. *Le Monitor et le Merrimac.* Paris: N. Chaix, 1862.

Swinton, William. "The *Monitor* and the *Merrimac,*" in his *Twelve Decisive Battles of the War: A History of the Eastern and Western Campaigns in Relation to the Actions That Decided Their Issue.* New York: Dick and Fitzgerald, 1867.

Trexler, Harrison Anthony. *The Confederate Ironclad "Virginia" ("Merrimac")*. Chicago: University of Chicago Press, 1938.

Welles, Gideon. *Diary of Gideon Welles*. Edited by Howard K. Beale. Boston: Houghton Mifflin, 1911.

———— "The First Iron-Clad Monitor," in *The Annals of the War*. Philadelphia: Times Publishing Co., 1879.

Wells, William S., comp. *The Original United States Warship "Monitor."* New Haven, Conn.: (Cornelius S. Bushnell National Memorial Assn.), 1899.

West, Richard S., Jr. "The *Merrimack* Threat," in his *Mr. Lincoln's Navy*. New York: Longmans, Green, 1957.

Wheeler, Francis Brown. *The First Monitor and Its Builders*. Poughkeepsie, N.Y.: Haight and Dudley, 1884.

———— *John F. Winslow, LL.D., and the Monitor.* Poughkeepsie, N.Y.: 1893.

White, Ellsberry Valentine. *The First Iron-Clad Naval Engagement in the World: History of Facts of the Great Naval Battle Between the Merrimac-Virginia, C.S.N., and the Ericsson Monitor, U.S.N., Hampton Roads, March 8 and 9, 1862*. New York: J.S. Ogilvie, (ca. 1906).

White, William Chapman, and Ruth (Morris) White. *Tin Can on a Shingle*. New York: Dutton, 1957.

Wilson, Herbert Wrigley. "The *Monitor* and the *Merrimac*," in his *Ironclads in Action: A Sketch of Naval Warfare from 1855 to 1895 with Some Account of the Battleship in England*. London: Sampson Low, Marston and Company, 1896.

Wise, John Sergeant. "The *Merrimac* and the *Monitor*," in his *The End of an Era*. Boston: Houghton Mifflin, 1899.

Worden, John Lorimer, Samuel Dana Greene, and H. Ashton Ramsay. *The Monitor and the Merrimac: Both Sides of the Story*. New York: Harper, 1912.

ARTICLES

Adams, W. Bridges. "The *Merrimac* and the *Monitor*," *Once a Week*, VI (April 12, 1862).

Allenson, George. "The *Monitor*," *Railroad Model Craftsman*, V (February, 1937).

Bartol, B.H. ("Remarks on the *Monitor*"), *Journal of the Franklin Institute*, LXXIII (April, 1862).

"Battle of Hampton Roads—Confederate Official Reports," *Southern Historical Society Papers*, VII (July, 1879).

Benedict, George Grenville. "The Builders of the First Monitor," *The Century Magazine*, XXXIX (March, 1890).

Bennett, Frank Marion. "The U.S. Ironclad *Monitor*" *Cassier's Magazine*, XIII (April, 1898).

———— "Ericsson's *Monitor*," *The Engineer*, CXXIV (August 24, 1917).

Bisset, G.A. "First American Iron-Clad—the *Merrimac*," *Marine Engineering*, XXV (December, 1920).

Bradley, Chester D. "President Lincoln's Campaign Against the *Merrimac*," *Journal of the Illinois State Historical Society*, LI (Spring, 1958).

Brooke, John Mercer. "The *Virginia*, or *Merrimac;* Her Real Projector," *Southern Historical Society Papers*, XIX (January, 1891).

Brooke, St. George Tucker. "The *Merrimac-Monitor* Battle," *The Transallegheny Historical Magazine*, II (October, 1902).

Bryan, Anna Semmes. "The *Virginia* and the *Monitor*," *Confederate Veteran*, XXXII (September 1924).

Butts, Francis Banister. "The Loss of the *Monitor*, by a Survivor," *The Century Magazine*, XXXI (December, 1885).

Campbell, Mrs. A.A. "The First Fight of Ironclads," *Confederate Veteran*, XXIX (August, 1921).

Catton, Bruce. "When the *Monitor* Met the *Merrimac*," *New York Times Magazine*, March 4, 1962.

Coates, Joseph Hornor. "The Advent of the Ironclads," *United Service*, I (October, 1879).

Coffin, Roland F. "The First Fight Between Ironclads," *Outing*, X (August, 1887).

Colston, Raleigh Edward. "Watching the *Merrimac*," *The Century Magazine*, XXIX (March, 1885).

Curtis, Frederick H. "*Congress* and the *Merrimac*," *New England Magazine*, XIX (February, 1899).

Davis, Charles H. "History of the U.S. Steamer *Merrimack*," *The New England Historical and Genealogical Record*, XXVIII (July, 1874).

Dawson, Lionel. "Starting Something," *Blackwood's Magazine*, CCLXXIV (September, 1953).

Eggleston, J. R. "Captain Eggleston's Narrative of the Battle of the *Merrimack*," *Southern Historical Papers*, n.s., III (September, 1916).

Ericsson, John. "The Monitors," *The Century Magazine*, XXXI (December, 1885).

"Ericsson's Revolving Turreted War Ship," *Scientific American*, LXIII (September 6, 1890).

Fiveash, Joseph Gardner. "The *Virginia's* Great Fight on Water. Her Last Challenge and Why She was Destroyed," *Southern Historical Society Papers*, XXXIV (July, 1906).

Foute, R.C. "Echoes from Hampton Roads," *Southern Historical Society Papers*, XIX (July, 1891).

Fowler, George L. "Ericsson's First Monitor and the Later Turret Ships," *Engineering Magazine*, XIV (October, 1897).

Gambrell, Herbert. "After the *Merrimac*," *Reader's Digest*. XXXI (October, 1937).

Gautier, Ange Simon. "Combat naval de Hampton-Roads (États-Unis), 8 et 9 Mars, 1862," *Revue maritime et coloniale* VI (April, 1862).

"The Grave of the *Monitor*," *Harper's Weekly* LVI (April 20, 1912).

"The Great Naval Revolution," *The Cornhill Magazine*, V (May, 1862).

Greene, Samuel Dana. "An Eyewitness Account: 'I Fired the First Gun and Thus Commenced the Great Battle,' " *American Heritage*, VIII (June, 1957).

———— "The Fight Between the *Monitor* and the *Merrimac*," *United Service*, X (October, 1893).

—— "In the *Monitor* Turret, March 9, 1862," *The Century Magazine*, XXIX (March, 1885).

—— "The *Monitor* at Sea and in Battle," *United States Naval Institute Proceedings*, XLIX (November, 1923).

Harper's Weekly, VI-VII (February 15, 1862–January 24, 1863).

Hislam, Percival A. "The Jubilee of the Turret-Ship," *Scientific American*, CVI (February 17, 1912).

Hollyday, Lamar. "The *Virginia* and the *Monitor*," *Confederate Veteran*, XXX (October, 1922).

Hovgaard. William. "Who Invented the Monitor?" *Army and Navy Journal*, XLVII (November 27, 1909).

Hughes, Robert Morton. "The *Monitor* Defeated the *Merrimac*—Myth," *Tyler's Quarterly Historical and Genealogical Magazine*, VIII (July, 1926).

"Ironclad Echo," *Newsweek*, XIV (August 21, 1939).

"John Ericsson's Deadly Cheese Box," *Life*, XXXIX (October 17, 1955).

Jones, Catesby ap Roger. "The First Confederate Iron-Clad the *Virginia*, Formerly the United States Steam Frigate *Merrimac*," *The Southern Magazine*, XV (December, 1874).

LaFaucheur, L.J. "The Fight Between the *Merrimac* and *Monitor*. Account by a Confederate Spectator," *Belford's Magazine*, VI (December, 1890).

Lamb, Martha Joanna Reade (Nash). "John Ericsson the Builder of the *Monitor*, 1803–1890," *Magazine of American History*, XXV (January, 1891).

Lewis, Charles Lee. "The Confederate Ironclad *Virginia*," *The Southern Magazine*, II (June, 1935).

McBlair, Charles H. "Historical Sketch of the Confederate Navy," *United Service*, III (November, 1880).

MacCord, Charles W. "Ericsson and His *Monitor*," *North American Review*, CXLIX (October, 1889).

McDonald, Joseph. "How I Saw the *Monitor-Merrimac* Fight," *The New England Magazine*, XXXVI (July, 1907).

McMaster, Gilbert Totten. "A Little Unwritten History of the Original U.S.S. *Monitor*," *United States Naval Institute Proceedings*, XXVII (December, 1901).

Martin, Harrison P. "When the *Monitor* Went Down," *United States Naval Institute Proceedings*, LXVII (July, 1941).

"The *Merrimac* and *Monitor*," *Southern Historical Society Papers*, XI (January, 1883).

"The *Merrimac* and the *Monitor*," *The Eclectic Magazine of Foreign Literature, Science and Art*, LVI (August, 1862).

"The *Merrimac* and the *Monitor*," *The Gentleman's Magazine*, CCXII (May, 1862).

"*Merrimack* and *Monitor*," *Chicago History*, III (Spring, 1954).

"The *Monitor* and the *Merrimac*," *Leisure Hour*, XIII (July 2, 1864).

"*Monitor-Merrimac*—Ericsson," *United States Naval Institute Proceedings*, LIII (February, 1927).

Morgan, William J. "The *Virginia* No Longer Exists," *The Iron Worker*, XXIV (Summer, 1960).

"A Naval Fight of '62. A Vivid Description of the Destruction of the Frigate *Congress* by the Merrimac. . . ." *The Quaker*, V (April, 1899).

Newton, Virginius. "The Ram *Merrimac*, Detailed Accurate History of Her Plan and Construction. . . ." *Southern Historical Society Papers*, XX (January, 1892).

"Officially, There's a *K* in *Merrimac*," *Civil War History*, VII (March, 1961).

Oliver, Frederick L. "The Officers of the *Monitor* and *Merrimack*," *Shipmate*, XXVI (August, 1963).

O'Neil, Charles. "Engagement Between the *Cumberland* and *Merrimack*," *United States Naval Institute Proceedings*, XLVIII (June, 1922).

Osborn, Philip Ransom. "The American Monitors," *United States Naval Institute Proceedings*, LXIII (February, May, July, 1937).

Parker, Foxhall Alexander. "The *Monitor* and the *Merrimac*," *United States Naval Institute Proceedings*, I (1874).

Phillips, Dinwiddie Brazier. "The Career of the Iron-Clad *Virginia* (Formerly the *Merrimac*), Confederate States Navy, March–May, 1862," *Collections of the Virginia Historical Society*, n.s., VI (1887).

—— "The Career of the *Merrimac*," *The Southern Bivouac*, V (March, 1887).

Porter, John W.H. "Origin of an Ironclad; How the *Merrimac* Came to Be Transformed—the Original Plans Still in Existence," *Confederate Veteran*, XXIII (May, 1915).

Preston, Robert L. "Did the *Monitor* or *Merrimac* Revolutionize Naval Warfare?" *William and Mary Quarterly*, XXIV (July, 1915).

Ramsay, H. Ashton. "The Most Famous of Sea Duels." *Harper's Weekly*, LVI (February 10, 1912).

—— "Wonderful Career of the *Merrimac*," *Confederate Veteran*, XV (July, 1907).

Ranson, Thomas. "*Monitor* and *Merrimac* at Hampton Roads," *Hobbies*, LXIV (September, 1959).

"The Revival of the *Monitor*," *The Engineer*, CXXIV (August 17, 1917).

Ryden, George H. "How the *Monitor* Helped the Army in the Peninsular Campaign of 1862," *The American-Swedish Monthly*, XXXI (March, 1937).

Sargent, Epes. "Ericsson and His Inventions," *The Atlantic Monthly*, X (July, 1862).

Say, Harold B. "Let the *Monitor* Steam Again," *True, the Man's Magazine*, XXII (January, 1948).

Selfridge, Thomas Oliver, Jr. "*Merrimac* and the *Cumberland*," *The Cosmopolitan*, XV (June, 1893).

"Shears that Built the *Merrimac*," *American Machinist*, LXXXV (May 14, 1941).

Shipp, J.F. "The Famous Battle of Hampton Roads," *Confederate Veteran*, XXIV (July, 1916).

Shippen, Edward. "Notes on the *Congress-Merrimac* Fight," *The Century Magazine*, XXX (August, 1885).

—— "A Reminiscence of the First Iron-Clad Fight," *Lippincott's Magazine*, XXI (February, 1878).

—— "Two Battlefield Pictures: A Reminiscence of the First Iron-Clad Fight," *United Service*, IV (January, 1881).

Sinclair, Arthur. "How the *Merrimac* Fought the *Monitor*," *Hearst's Magazine*, XXIV (December, 1913).

Smith, Alan Cornwall. "The *Monitor-Merrimac* Legend," *United States Naval Institute Proceedings*, LXVI (March, 1940).

Snow, Elliot. "The Metamorphosis of the *Merrimac*," *United States Naval Institute Proceedings*, LVII (November, 1931).

"Sobremennoe Obozrenie," *Morskoi Sbornik*, April, 1862.

"Some Further Particulars of the Fight Between the *Merrimac* and *Monitor*," *Once a Week*, VI (May 17, 1862).

Somerset, Henry Charles Fitzroy, 8th Duke. "The *Merrimac* and *Monitor*," *Southern Historical Society Papers*, XVI (April, 1888).

"Stevens Receives *Monitor* Drawings," *Marine Engineering and Shipping Review*, L (August, 1945); also in *Stevens Indicator*, LXI (May, 1945).

Still, William N. "Confederate Naval Strategy: The Ironclad," *Journal of Southern History*, XXVII (August, 1961).

Stimers, Alban C. "Aboard the *Monitor* in Hampton Roads," *Niagara Frontier*, III (Summer, 1956).

Tindall, William. "The True Story of the *Virginia* and the *Monitor;* an Account of an Eye-Witness," with an Introduction by Milledge L. Bonham, *The Virginia Magazine of History and Biography*, XXXI (January, 1923).

Tyler, Lyon Gardiner. "Virginia, Founder of the World's Navies," *Tyler's Quarterly Historical and Genealogical Magazine*, III (October, 1921).

"The *Virginia-Merrimac:* Behind the Scenes in the Confederate Navy Department, from the New York Sun," *United Service*, n.s., XIII (May, 1895).

Walker, Henry L. "CSS *Virginia*," *United States Naval Institute Proceedings*, LXXVIII (October, 1952).

Walton, Harry. "*Monitor:* History's Strangest Warship," *Popular Science*, CLXXVIII (March, 1961).

Webber, John. "The *Monitor* and the *Merrimac*," *The Collector*, XXV (October, 1912).

Weeks, Grenville M. "The Last Cruise of the *Monitor*," *The Atlantic Monthly*, XI (March, 1863).

Wood, John Taylor. "The First Fight of Ironclads; March 9, 1862," *The Century Magazine*, XXIX (March, 1885).

Woods, Helen. "Timby the Forgotten," *Harper's Weekly*, LV (February 11, 1911).

Young, Franklin K. "A Tale of Two Frigates. Unwritten History of One of the Most Peculiar and Well-Known Episodes of the Civil War, by an Eye-Witness," told to Franklin K. Young, *Nickell Magazine*, VII (May, 1897).

GOVERNMENT DOCUMENTS

Great Britain. *Hansard's Parliamentary Debates*. 3d series, vol. 166 (1862).

U.S. Congress. House. Committee on Naval Affairs. *Officers and Crew of the United States Steamer Monitor*. 48th Cong., 1st sess., H. Rept. 335, parts 1 & 2 to accompany H.R. 244. Washington: 1884.

U.S. Congress. House. Committee on Naval Affairs *Prize-Money to Officers and Crew of the United States Steamer Monitor*. 47th Cong., 1st sess., H. Rept. 144 to accompany H.R. 3840. Washington: 1882.

U.S. Congress. House. Committee on the Library. . . . *Virginia (Merrimac)-Monitor Commission*. 76th Cong., 1st sess., H. Rept. 1168 to accompany H. Con. Res. 327. Washington: 1939.

U.S. Congress. Joint Committee on the Conduct of the War. *Reports of the Joint Committee on the Conduct of the War*. 37th Cong., 3d sess., S. Doc. 108, part 3. Washington: 1863.

U.S. Congress. Senate. Committee on Naval Affairs. *Report (on the Relief of the Officers and Crew of the United States Steamer Monitor, Who Participated in the Action with the Rebel Iron-Clad Merrimac, on the 9th Day of March, 1862)*. 47th Cong., 1st sess., S. Rept. 394 to accompany S. 369. Washington: 1882.

U. S. Congress. Senate. Committee on Naval Affairs. *Report (on the Relief of the Officers and Crew . . .)*. 48th Cong., 1st sess., S. Rept. 153 to accompany S. 867. Washington: 1884.

U.S. *Congressional Globe*. 37th Cong., 2d sess., vol. 2 (March 11–27, 1862).

U.S. *Congressional Record*. 47th Cong., 1st sess., 13:1 (December 12, 1881–January 31, 1882).

U. S. Navy Department. *Destruction of the United States Vessels and Other Property at Norfolk, Virginia. Letter from the Secretary of the Navy, Transmitting in Compliance with a Resolution of the House of Representatives of July 16, 1861, the Correspondence Relative to the Destruction of the United States Vessels and Other Property at the Navy Yard at Norfolk, Virginia*. 37th Cong., 1st sess., H. Exec. Doc. 11. Washington: 1861.

U.S. Navy Department. *Letter of the Secretary of the Navy, Communicating . . . Information in Relation to the Construction of the Ironclad Monitor*. 40th Cong., 2d sess., S. Exec. Doc. 86. Washington: 1868.

U.S. Navy Department. *Official Records of the Union and Confederate Navies in the War of the Rebellion*. Washington: Government Printing Office, 1884-1904. 29 vols.

U.S. Navy Department. *Report of the Secretary of the Navy in Relation to Armored Vessels*. Washington: Government Printing Office, 1864.

U.S. Navy Department. Naval Amphibious School, Little Creek, Virginia. *Monitor and Merrimac; Re-Enactment—April 20–25, 1964*.

U.S. Navy Department. Office of the Chief of Naval Operations. Naval History Division. *Civil War Naval Chronology, 1861–1865*. Washington: Government Printing Office. (1961–1966).

U.S. War Department. *The War of the Rebellion: A Compilation of the Official Records of the Union and Confederate Armies*. Washington: Government Printing Office, 1885–1902. 128 vols.

UNPUBLISHED MATERIALS

Allen Collection. Harvard College Library, Cambridge, Massachusetts.

Brock Collection. Henry E. Huntington Library, San Marino, California.

Brooke, George Mercer, Jr. *John Mercer Brooke, Naval Scientist.* Unpublished Ph.D. dissertation. University of North Carolina, 1955.

Brooke, John Mercer. *Papers.* Private collection of George Mercer Brooke, Jr., Lexington, Virginia.

Buchanan, Franklin. *Letterbook, 1861–1863.* Southern Historical Collection. University of North Carolina Library, Chapel Hill, North Carolina.

"Civil War, 1861–1865." Mariners' Museum, Newport News, Virginia.

Daly, Robert Welter. *(The Battle of the Monitor and the Merrimac; an Historical Address Delivered March 9, 1962 at the Merrimac-Monitor Centennial Program, Mariners' Museum.)* Mariners' Museum, Newport News, Virginia. 24 leaves, title supplied.

Eldridge Collection. Henry E. Huntington Library, San Marino, California. Box 30 contains a three-page letter of H. B. Littlepage (November 28, 1876).

Ellet Papers. University of Michigan Library, Ann Arbor, Michigan.

Ericsson, John. *Papers.* American Swedish History Museum, Philadelphia, Pennsylvania.

Harbeck Collection. Henry E. Huntington Library, San Marino, California. (includes one letter from Fox to Ericsson, 8 January 1865.)

Jobson, J. Tyler. "Recollections of the *Monitor-Merrimac* Engagement as Seen from Pig Point." U.S. Naval Academy Museum, Annapolis, Maryland. (Typewritten.)

Monitor (Ironclad). *Log of the United States Ironclad Monitor.* Navy Archives, Washington, D.C. (Photostats.)

(Monitor Papers.) U.S. National Archives. War Records Branch. Navy Section. Naval Records Collection of the Office of Naval Records and Library, Washington, D.C. Record Group 45.

(Monitor Papers.) U.S. Naval Academy Museum, Annapolis, Maryland. Several manuscripts relating to the *Monitor,* among them a "personal log" kept by her paymaster, William T. Keeler, 1862–1865, and a letter by Lt. Worden giving an account of the battle with the *Merrimack.*

Pierce Collection. New York Public Library, New York, New York. Collection of pamphlets, magazine articles, relics, letters, and other manuscripts collected by Frank H. Pierce.

Porter, John Luke. "CSS *Virginia (Merrimack):* The Story of Her Construction, Battles, etc." Mariners' Museum, Newport News, Virginia.

Shankland, William F. *(Private Journal.)* Library of Congress, Washington, D.C. Journal of the commander of the U.S.S. *Currituck,* which escorted the *Monitor* to Hampton Roads.

Shoemaker, John J. "The Battle of the *Merrimac* and the *Monitor.*" Mariners' Museum, Newport News, Virginia.

Still, William Norwood, Jr. *The Construction and Fitting Out of Ironclad Vessels-of-War Within the Confederacy.* Unpublished Ph.D. dissertation. University of Alabama, 1964.

U.S. Ironclad Steamer Monitor, Designed by Captain John Ericsson, Built by Thomas F. Rowland, General Plan, Descriptive Sketch, and Contract. Mariners' Museum, Newport News, Virginia.

Welles Collection. Henry E. Huntington Library, San Marino, California.

Worden, John L. *Papers.* Lincoln Museum, Lincoln Memorial University, Harrogate, Tennessee.

Report of the Secretary of the Navy, Report of S.P. Lee, Acting Rear-Admiral, Commanding North Atlantic Blockading Squadron; January 3, 1863.

Campfire Sketches and Battlefield Echoes, "Life on the *Monitor,*" by Samuel Lewis (alias Peter Truskit), King and Derby, Springfield, Mass. 1887.

Aboard the U.S. Monitor: 1862, The Letters of Acting Paymaster William F. Keeler, Edited by Robert W. Daly. (Originals in Rosenbach Collection, U.S. Naval Academy Museum).

Report of the Secretary of the Navy, Report of J. P. Bankhead, Commander USS *Monitor,* January 1, 1863.

Atlantic Monthly, "The Last Cruise of the *Monitor,*" by Grenville Weeks, Vol. XI, Jan.–June 1863.

Report of the Secretary of the Navy, Report of Commander S. D. Trenchard, Commanding USS *Rhode Island,* January 1, 1863.

Logbook of USS Rhode Island, Record Group 24, Bureau of Naval Personnel, U.S. National Archives.

War Papers—Military Order of the Loyal Legion of the U.S., Maine Commandatory, "The Loss of the *Monitor,*" by Acting Ensign William Rodgers.

Reminiscences of the Old Navy, "Sinking of the *Monitor,*" by Stephen Decatur Trenchard (excerpts from his journal). Edited by Edgar Maclay, Putnam, New York 1898.

Report of the Secretary of the Navy, Report of Joseph Watters, Second Assistant Engineer, USS *Monitor,* January 1, 1863.

Report of the Secretary of the Navy, Report of Commander James F. Armstrong, Commander *State of Georgia,* January 3, 1863.

Battles and Leaders of the Civil War. "The Loss of the *Monitor*" by Francis B. Butts, Vol. I. Also same in *The Century Magazine,* Vol. 31, November 1885–April 1886.

Battles and Leaders of the Civil War. "The Building of the *Monitor,*" by John Ericsson, Vol. I.

Practice of Navigation and Nautical Astronomy, by H. Raper., Lt., R.N. 1864.

The Monitor and the Merrimac, Both Sides of the Story, "The Last of the *Monitor,*" Rear-Admiral E.W. Watson.

Harper's Weekly, "Wreck of the *Monitor,*" Vol. VII, New York, Saturday, January 24, 1863.

Battles and Leaders of the Civil War, Editor's Note, A. O. Taylor of *Rhode Island.*

Sequel to the story, *"The Loss of the Monitor,"* by D. Rodney Browne, ZC file, Division of Naval History, Washington, D.C.

Report of the Secretary of the Navy—General Correspondence, 3 January 1863.

Index

Note: Officers and men named are U.S.N., unless otherwise identified.

A. Colby, schooner, 80-83
airborne magnetic surveys, 91-96
Albany Iron Works, 23
Alden, James, Commodore, 17
Always Another Adventure, 89
Anaconda Policy, 21
Andahazy, William J., 90-1, 96-7
Anderson, Robert, Major, 16
Anjier, Richard, Quartermaster, 77
Arrogant, HMS, 8
Astor Hotel, 8
Atlantic Monthly, 57

Baker Wrecking Co., 18
Bankhead, John P., Commander, 56, 61-2, 64-70, 73, 75-8, 84, 87-8, 92
Bean, John H., 59
Beaufort, CSS, 40
Beauregard, P.G.T., General, CSA, 16
Belock, Sandra, 97
Benn, Nathan, 97
British Queen, steamer, 7
Braithwaite, John, 4
"Braithwaite" pump steam fire engine, 4
Broadwater, John, 103
Brooke, John N., Lieutenant, CSN, 18, 39
Brooklyn Navy Yard, 8
Browne, Rodney, Master's Mate, 73, 75-80
    letter to President, 80-4
Buchanan, Chester, 90, 97
Buchanan, Franklin, Flag Officer, CSN, 39-40
Bull Run, Battle of, 21
Bureau of Construction & Repair, 21
Bureau of Ordnance & Hydrography, 16, 21
Bushnell, Cornelius, 13, 22-3, 42
Butts, Francis B., Seaman, 54, 65-72, 77-8, 88

C. Vanderbilt, steamer, 49
caloric engine, 3, 14-15

Campbell, Albert B., 2nd Assistant Engineer, 56, 72
Cape Hatteras Lighthouse, 64, 87
Chase, Salmon P., Secretary of the Treasury, 16, 41
Christensen, Fred, Midshipman, 91
Coleman, James, Commander, 91
Congress, USS, 39-42
Continental Iron Works, 23
Crown, Joseph, Gunner's Mate, 43, 53
Cumberland, USS, 17-18, 39-40, 56

Dahlgren, John, Commander, 22, 42
Darden, William M., Professor, U.S. Naval Academy, 91, 93
David Taylor Model Basin, 94-5
Davidson, Bruce M., Academic Dean, U.S. Naval Academy, 93
Davis, Charles H., Commander, 22
Davis, Jefferson, President, Confederate States, 16-17
DeLamater, Cornelius H., 8, 13, 22
    Ironworks, 23
DeLancy, Charles D., 23
Delaware & Raritan Canal, 6
Demologos, USS, 7
Dent, Frederick B., Secretary of Commerce, 104
Diamond Shoals, 64
Drayton, Percival, Captain, 56
Drew, Daniel, 23
Duke University, 91, 103

Eastward, Duke University research vessel, 91-2, 95-7
Edgerton, Harold E., 91-2, 96-7
Ellison, Michael, Midshipman, 90-1
Elwood, Jim, 88, 90
Ericsson, Hjalmar, 3
Ericsson, John
    caloric engine, 3, 14-15
    early inventions, 3-7
    education, 3
    feud with US Navy, 10, 22
    "impregnable battery," 13, 22-4

military service, 3
Monitor drawings & work on, 24, 26-7, 33-4, 42, 48, 51, 87
steam warship design, 7-9
"subaquatic warfare" concept, 13
Ericsson, 13-14
"Ericsson gun," 8-9

Fadden, Bruce, 91
fire engine, steam, 4
floating battery, 17
"Flying Devil" *(Francis B. Ogden)*, 6
Fort Moultrie, 16
Fort Pickens, 16
Fort Sumter, 17
Fox, Gustavus, Captain, Assistant Secretary of the Navy, 17, 41, 48-9
Francis B. Ogden, tugboat, 6
Frederick, William III, 4
Fulton, Robert, 3, 7
Fulton II, USS, 7
funnel, telescoping, 9, 54

Galena, USS, 22, 51, 56
Galloway, Archie, 97
Gardner, Lt. Colonel, 16
Gassendi, French sloop-of-war, 40
Gilmer, Thomas W., Secretary of the Navy, 9
Goldsborough, Commodore, 39-40, 49
Gosport Navy Yard, 17-18
Gota Canal, 3
"Graveyard of the Atlantic," 87
Great Western, steamer, 9
Greely, Horace, 15
Greene, Samuel Dana, Lieutenant, 33, 38, 41-7, 49, 74, 76-7
Grimes, Senator, 21
Griswold, John A., 22-3
gun turret, revolving, 13

Hampton Roads, Battle of
Virginia vs Union fleet, 39-41
Virginia vs Monitor, 42-7
Hands, R.W., 3rd Assistant Engineer, 66
Harper's Magazine, 27
Harper's Weekly, 68-9, 71, 74
Harriman, H.D., 81-3

Harrison, William H., President, 8
Harwood, A.A., Captain, 21
Henshaw, Secretary of the Navy, 9
Hogg, William, 8
Howard, Sam, Acting Master, 41
Hribar, Midshipman, 98

Institute of Civil Engineers, London, 4
Ironclad Board, 22-4
ironclads
European developments, 13-14
proposed in U.S., 22
Isherwood, Benjamin, Engineer-in-Chief, 17

Jackel, Ed, 103
Jamestown, CSS, 40
Jeffers, William, Lieutenant, 49
Johnson-Sea-Link, 107
Joyce, Thomas, 1st Class Fireman, 77
Jones, Catesby ap Rogers, Lieutenant, 41
Jones, Collin M., Commander, 96-7

Keeler, William F., Paymaster, 33, 49, 54-6, 58, 61-8, 72-5, 84, 88
Keith, Harry H., Professor, U.S. Naval Academy, 90
Kelly, Fred, 92
Kennon, Captain, 9
Kidd, Isaac C., Jr., Admiral, 95

La Gloire, French ironclad, 14
LaMott, Mike, 91
Landahl, Charles, Lieutenant Commander, 88-9
Lee, Robert E., General, 17
Lee, S.P., Rear Admiral, 53, 57, 65, 84
Lewis, Samuel *(See* Truskitt, Peter*)*
Life Magazine, 89
Lilierkold, Carolina, 3
Lincoln, Abraham, President, 16, 21, 22-3, 41-2, 48-9
Liverpool and Manchester Railway, 5
Lockrane, Thomas, Seaman, 42
Logue, Daniel C., Surgeon, 47, 56

McCauley, Charles S., Commodore, 17
MacCord, C.W., 24, 34
drawings collection, 13, 24, 98

McMullen, Raynor T., 88
MacNeil, Ben Dixon, 89
McNish, Jack, Commander, 93
Mallory, Stephen R., Confederate Secretary of the Navy, 14, 18, 21, 39
Marston, Captain, 41, 49
Marx, Robert, USMC, 89-90
Massachusetts Institute of Technology, 91
Matthieu, Richard, Director of Research, U.S. Naval Academy, 93
Merrimack, USS, 17-18, 21, 23 *(See* also *Virginia*, CSS)*
metallurgical analysis, 102, 107
Miami, USS, 81-2
military strength, US, 17
Minnesota, USS, 39-43, 47
Mississippi, USS, 7
Missouri, USS, 7
Mizar, USS, 90
Monitor, USS, 13, 49, 51, 57-8
    action with *Virginia*, 42-8; alterations, 54-6; crew, 37, 53; daily routine, 55-6; design/construction, 22-4, 26-7, 33-4; launching, 33-4
Monitor, USS, loss of, 66-78, 84, 87-8
    as described by: Bankhead, 67-9, 76, 87; Browne, 77-84; Butts, 66-72, 77-79; Hands, 66; *Harper's Weekly*, 68-9, 71, 74; Keeler, 66-75; official reports, 87; *Rhode Island* log, 67-8; Rodgers, 69, 71, 75-6; Taylor, 72, 74-75; Truskitt, 73; Watson, 67, 76; Watters, 68, 75; Weeks, 66-71, 73-5, 77, 79
Monitor, USS, search for, 54, 87-103
    early searches, 88-90; "Project Cheesebox", 91-8, 102-03; *Rhode Island* navigational track, 89, 96
Monitor, USS, sinking of, 78
Monitor, USS, voyage to Beaufort, 59-65; to Hampton Roads, 37-9, 41
"Monitor Boys," 49, 51, 84, 107
Monitor Foundation, 88, 90, 97
Monitor Marine Sanctuary, 107-9
monitors, improved design, 51, 56
Montauk, USS, 56, 58
Moss, Robert, Commander, 91

NSRDC, 91, 94
Napoleon I, 3
Napoleon III, 13, 22
National Geographic Society, 91-2, 96-7
National Register of Historic Places, 104
naval officers, conservatism, 7, 21, 48

Naval Research Laboratory, 89-90, 92-3, 96
naval strength, US, 17
New Ironsides, USS, 56
New York Daily Tribune, 47
New York Times, 49
News American, 90
Newton, Isaac, 1st Assistant Engineer, 38, 44, 49
Newton, John, 91, 92, 97, 103
Nicholson, Dorothy, 91, 97
Nixon, Darrel, 91
North Carolina, USS, 37, 53
North Carolina Division of Archives & History, 89, 91, 104
North Carolina Tidewater Services, 89
"Novelty," steam locomotive, 5
Novelty Iron Works, 23

O'Brien, Jack, 73
Office of Coastal Zone Management (NOAA), 104, 107
Ogden, Francis B., 6, 8
Ogden (See Francis B. Ogden)
O'Leary, Michael, 90, 97
Outer Banks, 87, 89

P-3, aircraft, 91
Paixhans, Henri-Joseph, French General, 13
Passaic, USS, 56, 58-9, 64-5, 87
Patrick Henry, CSS, 40
Paulding, Hiram, Commodore, 22-3
Paulding, Leonard, Lieutenant Commander, 56
Pawnee, USS, 17
"Peacemaker" gun, 9-10
Pendergrast, Lieutenant, 40
Perry, Matthew C., Captain, 7
Perry, Sir William Edward, 6
Peterkin, Ernest W., Captain, USNR, 53, 89-90, 93, 96-7
Philadelphia Navy Yard, 8
Phoenix Foundry, 8, 13, 15
photogrametric survey, 105
photographic dimensioning, 102
Pook, Samuel H., 22
Porter, John L., Confederate Naval Constructor, 18, 39
Princeton, USS, 7-10
"Project Cheesebox," 91-8, 102-03 *(See* also *Monitor*, USS, search for)*

Radford, William, Captain, 40
Raleigh, CSS, 40
Raleigh Standard, 47
Rau, Midshipman, 98
Rechnitzer, Andreas, Dr., 97
Rhode Island, USS, 57-8, 87-9, 96
    rescue operations, 69-70, 73-84
    towing *Monitor*, 59-65, 67-72
Roanoke, USS, 39-41
"Rocket" steam locomotive, 5
Rodgers, John, Commodore, 18
Rodgers, Ensign, 58, 65, 69, 71-2, 75-7, 79
Rowland, Thomas F., 23
Royal Archives, Stockholm, 3

Sabine, USS, 37
St. Lawrence, USS, 39-40
Schneider, Kent, 97
Scott, Winfield, General, USA, 21
screw propeller, 6
Searle, W.F., Captain, 88
Seaward, Inc., 91
secession of states, 16
Selfridge, Lieutenant, 49
Seth Low, tugboat, 37-8
Seward, William H., Secretary of State, 16, 22, 41
Sewell's Point, attack on, 43
shell gun, development and naval use, 13-14
Sheridan, Robert, 91
Smith, Francis P., 6
Smith, Joseph, Commodore, Chief of Bureau of Yards & Docks, 22-4, 42
Smith, Joseph B., Lieutenant, 38
Smithsonian Institution, 96
Sea Probe, Alcoa research vessel, 95-7, 103-04
Society of Civil Engineers, London, 3
sonar, side-scan, 92
Sperry, N.D., 23
Stanton, Edwin M., Secretary of War, 41, 49
State of Georgia, USS, 59, 62, 64-5, 87
steam locomotive, 5
steam propulsion in vessels, drawbacks, 7
steam pumps, Braithwaite, 4
steam warship design, 7
Stephenson, George, 5

Stevens, Acting Master's Mate, 74-5
Stevens Battery, 14
Stevens Institute of Technology, 13-14, 24, 98
Stimers, Alban C., Chief Engineer, 33-4, 37-8, 42, 44-6, 87, 93
Stocking, John, Boatswain's Mate, 42, 69
Stockton, Robert F., Captain, 6, 8-10
Stockton, steamer, 6-7
Stodder, Louis N., Master, 42, 44, 69
Swedish Engineering Society, 3
"Swedish gunboat," 13
Symonds, Sir William, Surveyor of the Royal Navy, 6

Taft, William, President, 80
Taylor, A.O., Acting Ensign, 71-2, 74-5
Teaser, CSS, 40
Tecumseh, USS, 98
Tombs, Robert, Secretary of State, Confederacy, 16
Toronto, packet ship, 6
towing tank test, 93-5, 98
Townsend, Captain, 81
Townsend, Samuel P., 89
Trenchard, Stephen D., Commander, 57-63, 65, 68-9, 73-4, 78-9, 83-4, 88
Trident Foundation, 90, 97
Truskitt, Peter, Seaman, 53-4, 73
Turner, Thomas, Captain, 56
Tyler, John, President, 8-9

Underwater Archeological Associates, 90
Underwater Object Locator, 88-9
underwater video reconnaissance, 92, 107-8
U.S. *Monitor* Foundation, 88, 90, 97
U.S. Naval Academy, 90-1, 93
University of Delaware, 91
Upshur, Abel P., Secretary of the Navy, 8-9

Vanderbilt, Cornelius, 49
VanBrunt, Captain, 42-3
VanBuren, Martin, President, 8
Virginia, CSS, 22, 33, 37, 48-9, 51
    action at Hampton Roads, 39-47
    construction/conversion, 39

Walsh, Don, Commander, 93
Wardwell, Ed, 91

Warrior, HMS, 14
Washington Navy Yard, 51, 54
Watters, W.F., 1st Assistant Engineer, 61, 65-8, 72, 75
Watts, Gordon, 91-2, 97, 103, 109
Weeks, Grenville M., Assistant Surgeon, 53, 56, 59-63, 65-71, 73-5, 77, 79, 84
Welles, Gideon, Secretary of the Navy, 17, 21-23, 39, 41, 49, 51, 53
Willard's Hotel, 22
Williams, Peter, Quartermaster, 70, 76
Williamson, William P., Chief Engineer, CSN, 39
Wilson, Henry, Senator, 49
Winslow, John F., 22-3
Wommack, Roland, 90, 97
Worden, John L., Lieutenant, 16, 34, 37, 41-48, 56
Wright, H.G., Captain, 18

NOTES

NOTES

NOTES

NOTES